Spirituality and World Religions

January 20, 2000

To Bishop Tod Brown

May Christ fill you ever
more deeply with the mystery
of His death and Resurrection.
I hope that my book will be of
some assistance along your
spiritual path.

George E. Saint-Laurent

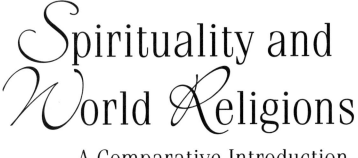

Spirituality and World Religions

A Comparative Introduction

George E. Saint-Laurent
California State University, Fullerton

Mayfield Publishing Company
Mountain View, California
London • Toronto

Copyright © 2000 by Mayfield Publishing Company

Library of Congress Cataloging-in-Publication Data

Saint-Laurent, George E.
    Spirituality and World Religions : a comparative introduction /
  George E. Saint-Laurent.
      p.   cm.
    Includes bibliographical references and index.
    ISBN 1-55934-962-X
    1. Religions. 2. Spirituality—Comparative studies. I. Title.
  BL85.S25 1999
  291.4—dc21   99-40348
                                                     CIP

Manufactured in the United States of America
10   9   8   7   6   5   4   3   2   1

Mayfield Publishing Company
1280 Villa Street
Mountain View, CA 94041

Sponsoring editor, Kenneth King; production editor, Julianna Scott Fein; manuscript editor, Joan Pendleton; design manager, Glenda King; text and cover designer, Jeanne M. Schreiber; manufacturing manager, Randy Hurst. The text was set in 10/13 Palatino by Archetype Book Composition and printed on acid-free 45# Highland Plus by Malloy Lithographing, Inc.

I dedicate this book to my beloved wife,
Michaeleen Saint-Laurent,
and to my dear daughters,
Marie-Louise Saint-Laurent and Jeanne-Nicole Saint-Laurent:
devoted family and faithful companions,
my best friends

Preface

Spirituality and World Religions focuses on a phenomenon that is central to every major world religion yet that textbooks on the subject often overlook: the experiential significance of these world views. It explores how we pursue personal transformation through religion and how we transcend ourselves in our relationships to the sacred and to other people. It also examines how we may embody spirituality in our everyday lives.

This is an unusual approach to the teaching of world religions. Because spirituality is so subjective it is particularly difficult to discuss in an academic setting. Yet it has a predominance in the human experience that makes such discussion vitally important to the student of religion. Given its approach, this book is intended to be a supplemental text for courses in the Introduction to Religion, Introduction to Comparative or World Religions, and any course that deals with the topic of spirituality.

The book consists of eight chapters that pursue insight into spirituality generally and also into the specific spiritualities of Judaism, Christianity, Islam, Hinduism, and Buddhism, respectively. We examine these five religious traditions and ask, "What is it like *inside* for most of the people much of the time, if they accept your worldview and actually walk according to your way?" We center our attention, then, not upon these world religions as such but upon the significant difference that they may make upon the lives of their adherents. We study personal belief in response to dogmatic teaching, subjective involvement in response to objective ritual, and moral activity in response to ethical law. Although we do consider themes, ideals, and motives in the abstract, we also attend to the devotional practices, festal observances, and symbolic rites of each religion.

Chapters 1 and 2 lay out the important distinction between the "spiritual" and the "religious" in their general senses. In Chapter 1, "Understanding Spirituality in General," we present spirituality in its secular guise, where it has expression in all aspects of human endeavor, including art, literature, music, ethics, and personal relationships. We discuss the multifaceted usage of the term in everyday life and come to a working and inclusive description of spirituality that incorporates its essential humanistic quality. In Chapter 2, "Understanding Religious Spirituality," we continue our discussion by looking at religion with an eye to understanding its relationship to spirituality. Our concern here is to develop a broad understanding of religion as a path toward spiritual growth. This chapter sets the stage for discussion about the specific spiritualities of the world's major religions.

In Chapter 3, "Religious Spirituality and Four Great Teachers," we examine the life and spirituality of four renowned persons in religious history: (1) Moses, the Prophet, the great teacher of Judaism; (2) Gotama, the Buddha, the great teacher of Buddhism; (3) Jesus, the Christ, the great teacher of Christianity; and (4) Muhammad, the Messenger, the great teacher of Islam.

In the five remaining chapters, we investigate in turn Jewish, Christian, Islamic, Hindu, and Buddhist spirituality. We organize the material for each tradition according to the same general pattern. After distinguishing the paradigmatic way to attain transformation within each religion, we explore successively (1) the experience of sacred reality, (2) growth through community, (3) formation through sacred scripture, and (4) response through worship, prayer, or meditation, individually or in combination. The meaning of technical and foreign terms is explained in parentheses whenever these occur for the first time. Each chapter concludes with some material for discussion and a brief annotated bibliography for further reading.

I have selected my quotations of sacred texts from published translations in contemporary English. Each of them is easily accessible for further study and reflection.

For my extracts from the Jewish and Christian scriptures, I have used *The HarperCollins Study Bible: New Revised Standard Version with the Apocryphal/Deuterocanonical Books* (New York: HarperCollins, 1993).

For my excerpts from the Islamic scriptures, I have called upon *Al-Qur'an: A Contemporary Translation by Ahmed Ali* (Princeton: Princeton University Press, 1988). I have drawn upon *The Sayings of Muhammad:*

Selected and Translated from the Arabic by Neal Robinson (Hopewell, N.J.: Ecco Press, 1991) in presenting the teachings of Muhammad.

In referring to the Hindu scriptures, I have culled from several sources. For verses from the Rig Veda, I have depended upon *The Rig Veda, an Anthology: One Hundred and Eight Hymns Selected, Translated and Annotated,* translated by Wendy Doniger O'Flaherty (New York: Penguin, 1981). For my citations from the Upanishads, I have utilized *The Early Upanishads: Annotated Text and Translation,* translated by Patrick Olivelle (New York: Oxford University Press, 1998). For my references to the Bhagavad Gita, I have called upon *The Bhagavadgita in the Mahabharata: Text and Translation,* translated by J. A. B. van Buitenen (Chicago: University of Chicago Press, 1981).

Finally, in order to present the remembered teachings of Gotama the Buddha, I have culled verses from the Pali Canon according to *The Sayings of the Buddha,* edited by Geoffrey Parrinder (Hopewell, N.J.: Ecco Press, 1998). For my quotations from *The Lotus Sutra,* I have selected verses from *The Lotus Sutra,* translated by Burton Watson (New York: Columbia University Press, 1993). For my citations from *The Description of the Happy Land* and *The Heart Sutra,* I have consulted *Buddhist Scriptures,* edited and translated by Edward Conze (London: Penguin, 1959).

I wish to express deep gratitude to my beloved wife, Michaeleen, and to my dear daughters, Marie-Louise and Jeanne-Nicole, for their patience and loving support through the several years during which I was preparing this book. I want also to thank Ken King, the editor of religion at Mayfield Publishing Company, together with his able assistant, for their continual encouragement and positive critiques. I am grateful for my departed parents, Louise and George Saint-Laurent; and for my sister, Louise McDevitt; and my brother, Andre Saint-Laurent; and for Bill Doucette—all of whom have embodied sterling spirituality for me by their lives. I must acknowledge my indebtedness to Rev. Benjamin Hunt, C.S.P., and Rev. John Carr, C.S.P., of St. Paul's College; to Rev. Henry Callahan, S.J., of Boston College; to Rev. Godfrey Diekmann, O.S.B., of St. John's Abbey; to the Paulist Fathers Community; and to Dr. Charles Frazee, Dr. Ananda Guruge, Dr. Benjamin Hubbard, Dr. Frank Stern, and Dr. Muzammil Siddiqi. Finally, I owe so much to my countless other teachers, friends, and students, who by word and example have taught me so much about spirituality in theory and in practice.

I would also like to thank the reviewers of the manuscript: Michael C. Brannigan, La Roche College; Dell deChant, University of South Florida; Kathleen M. Erndl, Florida State University; Nancy Falk, Western Michigan University; Linda Holler, San Diego State University; Margaret

Huff, Northeastern University; Dennis Lishka, University of Wisconsin at Oshkosh; Russell T. McCutcheon, Southwest Missouri State University; Guy Newland, Central Michigan University; David Panisnick, Honolulu Community College; Robert Platzner, California State University at Sacramento; Gordon E. Pruett, Northeastern University; and Gerald Michael Schnabel, Bemidji State University.

I am thankful to California State University, Fullerton, for the sabbatical leave during which I began this book and for the office, library resources, and equipment that this institution has made available to me.

Contents

CHAPTER FIVE
Christian Spirituality   97

CHAPTER SIX
Islamic Spirituality   129

CHAPTER SEVEN
Hindu Spirituality   161

CHAPTER EIGHT
Buddhist Spirituality   195

1

Understanding Spirituality in General

As we begin our reflections upon **spirituality,** we must first seek out some insight into the meaning of the concept itself, especially in practice. The topic of spirituality enjoys immense currency nowadays, especially in popular periodicals and books of fiction and nonfiction. Moreover, if we were to travel about the globe, we would discover that for many people of diverse traditions, spirituality is the central constituent of their life and culture. Busy financiers in Norway still make a priority of daily meditation. Nigerian entrepreneurs invite international lecturers to make presentations on topics such as "The Heart of Leadership." Homemakers in India perform their devotions daily at their household shrine. Nonreligious professionals in the United States retreat to the forests of Big Sur, California, to commune with nature and get in touch with their "inner being." Religious people everywhere set aside time for worship and prayer.

We commonly speak of spirituality in our informal exchanges. When we wish to acknowledge someone's capacity for warm relationships, we may well include spirituality along with other desirable traits such as upright character, compassionate tenderness, and sharpened listening skills. We can ascribe a dear friend's creativity and personal charisma to her depths of spirituality. We can attribute a leader's inspiring vision and ethical integrity to his resources of spirituality. On rare occasions, we may get together with intimate friends and unexpectedly attain a deeper level of conversation, as we share our insights into spirituality. The impressive list of those who have won the Nobel Peace Prize suggests that we esteem our heroes and heroines not only because of their nobility and fortitude but also because of their selfless spirituality in the service of the less fortunate. Of direct pertinence to our study is the fact that religious leaders finally demonstrate their credibility not by oratorical skill or administrative expertise but by authentic spirituality.

Modern bookstores and libraries devote ample space to their collections of books on spirituality, whose perspectives range from the psychological, inspirational, and ethical to the strictly religious. Some of these manuals proclaim a bold message about streamlined shortcuts to happiness. Such works promise success in the human enterprise, but the regimen they prescribe is relatively easy. They speak not about disciplined passions and the ultimate meaning of human life but about the satisfaction of every appetite, the winning of influential friends, and the speedy acquisition of material wealth. Some of them offer freedom from guilt not through redemptive forgiveness but through the cultivation of self-esteem. Thus they promote a narcissistic beatitude that is based not upon self-denying service to others but upon self-serving gratification.

Additional handbooks insist upon the lofty origin of their message, and they summon readers to an undivided commitment. They offer guidance not for glossing over the difficulties, disappointments, and frustrations of life but for confronting them steadfastly and enduring them with hope. Some of these challenging works propose a long and arduous path to liberation from the intellectual errors that delude us and entrap us on the wheel of rebirth. Other texts announce a narrow and difficult way to overcome the mystery of sin that alienates us from both God and one another, as it ensnares us in a mesh of iniquity that makes us liable to judgment. Many of these more rigorous books converge at one paradoxical truth: We can reach human fulfillment only through self-abnegation. We can receive only by giving ourselves; we can enter glorious life only through humbling ourselves and dying. These works call us to deflate or even to shatter our egos, convert our hearts, and adopt a radically new **paradigm** for human success. They offer us a personal salvation that may cost us all the vain accolades and empty pleasures that we have valued in the past, but they promise an unimaginable bliss for the future.

The concept of spirituality has become full and multifaceted in contemporary usage, and there is a growing consensus about its desirability.

Some of us think of spirituality as the thrust of self-transcendence, the energy of awareness, and the inspiration of grand ideals, values, and goals. Others relate spirituality to reverence for mystery, detachment from addictive cravings, and connectedness with all beings in the cosmos. Still others understand spirituality in terms of transformation by saving knowledge, enlightened understanding, and compassionate wisdom. In any case, we usually expect men and women of spirituality to manifest an inner discipline and a gracious availability to others. An authentic spirituality will mean fidelity to inner-directed conscience, a thirst for justice, an invincible hope, and a loving-kindness that is open to all. A genuine spirituality will involve an unaffected humility, a responsible stewardship for the world, and a generous service toward others. We would probably all agree that a balanced spirituality will disclose itself in a well-developed sense of humor (especially about oneself), coupled with a sense of personal peace and freedom.

Indeed, we do employ the word *spirituality* often enough in everyday conversation, but we apply it across a broad range of meanings, implications, and connotations. Social commentators use the term *spirituality*, but their underlying concept often remains vague, indistinct, and ambiguous. To what do we refer, for example, when we contrast a feminine spirituality to a masculine spirituality? It appears unlikely that sexual differences would preclude any common ground in matters of the human spirit. Should we separate active spirituality from contemplative spirituality? Even indefatigable activists often disengage themselves from their work to ponder its deeper meaning, while cloistered monastics have been known to write to others about the fruits of their reflection. How different are secular spirituality and religious spirituality? They may easily converge and overlap when people collaborate on projects of peace, ecology, and social justice.

Many people take it for granted that genuine spirituality (and ethical values, too) must connect with some religious affiliation. Indeed, spirituality and institutional religions have enjoyed a close historical bond, at least in the case of the so-called world religions that have taken shape during the past 3,000 years. For the greater portion of this book we shall engage directly in the comparative study of specifically religious spirituality—that is, the experience of Jews, Christians, Muslims, Hindus, and Buddhists. Nevertheless, we must note in passing that spirituality and structured religion are neither identical nor coextensive.

Many people understand themselves to be nonreligious, yet they demonstrate genuine spirituality by the motivation, style, and pattern of their secular lives. Other persons consider themselves both spiritual and religious, although they do not follow the defined creed or prescribed discipline of any particular religious institution. Still others deliberately place themselves outside of any religious institution, because they regard religious structures as counterproductive to the very health of their spirituality. Yet they are undeniably people of integrity, staunch values, and selfless benevolence in the service of others. By way of contrast, some individuals faithfully adhere to the tenets and practices of a particular religion, yet their hypocrisy, empty ritualism, and immorality preclude the development of any spirituality worthy of the name.

How, then, are we to understand the notion of spirituality so that our concept includes the entire spectrum of authentic spirituality yet excludes what is not genuine? We might as well attempt to define the love that all people feel for their parents, the value of ethical goodness, the delight of all children in a spectacular rainbow, or the grief of parents who have lost a child. Indeed, it is probably impossible to formulate a strict definition of spirituality. In any case, we shall be content for purposes of this comparative study to offer not a narrowly precise formula but only a broadly suggestive description.

A BROAD UNDERSTANDING OF SPIRITUALITY
An Approach to Spirit and the Spiritual

If we are to attain some general understanding of spirituality, we must first wrestle with the notions of **spirit** and the spiritual. We ordinarily use the word *spirit* (whether figuratively or literally) to express a dimension of our experience that is nonphysical and inaccessible to the senses. Yet the impact of this aspect of human life upon the visible world has been decisive and far-reaching. For example, we may praise the courageous spirit of a firefighter who risks his life in order to rescue a child from a blazing inferno. We may stand in awe of the creative spirit of an artist who expresses irrepressible vitality in her paintings. We may reverberate to the gentle spirit of an elderly professor who shares her wisdom with us after class hours. We may find the marvelous priest, minister, rabbi, or guru whose spirit empathizes with our difficulties of faith to be simpatico. We may feel gratitude toward a generous hostess because of her gracious spirit of hospitality. We may even experience the healing and elevating presence of a dear friend whose spirit reaches out compassionately to comfort us when we are sick at heart.

The lover in us likes to use corporeal images for the human spirit and its energy. For example, a virtually universal metaphor for the human spirit is the heart, that indispensable organ that reflects our every emotion. Obviously, our heart symbolizes the deepest core of our personal identity. If we protest that we are giving our heart to someone, we mean that we are binding our spirit to our beloved unreservedly and for the open-ended future as far as we can control it. The philosopher in us raises the great questions of birth, suffering, death, and the meaning of life itself and the role spirit plays in them. The psychologist in us instinctively fastens upon the eyes of another when we wish to attend to that person's spirit, because eyes are the windows of the human "spirit." The musician in us responds to stirring melody as the language of the spirit. That is why we meet songs of joy and sorrow in every culture, sacred hymnody and chant in almost every religious celebration.

With the notable exception of the Buddhists (who deny the existence of a substantial soul or self), religious people generally use the word *spirit* as a helpful synonym for the **soul.** They view spirit as the defining and humanizing factor in our experience as men and women. If this is true, then our spirit is the immaterial and immortal ground within us for all our mental and volitional activities, not only for our encounter with God or the Godhead but also for our relatedness to other human beings. From this perspective, our spirit is a noncorporeal entity that not only animates us but also empowers us for specifically human consciousness and activity.

Consequently, we often call upon the term *spirit* whenever we refer to our personal dignity, our inalienable rights, our intellectual endeavors, our volitional aspirations. We may think of the human spirit as the seat of mental consciousness, the psychic root of enduring continuity, the center of accountability, or the core of personal identity. From this perspective, our spirit is a subject (figurative or real) of attribution, direction, and energy. That is why religious people speak of the "spirit" in their analysis of the human predicament and their concern with their goals, their faith commitment, and their code of ethics.

By the same token, we may use the word *spiritual* (the adjective form of *spirit*) when we wish to highlight a nonphysical yet significantly human quality within our associates. We may acknowledge that a lawyer is a spiritual person because he serves the needy free of charge. We may describe a dedicated nurse as a remarkably spiritual person because she approaches her patients in their wholeness as human beings and not as numbers on a chart. We probably favor the term *spiritual* when our context is religious, as, for example, when we admire a traditional Jew or a Zen practitioner as a very spiritual person. By extension, we may apply the term *spiritual* to experiences, things, and places. We may reflect upon a lesson in spiritual wisdom, we may recommend a work on contemplation as a fascinating spiritual book, or we may describe an idyllic venue for contemplation as a "spiritual retreat house."

To sum up, the term *human spirit* apparently designates an important dimension of our experience, although it eludes our direct comprehension. We can hope to understand it only mediately and partially (analogously) through its concrete disclosure in human lives. Although spirit does, indeed, surpass our sensory knowledge, it appears to be not incidental but fundamental to our humanity as such. We use the term *spirit* when we are referring to what is specifically human within us and in all that we do. (Of course, many religious people would also apply the term *spirit* analogously to God and angels, who, they believe, exist with their own proper life and activity.)

Whether the human spirit is immaterial and incorruptible, or material and corruptible, we are investigating an indispensable dimension of the human person. Whether the human spirit is a substantial entity or a merely functional unity, we are concerned with a radical source of human experience. For our purposes within these pages, it will be sufficient to understand the human spirit in terms of a working description such as the following: *The term* human spirit *designates the inner foundation for human experience.* We may then call "spiritual" all those aspects of human experience that notably disclose this "inner foundation."

An Approach to Spirituality

Keeping the preceding interpretations of spirit and spiritual in mind, we can now suggest a broad description of spirituality as follows: *The word* spirituality *designates the inner meaning of human experience under the impact of a humane worldview.* Two elements compose this interpretation of spirituality. They are (1) "the inner meaning of human experience" and (2) "under the impact of a humane worldview." We shall now expand upon each of these phrases.

The Inner Meaning of Human Experience   To categorize spirituality as the inner meaning of human experience is to offer an admittedly vague description. We speak of inner meaning as opposed to the outer, or immediate, meaning of things in their material composition and extension. We can think of spirituality, then, as something qualitative rather than as something quantitative, such as corporeal structures and chemical reactions. Spirituality is the underlying explanation for such invisible realities as personal relationships, wisdom, and love. Spirituality constitutes that deeper realm of motives and principles, ideals and aspirations, reflections and sentiments—some of them, perhaps, only half-conscious or partly assimilated.

In our study of spirituality, we are focusing not upon human life and activity in themselves but upon the overarching purpose of that life and activity—a purpose that might be healing the wounds of humankind, for instance, creating a work of art, or accomplishing God's will. We are dealing not with something subject to microscopic analysis, but with the rationale for a mental disposition and attitude—a rationale that might be sensitivity to human misery, for example, a reverence for the mystery of the universe, or simply the awareness that one can breathe and is alive. We are concerned not with some concrete entity such as a book of readings, a kitchen, or a building, but with the reason for such objects—a reason that could be prayerful meditation, food for the poor, or a symbol of God's presence. As we explore particular religious spiritualities in later chapters, we shall review some of the major religious paradigms by which human beings have justified their lives and vindicated their actions.

Spirituality stems from the innermost roots of our personhood, and it may grow throughout our lives in its pervasive impact on everything we are and do. Spirituality is apt to manifest itself in symbolic things and actions that point beyond their materiality to a further, interior significance; an example is profound prostration of the body in adoration of God. Our spirituality may disclose itself in our contacts with other human beings—through gentle courtesy, attentive presence, or vulnerable availability, for instance. Our spirituality is not our individual autonomy, our self-consciousness, our conscience, or our relatedness to others; it is the factor that integrates all of these elements and makes them purposeful. Our spirituality can be, indeed, the spice that seasons our senses with zest for the banquet of life, the impetus that sparks enthusiastic engagement with the adventure of life.

If we admit the existence of a spiritual soul, we can view spirituality as the vitality that charges our soul with vision and energizes our activities with values and virtues. If we deny the existence of a spiritual soul (as do the Buddhists, for example), then we cannot root spirituality in anything, but we can still understand it as the dimension that directs our flow of consciousness and characterizes our actions. From either perspective, we are dealing with the interior thrust that informs human life with its fundamental significance. Our spirituality can define our criteria for genuine human success.

We can compare our spirituality not to the warmth that tans our skin but to the sun itself, not to the moist coolness that quenches our thirst but to the bubbling fountain, not to the sweet fragrance that intoxicates our olfactory nerves but to the exquisite rose in full bloom. Although spirituality is not our life or activity as such, spirituality does provide the values and virtues that inspire our achievements for the enrichment of others. That is why we can become wiser as we reflect upon Shakespeare's *Macbeth* and more joyful as we listen to the rousing chorale of Beethoven's Ninth Symphony. We can also become more recollected as we listen to Gregorian chant or more righteous as we imitate the life of Muhammad, for we have allowed their inner meaning to touch and nurture our own. Spirituality is like the light that envelops the saints of an *iconostasis* (a screen adorned with sacred images), a light that radiates outward for the edification of Eastern Christian worshippers: It is not the saints themselves but the sacred vision that transformed them.

Spirituality is not some rare attribute of scholars, mystics, clairvoyants, or saints alone; it is a basic gift of healthy and mature people everywhere. Nor is it some privileged luxury, refined taste, or hobby merely for the entertainment of an elite who have the leisure and inclination to cultivate it. On the contrary, a "spirituality-potential" awaits actualization within every human being, and we can look for its themes within any person's story. Spirituality can characterize all our nobler faculties, such as our intellectual power to conceive thought and articulate language, our capacity to make conscientious ethical judgments, and our social ability to create community. Our spirituality undergirds all our talents and intentions, needs and ideals, virtues and goals. It can also sharpen our therapeutic ability to laugh at life's incongruities and at ourselves.

Because there has never been anybody quite like us before and there will never be anyone quite like us in the future, each of us can nourish our own unique spirituality in terms of clarity, strength, and effective impact. Yet many of us have been born into a family that lives by a strong faith commitment, and we can also appropriate this tradition into our spirituality as we grow to adulthood. We can consciously claim a legacy of honor, for example, or fidelity to religious practices. Some of us may become involved enthusiastically at the outset but in the course of time grow weary of the effort, pursue an alternative vision, or simply become distracted by material concerns. Others among us may choose to cultivate our spirituality only after some crisis such as sickness, failure, or tragic loss. Or perhaps we find ourselves in a tunnel of darkness whose extension and direction we do not know, yet we persevere in seeking an answer to our basic question, "What is the ultimate meaning of human life?"

To affirm that spirituality is the inner meaning of human experience is to imply that it does not come ready-made and tightly packaged, with all its elements sharply delineated and ranked in proper order. On the contrary, it is more like a kitchen gadget that we ourselves must still assemble after purchase, piece by piece. Our spirituality can variously expand or contract, progress or regress, flourish or atrophy. We can opt for a spirituality that is pragmatic rather than idealistic, sensuous rather than ethereal, or energetic rather than enervated. We can assess another individual's spirituality as passionate or stoical, spontaneous or constrained, poetic or prosaic, inspired or pedestrian. We may even have to decide, unfortunately, that a person's spirituality is hypocritical, hollow, or dysfunctional.

Many individuals have probably contributed to the creation and development of our spirituality, from parents (and offspring?), siblings, sweetheart or spouse, teachers, and friends to colleagues, counselors, and, perhaps, religious figures. Education and the arts, vocational occupation and skill, triumphs and failures, joys and sorrows, hopes and disappointments along with countless experiences have also had an effect. Even geographical determinants such as city or country, mountain or desert, valley or seashore may have been critically influential. Of course, we are very likely to appropriate some elements into our spirituality from our culture, such as the priority of intellectual endeavor, the necessity of a vegetarian diet, or a provincial mistrust of strangers. Through self-examination, we can review our personal history in order to trace the components of our own spirituality so that we may interpret it to ourselves more accurately.

We may be among those who find a journal to be a beneficial tool for faithful adherence to a chosen path, or we may speak metaphorically of the walk, the journey, the spiritual pilgrimage, or the odyssey. We may then speak of following a guiding light, struggling in the spiritual combat, arriving at a crossroads, surviving a desert wilderness, or ascending to new plateaus. We may also draw our images from marine travel, and speak of crossing the stream, Mahayana ("a great raft"), an ark of salvation, a second plank after shipwreck, a new Exodus through the Red Sea, or a haven from the storm. Medieval Christian monks who never physically left their monastery used to go on spiritual pilgrimages into the interior recesses of their hearts, where they found God.

Our spirituality especially informs the uniquely human aspects of our life and activity (as distinguished from those functions that we share with animals and plants), such as our capacity for personal consciousness and relatedness to others in knowledge, freedom, and love. Some classical philosophers have stated that our specifically human orientation is toward intellectual cognition of the true, volitional choices of the good, and aesthetic contemplation of the beautiful. Indeed, religious theists (persons who believe in God) often insist that we have a profound hunger for God as absolute Truth, Goodness, and Beauty. Moreover, we human beings alone among the planet's inhabitants realize that we are going to die, ask philosophical questions about the meaning of our lives, practice religion, establish traditions of learning, and create projects for serving the vulnerable.

Our spirituality undergirds our intellectual life. That is why the major religious traditions through the centuries have supported learning and patronized research by providing libraries, schools, and universities. They have recognized the importance of education in the cultivation of a well-rounded spirituality. For example, we may come to recognize the presence of the Godhead as we study the natural world about us. We may even engage in exhaustive research until we learn the answer to some vexing question or attain insight into a mystery, and then we are filled with joy upon its discovery. We may intuit the dynamics of a personal relationship and reflect upon its potential for an enduring friendship. Our spirituality affects all kinds of intellectual activities, from understanding different kinds of people and grasping social issues to solving a myriad of problems and planning for the future. Many scholars understand the inner meaning of their lives preeminently in terms of the pursuit of truth.

Our spirituality also influences our volitional life with good habits that incline us freely to follow a better path. Our free will is our capacity to choose some portion of reality as good and desirable for us. For example, we can opt for one university among several academic institutions that have accepted our application, or we can decide upon one career out of several available opportunities. By the same token we can select certain persons to be our close friends. Our free will empowers us to connect with the whole world and at the same time make a determined preference for the poor and the marginalized. We can also relate in loving freedom to a sweetheart or spouse. On the other hand, we can turn away from a previously unsatisfying life pattern to a refreshing sobriety or a redemptive worldview. We can even be inspired to ultimate self-sacrifice for the love of the Absolute as we understand It, and we will not count the cost. Our spirituality can determine the direction of our whole lives for the open-ended future.

Our spirituality can influence the strictly ethical quality of our conduct, making it, for example, kind rather than cruel, forthright rather than deceitful, or humble rather than arrogant. It will also be of primary importance in the formation of our moral conscience. The vast majority of us develop at least some kind of ethical judgment, with some minimal convictions about the difference between right and wrong. We may fail to live constantly and faithfully according to our best convictions, but we do have a fundamental commitment to do what is good and avoid what is evil. Most of us want to be people of integrity, and, if we have children, we want them also to be good and decent. We sincerely want to make the right choices when seductive alternatives confuse us. We want others to respect us as persons of justice, and we instinctively admire these virtues in others. Many of us travel far along this road. We can even become passionately committed to the needy, and we may generously serve humankind at the sacrifice of our own possessions and comfort. Our spirituality can rule our lives ever more totally as we make conscientious choices. On the other hand, our spirituality can deteriorate to the extent that we compromise and betray our principles.

Our spirituality influences our aesthetic life as we pursue wholeness in our personhood. We have a deep thirst for beauty in our lives. By a combined movement of our intellect and will, we can respond aesthetically to delight in that beauty. We become more human as we create or enjoy literature, painting, sculpture, architecture, music, and the dance. Socrates, the ancient philosopher of Athens, was known to dance in his old age, because he felt a deficiency within his spirit. Lorenzo de Medici ("the Magnificent"), the medieval financial wizard of Florence, composed poetry in order to calm his turbulent emotions. Paul Tillich, a twentieth-century theologian, used to seek out the paintings in museum collections in order to cure his mental illness. Indeed, all the arts may be humanizing (and, therefore, spiritual) resources for our leisure hours. How gratifying it can be to learn to appreciate Brahms's Violin Concerto, T. S. Eliot's *The Wasteland*, Tchaikovsky's ballet *Swan Lake,* or Mont-Saint-Michel monastery in Normandy! We human beings would be woefully impoverished without the arts, and we would scarcely find the stamina for enduring life's ugly moments.

Moreover, a sense of cosmic connectedness in our philosophy of life can make us resonate to the splendor of nature's artistry. The exquisite glory of the tiny edelweiss flower, the might of snow-capped mountains, the sparkle of dancing brooks, and the vast glitter of the Milky Way can cause our hearts to dilate with joy. The sweet innocence of baby birds and animals as they cling to their mothers can arouse our tenderness. The fearsome power of giant whales frolicking in the ocean can fascinate us for hours on end. Some people give themselves to nature mysticism and commune with God in "cathedrals without walls." That is why so many persons commit themselves so passionately to preserving our earthly environment and protecting our wildlife.

Our spirituality and our personality are not identical and coextensive. Personality is the larger category that includes not only spirituality but also other aspects of human experience, such as the psychological. Our personality clothes everything that we do, including negative and involuntary behavior such as aggressive impulses, undisciplined appetites, irrational phobias, and destructive anxiety. Our personality develops out of every self-expression, whether it be responsible or instinctive, healthy or pathological, phlegmatic or forceful, boring or interesting, shy or aggressive.

Spirituality's connotations are broad and its implications are far-reaching, but this much is clear: Spirituality is a most significant dimension of our human experience, and it is surely a substantive issue worthy of our serious study. We are concerned here not with some mere convention, such as proper grammatical usage or good etiquette. Nor are we inquiring after some incidental talent, such as athletic prowess or computer skill. On the contrary, our spirituality sums up all those insights and convictions that make human life worth living.

The Impact of a Humane Worldview   We have described spirituality as the inner meaning of human experience under the impact of a humane worldview. A **worldview** is a perspective, or lens, through which we can approach and interpret global reality, a philosophy of life, as it were. A worldview provides us with a mental matrix of first principles and priorities within which we may situate every being and action according to its relative value and proportionate significance. A worldview functions as an intellectual compass for directing our journey of life, but it also serves as a moral yardstick for prudential judgment along the way. Worldviews in general accommodate us with an all-embracing horizon and context so that we can fit ourselves and all other realities into our universe. Many religious worldviews open out upon a sacred Reality that transcends this sensory world.

A worldview may be universal or ethnically confined. It may be dynamic or static, sophisticated or naïve, biased or tolerant. A worldview may draw upon a few folkloric axioms or upon mental abstractions of astonishing complexity. It may be secular or religious, self-centered or ordered toward others, undifferentiated or prioritized. Our personal worldview tends to be dominant, multileveled, enduring, and totally pervasive. It will modify our understanding of birth, health, marriage, and death, as well as our esteem for friendship, religion, art, education, vocation, politics, and society.

In our discussion of spirituality, we are concerned with worldviews that are humane as opposed to inhumane, humanizing as opposed to dehumanizing. The most humane worldviews provide for our complete success and fulfillment as human beings. Perverse worldviews diminish the very humanity of those who live by them. We do not expect evil ideologies to produce authentic spirituality, and there have been some ideologies that are base, vicious, and blatantly depraved as far as the most minimal standards of decency are concerned. The racist Nazism of Adolf Hitler (1889–1945) and the despotical Marxism of Joseph Stalin (1879–1953), for example, were evidently devoid of any redeeming traits, savagely brutal, murderous, and utterly depraved. Worldviews such as theirs are woefully corrupt, barbaric, and hateful. We stamp the monsters who subscribe to them as shamefully twisted or even diabolical and a disgrace to the human race.

The reference to "humane worldview" suggests that we are concerned here with a process of becoming noble human beings. We begin our lives as incomplete bundles of raw potentiality, and we must grow gradually toward our completed human stature. Indeed, very few of us appear actually to attain such a lofty perfection within our short lifetime. We have so much to do, so much to learn, and, above all, so much to become during our few decades on this planet. Our ideal of the completed man or woman usually awaits us up ahead, out in front, as a goal ever again to be pursued. Our spirituality flourishes or atrophies insofar as our worldview succeeds in summoning us to creative realization and effective action along our journey.

A humane worldview nourishes our moral fiber with elevating norms and inspires us with an image of what we ought to become. It affirms and reinforces our dominant concept of what it means to be a fulfilled human being, and we may give ourselves to it with enthusiastic generosity and passionate dedication. A humane worldview challenges us to be good and to do good. It provides us with incentives toward our betterment as men and women and orders us toward our ultimate success. A humane worldview furnishes us with a foundation for our preferential options, educates us with the standards of our ethical conduct, and holds aloft our goal of human success. It determines the form, style, and motives with which our spirituality unfolds in the concrete. A humane worldview sometimes provides heroes and heroines for our imitation, or it induces us to reproduce in detail the virtues of some relative, friend, teacher, mentor, or historic figure. It may rule our heart for a lifetime as our source of hope, despite many falls. Our spirituality will then be richly authentic and fruitful.

Many of us follow a religious paradigm in determining what it means to be a successful human being, and we pursue a supernatural goal within some established community of faith. If our life is a journey, then a humane worldview emanating from religion becomes the guiding light for our spiritual pilgrimage—what the Buddha would call "a lamp unto our feet." Others among us feel no need for religious guidance, although we do seek to become fully human in terms of this world and in accord, perhaps, with some humanistic model that makes sense to us. A saint, a philosopher, a statesperson, a philanthropist, or a scientist may embody our ideals. An artist, an entertainer, an artisan, or an academic may inspire us.

Often our ideal for completed humanity will lead to binding relationships with others, especially through caring and compassionate service. If we happen to be religious, we will also hunger for some sort of transcendent transformation, and we will probably long to express our aspirations through prayer and worship in a community. Whether we are religious or not, we will thirst to commune with dear friends through sharing and communication. We will move out beyond ourselves to focus upon others in the gentle openness of altruism—not because others gratify our needs or can do something for us, but because we value people in themselves and for their own sake.

The effective power of our humane worldview is critically significant for the lifetime process of total integration. Our worldview can make us whole, so that it heals, elevates, and transforms our total personhood. It can sharpen our awareness so that we become acutely sensitive to the feelings of others. It can vitalize the passion of our loving with selflessness, energize our creative labor with grand purpose, ennoble our freedom with moral values, and fortify our psyche with the joy of accomplishment. Our humane worldview can help us to keep our priorities clear, proportionate, and balanced, so that we faithfully respond to the demands of a delicate conscience.

Of course, it remains for each of us to determine the extent to which we will allow our humane worldview to affect the inner meaning of our human experience. That is why, in the last analysis, there are as many spiritualities as there are people. We might pay no more than lip service to our alleged worldview. Our merely formal and nominal conformity might allow us easily to be led by an alien set of principles in the secret recesses of our heart, while we fall short of our avowed goals. We might allow honesty, tenderness, love, and dedication to others to be eclipsed. We might stifle our moral conscience by self-centered indulgence that ignores any social obligations. We might commit ourselves to our worldview on a merely partial, temporary, occasional, or conditional basis. Our lukewarm, halfhearted involvement might make us vulnerable to several competing perspectives at the same time, each of them in its own way promising some sort of gratification. We might then compromise our spirituality in the interest of expediency or convenience. Our veneer of spirituality could then degenerate into an unscrupulous and hypocritical sham.

SPIRITUALITY CONCRETELY EXEMPLIFIED

We shall now consider some concrete models of the meaning and role of spirituality in the lives of people. We shall draw our examples from across a broad spectrum. We may imagine that a professor who is a Buddhist has achieved excellence in the art of communicating effectively with his students. He devotes all his skill and energy to his profession, since he seeks to imitate the Buddha, who is one of the towering teachers of all history. Because of his spirituality, he wants to share with others. A public servant who has a Jewish background devotes herself to promoting social justice for a nonreligious reason: She has derived a sensitized conscience about the demands of the common good from her study of social ethics. Because of her spirituality, she wishes to help others. An entrepreneur refuses to deliver a defective product, use deceptive advertising, or take unfair advantage of his competitors, not only because his Lutheran schooling has educated him in business ethics, but also because his parents have given him a family legacy of honor. Because of his spirituality, he is determined to deal justly with others. A woman who is a homemaker and mother of five small children learns that she has been stricken by a critical illness for which medical science has yet to discover a cure. Her pastor and three other members of her Catholic parish visit her regularly in order to encourage her and assist her with her chores. Because of her Christian spirituality, she is able to endure her sufferings with meaning and hope. A physician works tirelessly to alleviate the pain of patients whose bodies have been devastated by disease. He is not involved with any religion, but because of his spirituality, he longs to heal others. Albert Camus describes just such a doctor in his masterful novel *The Plague*.

Of course, countless figures in history have become heroes and heroines precisely because of their spirituality. It was their spirituality that energized their basic self-transcendence. They made the decision to be for others with all that they were and had, no matter how greedily the needs of other people might have consumed them. It was their spirituality that inspired their motives and provided moral principles for pursuing their life's work, no matter how attractive alternative ideologies might have been. It was their spirituality that illuminated their grasp of the intrinsic worth of all persons, no matter how wretched human bodies might become under the impact of oppressive poverty and terminal illness. It was their spirituality that drove them to empty themselves and identify with the lot of the diseased, the poor, and the oppressed. Needless to say, it was usually easy for their associates and other observers during their lifetime to detect the real significance of their actions. Several examples come to mind in this regard.

Mother Teresa of Calcutta (1910–97) won the Nobel Peace Prize in recognition of her tireless dedication to the needs of the destitute and dying in India. Her eyes always seemed to be flooded with compassionate love for all humankind. At the same time she challenged the conscience of the world, because she fearlessly defended the sacredness of all human life. Hers was a spirituality of loving.

Early in his career Albert Schweitzer (1875–1965) won wide acclaim as a Christian minister, a scholar of Scripture, a physician, and an organist. He probably could have achieved even greater fame, especially in biblical research. Yet he renounced his comfortable life in Europe so that he could give himself generously to the sick in Africa. His was a spirituality of healing.

Dorothy Day (1897–1980) cofounded the Catholic Worker movement, which is dedicated to granting food and shelter to the needy. She liked to quote the Russian novelist Fyodor Dostoevski, whose character Father Zossima insisted that love in action (unlike love in dreams) is "a harsh and dreadful thing." In her fidelity to Jesus, she generously took on the distasteful and exhausting work of nonviolent and unconditional love for the desperately poor. Because of her leadership, her Houses of Hospitality gleam forth from inner cities across North America, like torches of love that flame forth out of the darkness. Hers was a spirituality of serving.

Mahatma Mohandas K. Gandhi (1869–1948) nourished himself daily on the sacred writings of Hinduism, Christianity, and Islam. Gandhi astonished the whole world with his steadfast witness of prayer, fasting, and nonviolent action. He refused ever to regard or treat any human being as an enemy, even though he absorbed an opponent's violence into his own body. Again and again he suffered prolonged imprisonment, and finally he died a martyr. Through what he called *satyagraha* ("soul-force"), he succeeded almost single-handedly in liberating the subcontinent of India. His was a spirituality of leadership and peacemaking.

Martin Luther King, Jr. (1929–68), master orator, Baptist minister, and courageous leader, faithfully followed both the precepts of Jesus and the teachings of Gandhi on nonviolence and civil disobedience in protesting against all the injustices that oppressed African Americans. Cesar Chavez (1927–93), a devout Catholic who founded the United

Farmworkers Union, fulfilled a similar role on behalf of the Mexican American migrant workers. Theirs was a spirituality of leadership and social justice.

This is not to imply, however, that masterful spirituality characterizes only the few or the elite among us. Most of us can recall some people of remarkable spirituality whom we ourselves have known personally. They are, perhaps, those gracious and gentle persons whose kind presence we sought out and who have left an indelible impression upon our hearts. We may think at once of an affectionate grandfather, a gracious aunt, or an altogether benevolent friend who permanently altered our consciousness. We may cherish the memory of a particularly wise teacher who encouraged us to stretch ourselves for the pursuit of much higher goals than we had imagined possible for us. We may also recall that gentle nurse, that understanding counselor, or that generous mentor who was there at a critical juncture when we needed somebody to be kind to us. Perhaps we have enjoyed a solitary but unforgettable moment of privileged encounter, when we met an individual of "heightened consciousness" who opened our eyes to undreamt-of depth at our very fingertips.

Indeed, we do not have to abandon the world and escape to some remote cave at a distant mountain summit in order to discover spirituality in other persons. We do not have to consult a solitary recluse in order to gain critical insights into human transformation. We also experience spirituality in incidental and pedestrian ways, although we may not recognize their true import. We may be charmed by a person's delightful demeanor and write it off as merely her gentleness, sensitivity, or courtesy in collaborating with others. We may benefit from someone's self-giving and characterize it simply as his availability to the needy or his warm empathy with the heavily burdened. We may draw upon a friend's prudent advice and simply attribute it to his superior intelligence. We may think back upon the cheerful greeting of that hotel valet who parked our car at a certain hotel, or we may recall the affability of that maitre d' at the best local French restaurant, who somehow found us a table on a crowded Valentine's Day. There is nothing particularly uncommon or mysterious about such little kindnesses, and they may appear to be simply personality traits. Yet such happy occurrences in life often exemplify an advanced level of spirituality.

We can also discover some hints of spirituality within ourselves. We simply need to look at our daily routine and reflect upon the deeper significance of its details. Are we predisposed to be open and unbiased toward our own private world of people, animals, plants, and things? Do we respond kindly to those who intrude unbidden upon our carefully structured schedule? Is our facial expression authentic when we encounter others, and is our tone of voice respectful when we speak to them? Is our judgment merciful or even just, if we are asked to comment upon the lives of others? Are we patient with those who exhaust us with their complaints or with those who weary our ears with their chatter? Do we react generously when people make their demands upon us? Do we speak our words with sincerity and express our heartfelt convictions? As we confront the challenge of such questions, we begin to understand something about the spirituality that already exists or could exist within us and, therefore, something about spirituality as such.

It seems clear that we should rank the complete development of our spirituality among our primary goals as persons. Indeed, it is difficult adequately to distinguish our growth in spirituality from that basic journey through which we pursue our human wholeness. Certainly the great religions insist that our progress in spirituality and our growth to full humanization are mutually interdependent and coextensive processes. Each individual is to make his or her own choice of the appropriate means for attaining these goals. We can depend upon a religious institution for the nourishment and expression of our spirituality, or we can prefer to rely upon nature, philanthropy, or artistic creativity. We can always realize more insightful wisdom about the purpose and meaning of our sojourn on this planet. We can always become more generously loving within an ever-widening circle of relationships.

In the next chapter, we investigate the meaning of *religion* as such and how it may or should relate to spirituality or a religious spirituality in particular. In a later chapter, we study four great religious teachers as heroic models of spirituality who made an enduring contribution to our understanding of the human potential. For the greater portion of this book, we focus our investigation upon the five religious spiritualities of Judaism, Christianity, Islam, Hinduism, and Buddhism.

In those chapters where we investigate spirituality from an expressly religious perspective, we shall confront its vastly different expressions. We shall be drawing upon multiple sources from five distinct traditions, each of which has survived precisely because it has had so much to offer in terms of hope, meaning, fulfillment, peace, and other spiritual riches. We can all benefit immensely from our inquiry into each of them. We must give them not only our passive respect but also our actively sympathetic attention. Holy men in ancient India used to offer the following greeting to strangers: "From what sublime tradition have you come, noble sir?" They were themselves religious "professionals," yet they humbly claimed no monopoly on wisdom as far as the urgent questions about the human condition are concerned. Even though they themselves had much to share, they recognized that they could not teach anyone from whom they could not also learn. They knew their own limitations: Presumably, there were other languages and sacred visions that encapsulated dimensions of truth that had eluded their own.

MATERIAL FOR DISCUSSION

1. How would you describe the meaning of the word *spirituality* in terms of your own reflections upon human life and your own personal history?

2. What do you think is the relationship between spirituality and the fully human life?

3. Name those people who, from your personal experience or from your knowledge of history, have been heroes or heroines of spirituality for you. Why have you chosen them?

4. What characteristics would you expect to discover if you encountered a person of profound spirituality?

SUGGESTIONS FOR FURTHER READING

Carmody, Denise Lardner, and John Tully Carmody. *Mysticism: Holiness East and West.* New York: Oxford University Press, 1996. An introductory textbook for undergraduates that investigates in a substantive way the phenomenon of mysticism within every major religious tradition.

Jones, Cheslyn, Geoffrey Wainwright, and Edward Yarnold, eds. *The Study of Spirituality.* New York: Oxford University Press, 1986. A compendium of articles on spirituality from both theological and historical perspectives. While this volume is mostly concerned with the experience of Christians in both East and West, it also presents brief summaries of spirituality in each of the major world religions.

Van Ness, Peter H., ed. *Spirituality and the Secular Quest.* Vol. 22 of *World Spirituality: An Encyclopedic History of the Religious Quest.* New York: Crossroad, 1996. A most useful volume that investigates various dimensions of the search for spiritual fulfillment beyond the confines of the great religious traditions.

2

Understanding Religious Spirituality

In Chapter 1, we wrestled with the elusive concept of spirituality, and we had to settle for a practical, working description: *Spirituality* is the inner meaning of human experience under the impact of a humane worldview. In this chapter, we shall explore (1) a broad understanding of religion, (2) religion as concretely exemplified, and (3) the relationship between religion and spirituality. We shall then have a context within which to pursue our investigation of Jewish, Christian, Islamic, Hindu, and Buddhist spiritualities in particular.

A BROAD UNDERSTANDING OF RELIGION

Just what is religion? Our immediate problem is similar to the difficulty that we have confronted in regard to spirituality: **Religion** defies adequate, inclusive, and comprehensive definition. We may presume that we grasp what religion is in practice, and we readily distinguish religious phenomena from the secular. (Even then, many Muslims, Buddhists, and others in the East would insist that the distinction between *religious* and *secular* is an illusory and untenable dualism.) Our difficulty arises when we attempt to define religion in clear and precise terms. It is even a commonplace for textbooks in comparative religion to devote a whole chapter to summarizing the endless controversy among scholars regarding this issue.

Our challenge is to identify the essential meaning of religion in a way that includes all the religions we discuss: Judaism, Christianity, Islam, Hinduism, and Buddhism. For purposes of our study, the following working description of religion will suffice: *Religion is the pursuit of transformation under the impact of a sacred worldview.* This interpretation contains two elements: (1) "the pursuit of transformation" and (2) "under the impact of a sacred worldview." We shall examine each of these factors in turn.

The Pursuit of Transformation

Religion is a *pursuit,* and religious persons must be prepared to make a sustained effort throughout their life. Religion can be an idyllic search for absolute Truth, Love, and Beauty, but it can also demand a rigorous program of performance. An authentic faith commitment usually engenders a practical way of life and can even create a whole culture, as in the case of medieval Christendom. That is why Moses, the Buddha, Jesus, and Muhammad required that their disciples not only hope in the future but also apply themselves to virtuous conduct here and now. These men were teachers of uncommon vision, but they were also men of action who marshaled all their physical energy and inner resources toward their life's mission.

People practice religion in the more or less conscious quest for human significance. They often feel that they would be troubled, incomplete, and restless without their religion. Religious men and women seek satisfying answers to life's great questions: From where have I come, what does it mean to be a human being, why am I here, and what will happen to me after death? To the extent that practitioners faithfully adhere to the teachings of their tradition, they discover a new meaning in life. Of course, authentic faith should bear fruit in practice. Religious people have a framework of meditation and/or rituals of prayerful worship to purify their intentions and ethical criteria to discipline their activity. Devotees learn to interpret their daily experiences from a perspective of inspiring vision and lasting values. As their spirituality deepens and matures, they often feel a new conviction of purpose and mission, perhaps even a sense of vocation and election "from above."

Religion is the pursuit of *transformation*. Religious people want to integrate harmoniously all the levels of their humanity. They long for liberation from whatever traps and binds them. They seek healing from every scar of past brokenness, elevation to a new dimension of consciousness, and transfiguration according to their new ideal of complete personhood.

Jews, Christians, Muslims, Hindus, and Buddhists all teach a source of meaning not of this world: a confirmation in peace (Hebrew **shalom,** Greek *eirene,* Arabic *salam,* Sanskrit *shanti,* and Pali *santi*). They also agree that we initially find ourselves in a dehumanizing predicament of dis-ease. Human life, indeed, abounds with difficulties of every description, but human life itself is a major problem. That is why, they say, we feel ill at ease and alienated, as though we are strangers who do not quite fit into our own world. That is also why a haunting malaise troubles the most fortunate among us at the radical core of our being: our pervasive obsession with ourselves. We must, they insist, pass over from our systemic egocentricity to become reoriented about a new focal center.

Consequently, each of these world religions presents itself as a secure and trustworthy *way*. Each way is more than an ennobling concept to raise up the heart; it is also a path that guides behavior and a road that leads to salvation. Jews, therefore, speak of "the way of **Torah.**" Early Christians identified themselves as followers of "the way" (*hodos*). Muslims submit to God's will by following the "straight path" (**shariah**) of Islamic religious law. Hindus, with that broad tolerance for which they are famous, present no less than four major "ways" (*margas*) to *moksha* ("liberation"). Buddhists teach the "middle way" (*magga*) to **Nibbana** (or **Nirvana**) ("state of being blown out, cool"—that is, liberation from the wheel of rebirth), and some of them refer to each major interpretation of Buddhism as a *yana* ("vehicle").

These world religions proclaim ways to personal transformation for those who follow them, despite the affliction of moral evil, physical misery, and death. They announce a message of human fulfillment by which followers may conduct their lives with heartfelt purpose and an uplifting morality by which followers may devote themselves to others with compassionate service. Believers suffer frustrations, disappointments, and failures, of course. Yet each of these religions offers its adherents the strength to pick up the pieces after setbacks, go on in hope, and finally prevail, either within this world or, perhaps, within some further dimension in the future.

Of course, many people are born into a living tradition that nourishes them, and they spontaneously appropriate their parents' religion as their own. Other individuals deliberately choose a particular religion after careful reflection, because it enables them to make sense out of their confusion and wholeness out of their dividedness. They have found its teachings about human dignity and destiny, good and evil, health and pain, life and death to be uniquely persuasive. Both kinds of religious persons confidently root their hopes in a ground that is imperceptible to the senses, yet accessible through faith, enlightenment, or some sort of initiation into a "higher" level of existence. Their own belief system rings true for them and resounds in the deepest recesses of their hearts, while doctrines of other religions appear "less probable."

For Jews, Christians, and Muslims, our human problem is the moral ensnarement of **sin** that estranges us from a personal God, but the Creator in faithful and merciful love offers redemption. In Jewish thought, human beings must use their freedom responsibly and make the right choice between two strong inclinations: good tendencies (*yetzer ha tov*) and bad tendencies (*yetzer ha_ra*). They must obey the 613 commandments of God's instruction (Torah) in order to confirm their good inclinations and pass from dehumanizing self-will to the ennobling righteousness of God's holy people. In the Christian view, people must struggle against a state of sinfulness that they inherit from their first parents (**original sin**); they then aggravate this solidarity in sinfulness by their own transgressions (actual, or personal, sins). They must by Christ's assistance and empowerment (**grace**) die to self and pass over with him to resurrection as God's adopted children. In Islamic understanding, human beings must reject the temptations of the devil (**Iblis**) and choose freely to surrender (**Islam**) unreservedly to the will of God (**Allah**) as God's servants and finally, perhaps, as God's friends.

For Hindus and Buddhists, our predicament is not moral but intellectual: We human beings erroneously fail to see things for what they really are, and so we become trapped by the law of **karma** (action, consequence of an action) on the wheel of endless rebirth. Hindus identify our difficulty as the illusion of individual separateness, the false sentiment that we are discrete selves in our own right, distinct from one another and from the one universal and absolute Self (**Brahman-atman**). Hindus insist that we all possess the same Self (**atman**) and that all selfishness is, in fact, based upon pointless error. Therefore, we must adopt one of the approved *marga*s and pass over from the state of error that constrains us in rebirth to a liberating realization of our true identity in the universal Self. Buddhists, on the other hand, view our difficulty as the delusion and ignorance of permanent selfhood as such. This ignorance leads to craving desire, and craving desire causes rebirth to further suffering. In fact, the notion of self, whether individual or universal, is empty and void of any reality. Therefore, we must follow the "middle way," with its Noble Eightfold Path, in order to pass over from our state of ignorance that causes craving desire, rebirth, and suffering to a state of enlightenment and Nibbana.

The Impact of a Sacred Worldview

Religion is a pursuit of transformation under the impact of a sacred worldview. We have described worldview as a perspective, or lens, through which we can approach and interpret global reality. The term *worldview* recalls all that we have seen in Chapter 1 about the effect of our philosophy of life upon all that we are and do. Our worldview directs our activities by determining our primary goals and motives as we perform our daily tasks. Our worldview provides us with the solid values that we need in order to develop both individually and socially. Our worldview also furnishes us with principles for discerning what is really true, norms for performing what is authentically good, and criteria for appreciating what is genuinely beautiful. To categorize religion as a worldview, then, is to place religion among the most decisive factors in human experience.

Religion is the pursuit of transformation under the impact of a **sacred** worldview. The notion of the sacred is utterly decisive here (although problematical and resistant to discrete analysis), and we must work out at least some general understanding of its meaning. Jews, Christians, Muslims, and Hindus acknowledge the sacred as existing in an ultimate and absolute reality such as God or the Godhead (Brahman-atman). Buddhists recognize the sacred in the ceaseless process or flow of being, although many of them reject any dualistic distinction between the "sacred" and the "profane" (just as the flow of this-worldly experience and absolute Nibbana are really inseparable and the same). All of these religious people further recognize the sacred as an awe-inspiring dimension of whatever symbolizes and/or communicates the **numinous** ("pertaining to the divinely Other"). For example, devotees encounter the numinous in consecrated shrines, seasons of celebration, inspired books, and rites of passage. All religious people experience the sacred as beyond all comprehension, impossible to define, and very difficult to describe. Yet they insist that the sacred is incontestably real, irresistibly attractive, wondrously provocative, and enduringly fascinating. They know that they can approach the sacred only with the utmost reverence.

The sacred transcends every limitation and overflows every boundary. The whole universe cannot fully contain the sacred and its phenomena, because it exceeds our every ordinary horizon. If the ultimately sacred is a divine being, it may be at once deeply **immanent** (abiding within) and absolutely **transcendent** (exceeding limits, transcending). The God of the Jews, Christians, and Muslims is distinct from all creatures, yet God pervades them all in immanence and surpasses them all in transcendence. For many Hindus, the ultimate divine principle (Brahman-atman), is identified with all things as It pervades them all in immanence and surpasses them all in transcendence. The divinity contains the cosmos, but the cosmos does not contain the divinity.

Since the sacred is intrinsically mysterious, we are incapable of grasping it directly, whether by our senses or by our intellect. Since the sacred exceeds all that we encounter in our natural and ordinary experience, it is **ineffable** (beyond adequate human expression). That is why theological language, for example, can at best be no more than indirect and analogical or negative. Even Thomas Aquinas (1225–74), a philosopher-theologian of extraordinary acumen, affirmed that we know what God is not rather than what God is. Our clouded knowledge of the sacred can be no more than a distant reflection, and our stammering speech about the sacred can be no more than a metaphorical suggestion. Our words may point toward the sacred from afar, but they cannot encompass it. Still, religious people have always tried mentally to probe the meaning of the sacred and have attempted verbally to articulate its significance. They have often created **myths** (vividly imaginative stories) in order to pass on their experience to the next generation. These colorful narratives form the core of their nonwritten and scriptured traditions, creeds, and texts for worshipping communities.

It is very important to realize that religious persons may persevere in their religiosity whether or not they have any emotional feelings in the presence of the sacred. Religion is not essentially a matter of sensibility and sentiment. Some people are certain that they have somehow encountered the sacred, although they have perceived little or nothing on an emotional level. Others may engage themselves with enthusiastic and even passionate commitment to the sacred. Even these people recognize, however, that their faith or enlightenment has to sustain them even when all the sweetness of sensible consolation dissolves into the bitter darkness of aridity.

Most religious persons are not mystics who frequently or habitually experience the sacred as immediately available. Some do speak poetically of savoring the supernal delight of the divine presence or hearing the melody of the divine voice. Others recount how the ecstasy of spiritual betrothal has drawn them up out of themselves into the divine embrace. Nevertheless, the vast majority of religious people lead humdrum lives of unspectacular but faithful practice in an earthbound and uninspired context.

Religious people engage in numerous kinds of activities. For example, they likely pray and worship, meditate upon scriptures, engage in ritual celebrations, fast, give alms, go on pilgrimages, or serve the needy—and maintain some sort of contact with the sacred through it all. They all seek to commune with awe-inspiring Reality, and they hope that their particular way will lead them to final transformation, enlightenment, or salvation.

The defining dimension of all religious exercises is the sacred connection. Buddhists of the **Theravada** ("teaching of the elders"—that is, the Buddhism of Southeast Asia), for example, deny the existence of both a personal God and a human soul, yet they are certainly religious, since they acknowledge the sacred. Reform Jews are often agnostic in regard to afterlife, but they too are undeniably religious, since they are committed to the sacred. Members of the Society of Friends (**Quakers**) and practitioners of **Zen** give no place to ritual, but they are religious beyond doubt, since they pursue communion with the sacred. Moreover, religious traditions differ from one another in their descriptions of the sacred. They may attempt to speak of the sacred literally, figuratively, or mythically—or not at all. In the last analysis, however, the sacred still remains pivotal and indispensable.

RELIGION CONCRETELY EXEMPLIFIED

The religious activities of others may appear to us as alien, bizarre, incredible, scandalous, dehumanizing, or utter nonsense when we judge them in the light of our own bias or through the filter of our own religious or nonreligious lens. It is important for us to realize that others may judge our point of view just as harshly and unsympathetically as weird, strange, or dangerous. Our holiday for recreation and fun may be another's holy day for fasting and repentance. Our spontaneous gesture of offering hospitality to a friend may be another's ritual symbol for worshipping a goddess.

Nonetheless, it is usually easy for us to identify a phenomenon as religious, especially if it is public. We may come in contact with the religious impulse across a broad spectrum of traditional structures. Since, however, we are focusing in this book upon the spiritualities of Judaism, Christianity, Islam, Hinduism, and Buddhism, we shall draw our examples exclusively from those five traditions.

We may not be aware of a Jewish associate's religion when he is away from work, fasting all day on **Yom Kippur,** but we surely witness a religious practice if we attend his adolescent son's solemn **bar mitzvah** (the ceremonial admission of a Jewish boy to legal adulthood). We may not notice that a Catholic co-worker punctuates her workday with silent memorized prayers, but we will collide head on with her prayer life if we are guests at her Nuptial **Mass.** We are probably oblivious of the Muslim who recites verses of the **Quran** ("recital") in his home, but we experience the full impact of his Islamic faith if we are guests at his sacrificial-lamb banquet on **Id al-Adha** (Feast of the Sacrifice). We may unknowingly pass a Hindu who meditates as he waits for a bus, but we cannot fail to observe members of the Society for the Promotion of Krishna Consciousness as they dance for joy in an airport and chant their mantra to Lord **Krishna,** *"Hare Krishna, hare, hare!"* We might be uninformed about a Buddhist teacher's practice of deliberately measured breathing and awareness before she begins her day, but we would certainly experience the sacred if we were invited to witness her ordination as a nun.

If we take a vacation trip, we may confront a bombardment of fascinating religious events. We can observe a handful of traditional Jews as they pour forth their hearts in prayer in an ancient synagogue of Safed, not far from the Lake of Galilee in Israel. We can breathe in the sweet aroma of soaring incense while the Ecumenical Patriarch of Eastern Orthodoxy leads the celebration of solemn **vespers** in his chapel at Istanbul. We can visit a nondenominational chapel at Amsterdam International Airport and find a Muslim prostrating himself in surrender over in a corner because it is time for evening prayers. We can drift gently in a boat on the Ganges River near Varanasi at sunrise while Hindu pilgrims bathe devoutly, sons arrange for the cremation of their parents' remains on a ghat, and a holy man circumambulates a nearby tree in homage to its spirit. We can explore the suburbs of Bangkok and see lines of Buddhist monks in their saffron robes leaving their monastery with eyes downcast and bowls in their hands as they go forth silently to beg for that day's food.

Christianity places a strong emphasis upon **orthodoxy** ("right faith") in God's self-disclosure, together with correct interpretation and formulation of what that revelation implies. **Evangelical** Protestant Christians, for instance, devotedly accept in all literalness the Word of God that they discover in the pages of their **infallible** Bibles. Catholic Christians accept without reservation the **dogmas** (doctrinal formulations) of their Church's infallible **magisterium** (teaching authority). Non-Christian religions stress **orthopraxis** ("right action") in regard to what adherents believe to be a sacred plan for human living. The traditional Jew, for example, considers someone who does not do God's will in his or her life as more objectionable than the atheist, who only denies God's existence on a theoretical level. Islam takes its proper name from the very word *Islam* ("submission"), and it is the foremost duty of every Muslim obediently to perform Allah's will. For the Hindu, **Dharma** ("eternal religious law") is preeminently a practical law that encompasses the whole of human action, so that Hinduism is scarcely distinguishable from Indian culture. Hindu Dharma constitutes an everyday way of life for home and marketplace as well as for temple. The Buddha rejected speculative questions about the existence of the gods or the nature of Nibbana as irrelevant to religion and a distraction, since religion involves determination to work out your own salvation. He concentrated upon transmitting his practical **Dhamma** (the Buddha's message of universal truth) as the technique for achieving liberation from suffering and rebirth.

All of the world religions in their earliest history nourished their adherents on a living stream of oral tradition. Priests, prophets, or sages passed on their messages of salvation from generation to generation. The old initiated the young into their belief system and all that it demanded of them. In the course of time, sacred writers committed the distilled essence of their tradition to written form (scriptures), in order that their liturgical leaders might communicate it to believers during communal worship. Thus hearing and celebration nourished communities of faith.

After many centuries, the Jews recorded their traditions in the thirty-nine books of the Hebrew Bible. The Christians appropriated the **Hebrew Bible,** reinterpreted it as **Old Testament** in light of their faith in the risen Jesus, and gradually composed the twenty-seven books of the **New Testament.** The Muslims determined the **canon** (definitive edition) of the Quran, with its 114 **suras** (chapters), less than twenty-five years after the death of Muhammad (632 C.E.), and it has constituted the heart of Islamic life and worship practically from the beginning. The Hindus also entrusted their tradition to writing over many centuries in an immense body of scriptures known as the **Vedas.** The Buddhists, several centuries after the death of the Buddha, created the **Tipitaka** ("three baskets") of the **Pali Canon.**

Religion is always comfortably at home in the world of the symbolic and the intuitive, and virtually every religion has created sacred gestures. These nonverbal yet communicative signs serve as bridges to establish communion with the divine Other. Thus, the history of religions discloses an extensive reservoir of sacred tokens, places, persons, objects, and times, all of which have become channels to the world of the numinous. Rites of passage that celebrate critical stages of life such as birth, puberty, marriage, and death are particularly prominent ceremonies in religious life.

The bodily sign is perhaps the most spontaneous and natural of all religious symbols. Frequently it possesses much more content than the spoken word, even if it occasionally requires the accompaniment of interpretative speech. For example, individuals at prayer can bow the head, incline the torso, or lie face down upon the floor in prostration. A whole community can walk solemnly in procession, or a solitary celebrant can lead a congregation with stylized postures and bodily movements. Devotees can lift up their eyes, extend their arms, and fold their hands or turn them upward. People can pray while kneeling, give testimony while standing, or meditate while sitting in the lotus position with eyes half-closed, hands on the lap, thumbs gently touching, and legs crossed over each other.

Pentecostal Christians firmly impose their hands upon the heads of the sick for whom they pray. Muslims who make the **hajj** ("pilgrimage") to Mecca walk rapidly back and forth in memory of Hagar, because she ran frantically in search of water for her son, Ismail. Eastern Orthodox priests trace the sign of the cross from right to left over their congregations as they invoke the blessing of the **Trinity** in the name of the Father, of the Son, and of the Holy Spirit. Buddhist laypeople in Sri Lanka celebrate joyously every year when an elephant carries a relic of the Buddha's tooth publicly through the streets. The Catholic pope follows at the end of a solemn and colorful procession of attendants, clerics, abbots, bishops, and cardinals into St. Peter's Basilica in Rome. Traditional Jews rock back and forth in a gentle enthusiasm as they pour forth lengthy prayers in their synagogues.

Religious traditions also take shape about sacred places where the numinous has disclosed itself. Some of these settings are naturally evocative, even for observers of other persuasions. A Jew can feel the sense of sacred space in a Gothic cathedral. A Muslim can reverberate to a massive statue of the god **Shiva** on an island near Bombay. A Christian can be genuinely awestruck by the exquisite serenity of Buddhism's **Daibutsu**, "the Great Buddha" at Kamakura, Japan.

It is not difficult to intuit the deeper significance of geological features that centuries of arduous pilgrimage have hallowed: Croagh Patrick in Ireland, Mount Tabor in Israel, or the Meteora in Greece. We do not need to believe in Hinduism in order to appreciate the purificatory impact of the Ganges River as it glows magnificently in the radiance of a new dawn. Even casual tourists in Paris who visit Notre Dame cathedral may gasp and feel themselves irresistibly borne aloft by pointed arches that soar ever upward, seeking out heaven itself. Explanation is often not possible, but neither is it always required.

Transcendent meaning has informed other places, because believers associate particular historical events or nonhistorical myth with them. For Muslims, the **Kaba,** a large cube with a black rock in one corner, is the "center of the world" since Islam teaches that Ibrihim and Ismail built it long ago for the glory of Allah. Jerusalem is "the Holy City" because of its enduring meaning for Jews as the location of David's city and Solomon's Temple, for Christians as the site of Jesus' death and resurrection, and for Islam as the place from which Muhammad ascended by night to heaven. Rome is "the Eternal City" for Catholics since Rome possesses the tombs of Christianity's foremost apostles, Peter and Paul. A surviving Bodhi tree at Bodh Gaya in India marks the hallowed spot where Siddhatta Gotama once sat, received his enlightenment, and arose as awakened, the Buddha. Eastern Orthodox monks have for 1,600 years inhabited St. Catherine's Monastery on Mount Sinai, which they built in this remote place precisely because they wished to commemorate Moses' giving of the Torah to the Israelites.

Religious people can also encounter the sacred through a person or object that embodies it. The Buddhist accumulates merit by feeding the monk who appears at her door daily. The Hindu seeks out a guru for guidance in Vedic wisdom. The Catholic confesses her sins to Christ through a priest and receives Christ's forgiveness through the priest's mediating absolution. The Muslim reads the Quranic Word of Allah in the beautiful calligraphic inscriptions that adorn the walls of his mosque. The Eastern Orthodox Christian views her holy icons as windows opening out into the world of the resurrection and also as channels of the divine breaking back into this world. Tibetan Buddhists view the Dalai Lama as a living conduit of holiness, and they find aid for prayer through bells, mandalas, flags, and wheels. A Jewish family claims as their own the saving meaning of Israel's Exodus by eating the Passover meal. An extended Hindu clan sets aside a whole week in order to walk on pilgrimage to a revered temple of the beautiful goddess **Parvati** in Varanasi.

Religious symbols of the sacred appeal to all the senses. Catholics respond to liturgical colors such as violet during penitential seasons and then to white or red during major festivals. Protestants resonate to the sound of scriptural readings, sermons, and stirring hymnody. Eastern Orthodox Christians are uplifted by the aroma of incense and clinking of bells when the deacon swings his thurible aloft. No Jew can describe the taste of sweet Sabbath wine and all it connotes from a thousand celebrations. No Hindu can account for the sober inebriation of her con-sciousness upon offering the gift of fragrant flowers to the god Krishna at her favorite shrine. No Muslims can communicate the deep spiritual feel-ings experienced when they observe the strict fast of **Ramadan.**

Even time itself may manifest the sacred. Profane time and sacred time lie parallel to each other, and the religious festival or fast creates a bridge between the two. There is an acute difference between the ordinary time that ticks on routinely and the peak moments of *kairos* ("decisive op-portunity"), when the divine implodes into the secular for a few precious instants that defy all telling. Consider how other is the experience of time for the Pentecostal who gives herself to a prayer service far into the night. The Muslim who stands before Mount Arafat all afternoon is not on ordi-nary time, because he is sharing in a foretaste of Judgment. Fourteen hours of sitting and practicing Zen do not seem like fourteen hours to the Buddhist monk. The hours from 12:00 to 3:00 P.M. on Good Friday have a different texture for the Christian who meditates upon the crucifixion of Christ. For the Jew, the high point of the week is the seventh day, the Sabbath Queen, when God's eternity breaks through into human time and transforms the very meaning of its hours.

Religion can be a profoundly communal experience. For example, there is the psalmody of Catholic nuns, assembled by the dozens for monastic choir in the Rhineland, and there is the joyous enthusiasm of Muslims, gathered by the millions for the pilgrimage at Mecca. There is the affection of a Jewish family with a small group of friends, celebrating a marriage in Brooklyn, and there is the hope of a large Hindu community that shares life in an **ashram** outside of Madras. Yet religion can also be as individualistic as the asceticism of a Hindu holy man who wanders silently amidst the teeming crowds of Calcutta or the "skill in means" of a Buddhist laywoman in Burma as she provides food and clothing for her family.

Religion can be as public as the midday prayers of Muslims in the streets of Tangiers, the coronation of the queen by the Anglican Archbishop of Canterbury, or the quasi-martial hymnody of a Salvation Army band in San Francisco. It can also be as private as the Bible study of a born-again Christian in her bedroom in Dallas, the devotion of a Hindu homemaker at her *puja* shrine in New Delhi, or the practice of Zen by of a busy chief executive officer in his Tokyo office.

It is a commonplace for many of us to observe that life is plagued by interior disquiet. Although we may enjoy a modicum of success at var-ious levels of our experience, many of us still feel a spiritual malaise deep within ourselves at the core of our being, an anonymous perception that all is not quite right. Although we may enjoy fleeting satisfactions of mind and body from time to time, some of us still remain men and women of "quiet desperation" in our heart of hearts. We often confront a disheartening burden of stress, discordance, and alienation. Many of us conclude that there must be something radically "out of whack" within us. Others among us are troubled by a lack of connection, an existential *angst*, a wrenching of the spirit—even a vague disquiet because we do not quite fit into the universe.

Yet we thirst for the fullness of life and truth and love unendingly. Although we can experience our personal history only in a piecemeal way from moment to moment, we still want to live forever. Although we feel victimized by Madison Avenue "hype," journalistic manipulation, political equivocation, and institutional deceit, we still hunger to grasp the whole truth. Although we sometimes feel trapped in a narcissistic nightmare, we still long for a liberating love of the unmitigated good.

Religious persons among us sometimes determine that it is futile to retreat into the prison of their own egos. They decide that they must turn upward, outward, and beyond themselves, because nothing short of the boundlessly absolute can slake their thirst. They have become convinced that human life is essentially a quest for ultimate serenity through self-transcendence—at least through self-donation in service of others. They long finally to cross over from distress to a calm haven—from tormenting conflict of soul, spirit, and body to an all-pervasive peace.

The world religions offer their various ways for fulfilling this human need, and they each proclaim union with an ultimately sacred Reality as the sure and proved remedy for the human predicament. Each world religion presents a well-trodden path by which people may pass from self-centeredness to other-centeredness, where a transcendent "peace of mind," or "peace of soul," awaits those who persevere. All the world religions insist that without religion we cannot be integrally whole, because we are in trouble at the deepest level of our fragile and mortal being. Judaism, Christianity, and Islam emphasize saving faith; believers try to appropriate what prophets have received from God. Hinduism and Buddhism focus upon enlightenment; believers try to attain what sages have realized within themselves. No matter how the various religions may categorize the existential challenge of being human, however, they all agree that we desperately need the saving assistance, redemption, or liberation that only religion can provide.

All world religions, therefore, offer peace to those who faithfully follow their "way." This peace surpasses human comprehension, yet it lies as a core value within each world religion, not only as a treasure to be pursued but also as a gift to be possessed and enjoyed even now by way of foretaste. Peace is often the priceless treasure to which many religious people appeal when they wish to proselytize others or to vindicate their own conversion and perseverance in the first place. Religion's peace may be the serenity of reconciliation after estrangement, the repose of understanding after chaotic darkness, or the calm of self-possession after inner tumult and division. From other perspectives, religion's peace can be the conviction of personal dignity after just vindication or the tranquility of hope after the death of a loved one. In its finest hour, religion's peace can be the happy resolution of dangerous conflict among individuals or nations, when people accept the demands of a powerful religious theme such as covenant, love, submission to God, truth, nonviolence, or compassion. For this reason, every religion offers its vision or worldview as an indispensable light for wayfaring human beings, who must complete life's often dark and uncharted journey.

Those who follow theistic religions believe that it is the Creator's will that every individual should become fully human. In this case, human completion redounds to the Creator's good pleasure. Those who follow nontheistic religions depend upon their own resources as they seek their fulfillment through liberation from all the chains that enslave them to the wheel of rebirth. In this instance, human fulfillment involves unimaginable bliss apart from a divine Being.

Religious people often wish to express the feelings of their soul through the body in sacred dance. In the Bible, we read that "Then Miriam, the prophetess, the sister of Aaron, took a timbrel in her hand; and all the women went out after her with timbrels and dancing" (Exod. 15.20). Later in the Bible, we learn that "David and all the House of Israel were making merry before the Lord with all their might, with songs and lyres and harps and tambourines and castanets and cymbals" (2 Sam. 6.5). In some instances, the dancing is obviously a movement of the body in response to music and rhythm, such as we observe among the **Sufis** of Islam, the **Shakers** of Christianity, or the **Hasids** of Judaism. In other cases, it is more subtle, modest, and ritualized, as we notice in the solemn liturgical processions of Catholic and Eastern Orthodox Christianity and in the monastic ceremonies of both Theravada and **Mahayana** Buddhism.

All the world religions regard marriage in its earthy physicality as a sacred relationship, and they usually celebrate it with a religious rite. For this very reason, the world religions teach reverence for sexual relations between a man and a woman as a holy event that is restricted exclusively to married people. For Eastern Orthodox and Catholic Christians, matrimony is not only a sacred relationship but also a **sacrament,** or **mystery;** and grace (God's sanctifying action) informs the act of marital love. Religious couples commonly speak of "marital spirituality" or "the spirituality of married love."

Buddhists speak of the **arahat** (a person who has become transformed through enlightenment) or the **bodhisattva** (a person who enjoys the transcendent powers of an enlightened being and is destined for Nibbana). Hindus revere the *sannyasin* (itinerant holy man) who has become a realized being. Catholics venerate the saint in whom the risen Christ has completed his sanctifying work through the Holy Spirit and his Seven Gifts: wisdom, understanding, knowledge, counsel, fortitude, piety, and fear of the Lord. They view these endowments as dynamic faculties for action under the overshadowing inspiration of the Holy Spirit. Eastern Orthodox Christians see the graced believer as a new creature, empowered by the divinizing action (**theosis**) of the Holy Spirit. The holy man or holy woman becomes a living conduit of God's power, and both miracles and oracles are to be expected upon encounter with such a person.

RELIGION AND SPIRITUALITY DISTINGUISHED

Religion and spirituality are the two principal topics of this book, and we are now in a position to distinguish them. The two are closely related to each other as natural correlatives, and they are often found together in the same individual. Yet it is clear that they cannot be the same reality, since we can on different occasions find each of them existing somehow apart from the other. We meet people who are religious persons of deep spirituality. We also know that some people can have a genuine spirituality without being religious, while other people can be very religious without having much spirituality.

In the previous chapter, we described spirituality as "the inner meaning of human experience under the impact of a humane worldview." In this chapter, we have come to understand religion as the pursuit of transformation under the impact of a sacred worldview. Religion is clearly a humane worldview: It can lead human beings to become reconciled with one another in righteousness, compassion, and loving service as they journey toward peace. Our next step is to combine both explanations in terms of religious spirituality: *Religious spirituality,* then, *is the inner meaning of human experience as shaped by the pursuit of transformation according to a sacred worldview.* In this light, those who pursue transformation according to a worldview that is humane but not sacred may categorize the inner meaning of their experience as secular spirituality.

Religious spirituality can involve the healing, elevating, and transforming effects of a sacred tradition upon its practitioners. Religious spirituality can work for the human completion of those who practice a religion and seek the fulfilling relationship that it promises. Religious spirituality can be the realization of personal redemption or salvation. All the great world religions understand the production of spirituality to be a central focus and one of their principal goals. The cultivation of spirituality among people is one of the chief reasons why world religions exist and why they do what they do.

As we study each world religion in turn, we need to bear in mind the important distinction between what each religion ideally represents and requires from all its adherents throughout the ages and what individuals concretely appropriate from that religion. We must distinguish between what mainstream authorities claim as faithful to their tradition and what particular folk from different times and regions actually do in apparent ignorance of official canons and dogmas. We are concerned with the approved streams of spirituality that flow from what we may call orthodoxy rather than **heterodoxy,** authenticity rather than aberration.

World religions offer their sacred scriptures and creeds of belief in order to provide guidance, vision, and opportunities for liberation and growth. They also hold up their legal and ethical codes, their holy and heroic figures, their works of devotion and exercises of **asceticism,** their ministerial structures and traditional customs, and much else besides for the expression of the religious impulse. All of religious life, however, is ordered ideally toward a more complete spirituality and a more perfect humanity. Indeed, for most persons it constitutes the privileged method of choice for realizing life's meaning.

Many religious people of all persuasions believe that they must lead lives inspired by love (or its immediate correlatives such as compassion, nonviolence, or mercy). They are convinced that love is the most creative and productive power in the universe. Love is the soul of self-abnegation and the thrust of self-donation. Love is the communion of life that symbols seek to embody, married people long to consummate, and children must receive before all things. Love is the core of forgiveness, the universal medicine, and the nourishment of hope. Love initiates conversions, reconciles the estranged, and crowns all virtues. Jews, Christians, Muslims, Hindus, and Buddhists in their best moments can estimate the depth and authenticity of their spirituality in direct proportion to their loving service of others.

World religions have endured and flourished only because their leaders have on the whole provided viable channels and supportive structures toward authentic spirituality. The great prophets and reformers ultimately have exposed anything short of this as empty formalism and hypocrisy. The whole point of reformation movements has been to reunite spirituality and religion in reciprocal dependency as ideal and reality, vital power and active outpouring, interior meaning and exterior structure.

Religion needs spirituality for its health and authenticity. Otherwise, religion's practice degenerates into ritualistic formalism. Its institutional allegiance is reduced to ethnocentric tribalism, and its faith commitment becomes indistinguishable from social convention, pragmatism, magic, tabooism, or superstition. Without spirituality, individuals may act out their religion merely for the sake of privilege and economic advancement.

There is a marvelous consensus among the world religions about the necessity of human conversion, beginning again, starting anew toward one's ideals. They all insist that we must transcend our limitations and center ourselves knowingly, lovingly, and freely upon the sacred, however we may understand that mystery. Our birth into this world signals the beginning of a lifelong process of becoming fully human through death to self (or the illusion of self) and life for others. Completed humanity, religious development, and a transforming spirituality coalesce within a single vision.

MATERIAL FOR DISCUSSION

1. Give an example from your own experience or from your historical knowledge of someone who in your judgment is very spiritual, although not professedly and actively religious. What are the outstanding qualities of this person?

2. Give an example of an acquaintance who in your judgment is a very spiritual person precisely because he or she is professedly and actively religious. What are the outstanding qualities of this person?

3. From your own experience of religion and of religious people, develop your own practical description of religion as such.

4. What do you think is the relationship between spirituality and religion? Is it direct and immediate or merely incidental?

SUGGESTIONS FOR FURTHER READING

Cunningham, Lawrence, et al. *The Sacred Quest: An Invitation to the Study of Religion.* 2d ed. Englewood Cliffs, N.J.: Prentice-Hall, 1995. A particularly readable introduction to religious studies, treating such topics as "The Nature of the Sacred," "Ritual," and "Sacred Communities."

Schmidt, Roger. *Exploring Religion.* 2d ed. Belmont, Calif.: Wadsworth, 1988. A well-organized undergraduate textbook that presents all the various facets of religion in a most interesting way.

Smart, Ninian. *Worldviews: Cross-Cultural Explorations of Human Beliefs.* 2d ed. Englewood Cliffs, N.J.: Prentice-Hall, 1995. An excellent study of religion in terms of its multiple dimensions: experiential, mythic, doctrinal, ethical, ritual, and social.

Wilson, Andrew, ed. *World Scripture: A Comparative Anthology of Sacred Texts.* New York: Paragon House, 1995. A handy anthology of sacred writings drawn from all the world's religions and arranged according to themes such as "Ultimate Reality and the Purpose of Human Existence," "Evil, Sin, and the Human Fall," and "Salvation and the Savior."

3
Religious Spirituality and Four Great Teachers

Moses was keeping the flock of his father-in-law Jethro, the priest of Midian; he led his flock beyond the wilderness, and came to Horeb, the mountain of God. There the angel of the Lord appeared to him in a flame of fire out of a bush; he looked, and the bush was blazing, yet it was not consumed. Then Moses said, "I must turn aside and look at this great sight, and see why the bush is not burned up." When the Lord saw that he had turned aside to see, God called to him out of the bush, "Moses, Moses!" And he said, "Here I am.'" Then he said, "Come no closer! Remove the sandals from your feet, for the place on which you are standing is holy ground." He said further, "I am the God of your father, the God of Abraham, the God of Isaac, and the God of Jacob." And Moses hid his face, for he was afraid to look at God.

—Exod. 3.1–6

The Buddha was staying at a cottage in a wood and he overheard his disciples discussing births. He said: In this fortunate eon the Exalted One has now arisen in the world as a Supreme Buddha. He is of noble birth, born in a clan of nobles, in a family with the surname of Gautama. His chief attendant is Ananda, and two chief disciples Sariputta and Moggallana, a glorious pair. His father is

41

the rajah Suddhodana, whose wife Maya is his mother, and their seat is the town of Kapilavastu. His leaving the world, becoming a recluse, his travail, his enlightenment, his setting the Wheel of Truth rolling, are each on such and such wise.

—Digha 2.1.51–52

Now when all the people were baptized, and when Jesus also had been baptized and was praying, the heaven was opened, and the Holy Spirit descended upon him in bodily form like a dove. And a voice came from heaven, "You are my Son, the Beloved; with you I am well pleased."

—Luke 3.21–22

Read in the name of your Lord who created, created man from an embryo; read, for your Lord is most beneficent, who taught by the pen, taught man what he did not know. And yet, but yet man is rebellious, for he thinks he is sufficient in himself. Surely your returning is to your Lord.

—Quran 96.1–8

In Chapter 1, we arrived at a broad explanation of *spirituality* as the inner meaning of human experience under the impact of a humane worldview. In Chapter 2, we worked out a practical understanding of *religious spirituality* as the inner meaning of human experience as shaped by the pursuit of transformation under the impact of a sacred worldview. In the present chapter, we shall trace the portraits of Moses, called God's man (circa 1350–1230 B.C.E.), Siddhatta Gotama, called the Buddha (circa 560–480 B.C.E.), Jesus, called God's Son (circa 4 B.C.E.–30 C.E.), and Muhammad, called God's messenger (circa 570–632 C.E.), each of them an uncommon master of religious spirituality who stands at the origin of an enduring tradition. (No founding teacher stands at the head of the Brahmanist, or Hindu, tradition.) For each of these teachers we shall present a brief biographical outline and a summary of spirituality in terms of vocation, vision, values, and virtues.

We must acknowledge from the outset, however, that even sympathetic and respectful observers who seek to appreciate religious heroes or heroines other than their own confront an insurmountable difficulty. Personal faith is an indispensable prerequisite for full understanding, and only those who actually follow religious teachers and believe in their authority can grasp every facet of their significance. The more that religious persons believe, the more they understand; the more that religious persons give themselves to personal engagement, the more profoundly they comprehend the implications of their religious commitment. On the other hand, our best efforts to appreciate religious leaders without the appropriate faith will prove inadequate to the task. There is simply no way for us fully to penetrate into their significance from the "outside."

Granting that our best efforts at understanding will fall short, we must still try our best to imagine the traditional context that gives them meaningful perspective. We must seek, in other words, to appreciate these four men as clothed by living belief systems. Thus, we shall treat Moses' encounter with God in the desert near Mount Horeb in terms of Jewish faith as a valid **theophany** ("appearance of God"), and we shall regard Gotama's experience under the Bodhi tree in terms of Buddhist belief as an authentic enlightenment. By the same token, we shall grant the significance of Jesus' death and resurrection in terms of Christian faith as redemptive, while we shall accept Muhammad's call to be God's messenger in terms of Islamic faith as unquestionably true. In this way we shall not need to qualify each belief system with such clumsy and neutral disclaimers as "so it is believed," "according to their point of view," "supposedly," or "allegedly." We shall simply relate the remembered story of each great teacher as his followers cherish it.

MOSES, THE PROPHET: THE GREAT TEACHER OF JUDAISM

The Life of Moses

The Jews speak of Moses as *Moshe Rabbenu* ("Moses, our teacher"), the greatest of the prophets and the most memorable figure in Jewish history. His life was uncommon from the beginning. He grew up not among his own Israelite people (the Twelve Tribes of Israel), who were enslaved in Egypt, but as the adopted son of an Egyptian princess, who gave him the opportunity to study "all the wisdom of the Egyptians." After Moses reached adulthood, however, he killed an Egyptian guard who had been beating an Israelite slave. Moses thereupon escaped from Egypt into the harsh desert of Midian, where he became a shepherd in the employ of Jethro, his father-in-law. It was while keeping his solitary watch one day in the desert that he had an enlightenment-conversion experience that would radically affect both his own life and the subsequent history of religion. Moses beheld an apparition of the living God of Abraham, Isaac, and Jacob, blazing up through the flames of a burning bush.

It was on this never-to-be-forgotten occasion that God revealed his proper name, *YHWH*. (Authors occasionally provide vowels to this **tetragrammaton,** or "word of four letters," so that it reads in Roman letters as **Yahweh.** Traditional Jews in their reverence avoid pronouncing the sacred name. Consequently, they substitute the title **Adonai,** or "LORD," when they address God in prayer or worship and **Ha Shem,** or "the Name," when they refer to God in other circumstances.) God then commanded Moses to lead the Israelites out of Egyptian slavery into the Promised Land of Canaan. Moses knew his limitations as a speaker, and he felt that he sorely lacked the leadership skills that he would need if he was to command the Twelve Tribes of Israel. Yet God promised God's providential presence to Moses at every step, and so Moses finally accepted his extraordinary commission.

Moses returned to Egypt, where, after many divinely wrought wonders, he was able to liberate the Israelites from the pharaoh's cruel oppression. Moses then led them out of Egypt through the Red Sea (or Reed Sea), which miraculously parted for the safe passage of the Israelites but swept back to entrap the Egyptian soldiers in their chariots. Three months later, Moses entered into extended dialogue with God on Mount Sinai. Thus Moses gradually learned the way of the Torah that would lead to the salvation and sanctification of the Jews as God's holy people.

God authorized Moses to mediate the **covenant** (an alliance or agreement) whereby Israel became God's own precious possession—not because the Israelites were a great people, because, in fact, they were the "smallest of peoples," but just because God loved them. The Twelve Tribes of Israel (from whom the Jewish people and their religion, Judaism, later emerged) for their part were to become holy as the LORD, their God, was holy. The Israelites were to commit themselves to the faithful observance of the Torah with its 613 *mitzvot* (commandments). By following the way of the Torah, the Israelites were to bear witness among all the nations to God's holiness. In particular, the Israelites were to keep the Sabbath rest every week and celebrate the Passover meal annually as a perpetual memorial for all that God had done for them. Moses' pinnacle experience occurred while he was standing in the cleft of a rock on Mount Sinai: Moses beheld God's glory, and yet Moses lived!

When Moses descended from Mount Sinai, his skin glowed radiantly with blinding light, so that the Israelites could not bear to gaze upon him. Michelangelo's marble carving of Moses (to be found today in the Roman church of San Pietro in Vincoli) remotely suggests the awesome power of Moses' newly transfigured presence. Moses' gravest trial extended over the next forty years, during which he had to endure the continuous rebellion of his "headstrong" people. Joshua was his special friend and lieutenant. God accompanied the Israelites constantly, manifesting the divine presence as a pillar of cloud by day and a pillar of fire by night. God cared for them, supplying them with water from a rock and miraculous **manna** (a breadlike substance) from heaven. Despite God's wondrous provision for their needs, however, the Israelites never ceased to complain to Moses about the hardships that they had to suffer in the inhospitable desert. Again and again, Moses had to plead with God to demonstrate merciful love and forgive the rebellious people.

Finally, Moses died in advanced age, shortly after he had guided his people to the very threshold of the Promised Land. The Israelites buried him in an unmarked grave on Mount Nebo. Moses has lived on in the collective memory of the Jewish people, however, as their unparalleled leader, their teacher of the Torah, and their mediator before God. Moses became the instrument through whom God transformed a horde of runaway slaves into Israel, God's holy people. Moses became the prophet of God's self-disclosure. Consequently, Moses became the source of an oral and literary tradition and provided a new paradigm for divine-human relationships.

The Spirituality of Moses

Vocation   God called Moses to be the prophet of the Sinai covenant. Moses somehow experienced the awe-inspiring presence of God and "heard" God speaking. We cannot begin to imagine the other-worldly psychology of such an encounter. Even the biblical author falls back upon mythic language. The image of blazing fire with its effulgent light and radiant heat poignantly suggests a revelation of the absolutely sacred, ultimate, and transcendent One, somehow becoming humanly accessible. Moses came to see the cosmos in a new way, illumined by a radically different light. Thereafter, Moses was a chosen vessel of God, a man who belonged to God, and Moses could never be the same again. His single passion became a jealousy for God's exclusive claim upon Israel's worship, and his all-consuming desire became the performance of God's will. Moses proclaimed God's Word indefatigably without counting the cost and became the quintessential prophet, the man totally at God's disposal.

Vision   Moses' sacred worldview found its roots in the way of the Torah, the saving plan of God for Israel to become a covenanted people who would bear corporate witness to God's holiness. Moses became a man immersed in God's enveloping presence, a privileged servant who could commune with God as friend communes with friend. Moses spoke God's Word with boldness and challenged God's people to respond obediently. A vessel of election, Moses passed from his state of egocentricity to a transforming God-centeredness.

Moses fulfilled God's will by faithfully walking the way of the Torah and all its commandments. The Torah became Moses' spiritual center of gravity for every thought, word, and deed. The Torah provided the fundamental orientation for Moses' activities, infusing them with vital purpose and meaning. Through the Torah, God changed Moses from a retiring shepherd of halting speech into one of the most forceful personalities the world has ever known.

Values   God had disclosed that he is immanently present within the forces and rhythms of nature, yet transcendentally distinct from them all. Moses came to realize that the Lord who was the God of Abraham, Isaac, and Jacob was now also the covenanted God of Israel, the one (*echad*) Creator of all that is, the God of steadfast love (*hesed*) and fidelity (*'emet*). Moses encountered the ineffable God, and reverential fear enveloped his heart. Moses realized God's all-encompassing presence, and a vivid mindfulness flooded his mental faculties. Moses met the all-holy God, and the experience intoxicated his senses, purifying and expanding his horizon forever. Moses heard the voice of God thundering within his consciousness, and he somehow survived to recount this mind-shattering event to Israel. Moses wholeheartedly chose God as the First and the Last, the absolute Priority who put every other concern in its place and brooked no rivals.

Moses' preeminent value was God, that absolute Value because of whom all else is valuable, that timeless and unconditioned Value without whom nothing else can possibly be valuable at all. Moses believed that God is eternal Wisdom, and he regarded all that God has made as wondrously true because of God. Moses learned that God is boundless Goodness, and he embraced all that God has produced as very good because of God. Therefore, Moses valued all creatures as reflections of God, their single source: human persons as God's personal image, the entire universe as God's handiwork, and Israel as God's holy people.

Virtues   Moses achieved his full humanity by living "God-wardly." Moses became God's man, who burned with zeal for achieving God's will, the consummate man of God who spoke on behalf of God, labored for the sake of God, and fastened his heart upon God. Moses committed himself unreservedly to the service of God and to the leadership of Israel, God's holy people. Since Moses not only taught the Torah to the Israelites, but also himself walked faithfully in its way, he reaped the fruit of *tzedakah* ("righteousness") that reflected God's holiness. Thus Moses became the preeminent model of *tzedakah* for all later generations of the Jewish people. Moses vindicated God's confidence in him. Moses became a mystic (someone who "directly" experiences the divinely Other), a preacher, a legislator, a diplomat, and an extraordinary leader of human beings. Moses became the instrument through whom God founded a tradition that has already endured for over 3,000 years. Indeed, Moses changed the course of history for all later generations in the Western world.

As the years passed after that first encounter with God in the burning bush, Moses developed all those qualities so necessary for his prophetic vocation: fortitude, decisive judgment, single-minded vision, determination, relentless effort, faithful commitment, and selfless service. He became a servant-leader of moral integrity, interior discipline, humility, and prayerfulness. As God's people passed over from Egypt through the desert to freedom in the Promised Land, God's prophet passed over internally from self-centeredness to transforming union with the transcendent God.

GOTAMA, THE BUDDHA: THE GREAT TEACHER OF BUDDHISM
The Life of Gotama

Siddhatta Gotama, or **Shakya-muni** ("sage of the Shakyas"), was born of royal blood in the Indian city of Kapilavastu at the foot of the Himalayas. Gotama's father deliberately prevented Siddhatta from discovering the pain and misery of the human condition by surrounding him with the lavish luxury of a petty Indian prince. Upon reaching the age of twenty-nine, however, Gotama ventured forth from his palace. To his utter astonishment, he discovered the pains of old age, the sufferings of disease, and the corruption of death that afflict humankind. Gotama was filled with compassion when he realized that pain pervaded every dimension of human life. Therefore, he renounced all self-indulgence, donned the lackluster garb of the seeker, and plunged into the forest. Gotama went on to devote himself for six years to a concentrated quest for religious peace. He experimented with extreme techniques of meditation and physical austerity but he discovered no path to true wisdom and Nibbana.

Shakya-muni finally sat down beneath a Bodhi tree at Bodh Gaya, south of the Ganges River near Varanasi, and he resolved that he would not rise until he had attained enlightenment. When Mara, the evil spirit, assaulted Gotama violently from within, the seeker had to confront soul-searing temptations to abandon his quest. Yet Shakya-muni was victorious over all his trials by the strength of his *maitri* ("friendly love"). He reviewed all his thousands of previous lives and was able to diagnose the root cause of the human predicament as conditioned arising. By "conditioned arising," Gotama meant that everything exists relatively and interdependently with something else; everything proceeds from some previous condition, and nothing exists of itself or without qualification. He concluded that nothing whatever exists absolutely, not even the Godhead of contemporary Indian religion, Brahman. Consequently, it is an ignorant delusion to suppose that we have a permanent soul or self. Indeed, our persistent error about having substantial selfhood (the presumption that we are "somebody" subsistent, a subject separate from the others we encounter) underlies all our cravings and brings about our rebirths. We have no soul or self within us; rather, we are actually *anatta* ("no-self"). Gotama carefully discerned the sure way to cessation of suffering and liberation from the relentless wheel of rebirth. Finally, Gotama passed through a night of ecstasy and arrived at full, penetrating insight into his Dhamma ("the message of universal truth").

When the sun shone the next morning, Shakya-muni arose from his rapture as the triumphant **Buddha** ("the enlightened one"), a master of wisdom who overflowed with compassion for every sentient being. Gotama had discerned the wondrous path to liberation from every fetter. He had come to know the Dhamma, the ultimate truth about the fundamental meaning of life and the certain path to deliverance from life's sufferings. Henceforth, Gotama referred to himself not by his surname but as **Tathagata** ("one who has been thus perfected"), a synonym for *Buddha*.

The Buddha was initially tempted not to teach his Dhamma, since he recognized that it was subtle and difficult to understand. Yet the God Brahma intervened to plead with him to preach the Dhamma for the sake of gods and human beings. Shakya-muni was then able to see that some persons, at least, would accept the Dhamma with joy. In his boundless compassion, therefore, the Buddha agreed to remain and serve his fellow human beings. He resolved to proclaim his Dhamma for their deliverance.

Entrance into the enlightened state had radiantly transformed the Buddha, so that he exuded an irresistibly powerful presence. When passers-by met him on the road, they asked him if he was a magician or, perhaps, a god. Shakya-muni replied, "I am awake." The Buddha made his way back to a cave near Varanasi and found some seekers who had been his earlier companions in austerity. Thereupon, he proclaimed his Dhamma for the first time in a history-making address.

This pivotal discourse of the Buddha (known as the Sermon in the Deerpark) outlined his Four Noble Truths. First, all of life abounds in suffering (*dukkha*). Second, craving desire (*tanha*) causes suffering. Third, suffering ceases if craving desire ceases. Fourth, the middle way to the cessation of craving desire demands right knowledge, right intention, right speech, right conduct, right livelihood, right effort, right mindfulness, and right meditation.

The Buddha went on to institute his **Samgha** (monastic community) as a congregation composed of monks and nuns, with laymen and laywomen as affiliates. The Samgha would be the traditional repository for preserving the Dhamma for generations to come. His closest friend and associate for the rest of his life was to be his cousin, Ananda. Gotama devoted himself tirelessly to preaching his Dhamma for forty-five years; at the advanced age of eighty, he passed over into **Parinibbana** (the state of Nibbana that an enlightened being realizes after death).

The Spirituality of Gotama

Vocation   All the benevolent energies of the universe summoned Gotama through his successive lives to become the Buddha. When he was born for the last time and achieved his saving wisdom, it was a momentous victory for all gods and human beings. Gotama had come into the world for one reason only, and even his father with all his wealth and clever plotting could not prevent Shakya-muni from acknowledging his true vocation. This profound sense of sacred destiny and mission colored his personality totally from the time he began his quest until the time he so wondrously completed it.

Therefore, Gotama, now transformed as the Buddha, was enveloped in a serenity not of this world. He became wondrously disciplined in his passions and detached from all material things. He had clearly entered into a higher dimension of acute awareness, total freedom, and consummate humanity. As Shakya-muni preached his Dhamma and fulfilled his vocation, his spirituality blossomed magnificently. His single purpose in every action and his exclusive focus in every word were to preach his saving message to all who would listen. Over the twenty-five centuries since then, billions of human beings have "taken refuge" in the Buddha, in his Dhamma and in his Samgha, and they have found their life's fulfillment.

Vision Gotama's vision was the middle way of his Dhamma. This worldview was nontheistic on the practical level, since the gods and goddesses were irrelevant to the critical goal of religion: salvation from the wheel of rebirth with its consequent burden of pain. He judged that deities can be of no assistance to human beings seeking salvation, since the gods and goddesses themselves are subject to the wheel of rebirth. Yet Gotama did pursue Nibbana as the one sacred, ultimate, and absolute dimension of reality, and he did propose a nontheistic method by which all people could achieve it for themselves: the Four Noble Truths. If people were willing to enter into what the Buddha had experienced, they would also be enlightened and set free from the craving desires that cause rebirth into the sufferings of this impermanent world. They could then enter into a state of unconditioned peace, serenity, and bliss (Nibbana).

Gotama formulated his unique pursuit of transformation in terms of a middle way, the Noble Eightfold Path. An eminently pragmatic man, he focused upon a most practical method for attaining dispassion, peaceful detachment, and Nibbana. Shakya-muni saw no point in speculating about the nature of Nibbana. People who confront a flooded stream must not distract themselves with questions about the opposite shore; they must concentrate upon crossing the stream without mishap. People who are chained to the wheel of rebirth must not waste their time with discussions about the nature of Nibbana; they must devote all their energies to reaching Nibbana without entrapment. Gotama accepted nothing on faith in the Vedic scriptures or the ministry of the Brahmanical priesthood but assented only to what he could rationally deduce for himself. He placed no trust in gods or goddesses, prayers, rituals, or caste privilege but relied solely upon what he could accomplish by his own efforts. Nor did he demand faith from the disciples who looked to him for guidance; he simply urged them to work out their own salvation with diligence and realize the truth for themselves within themselves.

Gotama was one of the world's greatest pathfinders, a solitary pioneer who forged a tested road to the realm of peace, a pilgrim on a perilous quest for the sacred center, a cosmic wayfarer to the real. Gotama's progress to Nibbana was an odyssey of the spirit: an emancipation from error and a release to the truth, a passing from the conditioned to the unconditioned, a deliverance from suffering to bliss, a liberation from delusion to reality, a transformation from ignorance to wisdom. Shakya-muni himself journeyed from illusory self-preoccupation to a new center of gravity in the ultimate and only Absolute, Nibbana. Having attained his enlightenment, however, he willingly postponed his final entrance into Nibbana and lived on in this world so that he could point the way for others.

Values   The sacred foundation for all of the Buddha's values was Nibbana, the only permanent Reality. Therefore, his primary value was his Dhamma, the correlative truth about Nibbana and how to achieve it. The Buddha esteemed everything else only insofar as it pertained to the Dhamma. He preached the Dhamma to others so that they could receive enlightenment. He gathered disciples and founded the Samgha so that other human beings could follow the Dhamma with its middle way and Four Noble Truths toward their own liberation from suffering. Gotama formulated the Five Precepts in order to promote the moral values implied by the Noble Eightfold Path. He presented them not as abstract formulas for a belief system but as ethical commandments for practical observance: (1) Do not kill, (2) do not take what is not freely given, (3) do not commit unchaste acts, (4) do not lie, (5) do not drink intoxicants. The Shakya-muni himself embodied the Dhamma, and he has always been its foremost exemplar. Nevertheless, Shakya-muni could not do for disciples what they had to do for themselves; buddhas (there have been others during other eons) serve only as beacons that light up the way.

Virtues   Gotama's supreme virtues were his wisdom and its correlative, compassion for all sentient beings. In his wisdom, he realized that things are not separated from one another but are necessarily interrelated and interdependent. Therefore, Shakya-muni encompassed all sentient beings in his compassionate embrace. We must appreciate the crucial difference between *pity* and *compassion*. To feel pity is to maintain one's own secure position as one looks down with cool detachment upon another's misery. To have compassion is to share the pain of another by entering into that anguish and assuming it as one's own. Pity is a matter of intellectual concern, while compassion is a matter of heartfelt love.

Gotama consciously identified himself with the suffering of every sentient being, because he knew that he was part of all of them and they were all part of him. He was determined to save not only himself but also as many others as possible. That is why the Buddha decided remain and to remain and teach the Dhamma in this world for forty-five years after he had attained his enlightenment. That is also why he sent missionaries far and wide to proclaim the Dhamma to all who would listen. Gotama's compassion included loving-kindness and sympathetic joy upon the happiness and equanimity of others.

Shakya-muni was a man of compassionate mind and wise heart; his interior bliss radiated through his benevolent gaze. He lived in complete self-possession, dispassionate calm, tranquil serenity, and imperturbable peace. Gotama totally negated any illusion about permanent selfhood with its consequences of self-centeredness, self-importance, self-service, self-defense, self-pity, self-aggrandizement, and self-seeking. He cleansed all greed, hatred, violence, covetousness, jealousy, envy, anger, and deceit from his heart as he attained ethical purity. Shakya-muni was a man altogether liberated in every dimension of his being. He enjoyed this most remarkable freedom because of his selflessness and non-attachment, and his liberty engendered an extremely attractive charisma. Gotama was also a genius of practical skills, a founder of a religious tradition, and a beloved friend to all who approached him. He was teacher, organizer, reformer, founder, abbot, counselor, psychologist, and spiritual physician, all in one. Above all, the Buddha was a man of wisdom, and he shared that wisdom in boundless compassion. Buddhists see in Shakya-muni the greatest man who ever lived.

JESUS, THE CHRIST:
THE GREAT TEACHER OF CHRISTIANITY
The Life of Jesus

As in the case of Moses and Gotama, we have little knowledge of Jesus' youth, which is known as his "hidden life." His mother, Mary, a young Jewish virgin, gave birth to him in Bethlehem in the Roman province of Judea. As a young boy, Jesus subjected himself obediently to Mary and Joseph, his foster father, and he grew up in poverty at Nazareth, an obscure village of Galilee from which no noteworthy person was to be expected. When Jesus was about thirty, he submitted to **baptism** (symbolic washing with water) by his cousin John in the Jordan River, emerged from the water, and heard the voice of God proclaiming: "This is my Son, the Beloved, with whom I am well pleased" (Matt. 3.17b). Jesus then retreated to the Judean wilderness, where he fasted for forty days and meditated upon God's plan for him.

Jesus gradually became convinced that God had called him to be the **Messiah** ("anointed one"), the agent of God's redemptive plan for the Jews. Jesus' first trials revolved about the nature of this messianic role. Was it to be terrestrial, military, and political, or was it to be otherworldly, nonviolent, and spiritual? **Satan,** the evil tempter, tried to convince Jesus that he should follow the easygoing path of a self-serving magician, a wonder worker who would seduce the crowds, or a warrior-king who would achieve political mastery of the world. Jesus resisted Satan, however, and opted for the humble role of a defenseless prophet, dependent upon the gentle persuasive power of the Word.

Jesus seems to have reflected still more deeply upon his full identity, so that he arrived at the most amazing conclusion. In some mysterious way he began to perceive that he enjoyed a unique community and communion of life with God, a connection that other human beings did not and could not completely share, yet a bond so familiar it could only be called filial. Jesus gradually interpreted his intimacy with God as the tender relationship of a son with his loving father, and he learned confidently to address the all-holy Creator of heaven and earth as **Abba** ("Daddy"). Christian disciples have been plumbing the depths of Jesus' mysterious identity ever since.

Jesus went from village to village, preaching his **gospel** ("good news"), usually by narrating stories known as **parables.** He announced that God is a father of incredibly forgiving and compassionate love, whose saving reign has arrived among humankind. Jesus proclaimed that a new era had dawned, and the signs were his wondrous acts of miraculous power. He discerned secrets of the human heart, he calmed the wind and the sea, he multiplied a few loaves of bread and fish so that thousands could eat, and he exorcised demons from those possessed. Jesus became famous particularly as someone who could heal the sick, and, of course, afflicted people flocked to him in large numbers. He relieved all the impairments of those who could not see, could not hear, could not speak, or could not walk. Jesus even cleansed lepers completely of their "living death" and restored them to society. Most impressive of all, he raised the dead to new life in this world on at least three occasions.

Jesus granted even greater joy to people by forgiving them their sins and celebrating meals of friendship with the outcasts of society. In his Sermon on the Mount, Jesus proclaimed that the truly blessed are the poor and the gentle, the merciful and the pure of heart, the peacemakers and

those who mourn, those who hunger for justice and those who are persecuted in the cause of right. Jesus promulgated internal criteria for moral
living, recognizing the central role of the mind and heart as the source of
motive and intention in sinful behavior. Jesus called for a radically new
spirituality of self-denying and indiscriminate love for every member of
the human family, even one's enemy.

Jesus made it clear that the only appropriate response to his message
was to rejoice and convert to a new life according to his revolutionary system: The first will be last, the last will be first, and guests should sit at the
end of the table. It is better to give than to receive. People can find self-
completion only through self-denial. Men and women will know exulta-
tion through humiliation, and they will enter genuine life only through
death. Jesus' disciples would later ponder the actual passage of Jesus himself through crucifixion to resurrection as the ultimate and all-persuasive
validation of this paradoxical doctrine.

Jesus of Nazareth gave himself for the most part to the rural communities of the hard-working poor, the disabled, the disreputable, the rejects
of society, the disenfranchised, and all those whom the social mainstream
had marginalized. He became known as a man who frequented the company of sinners and enjoyed meals with them. Jesus gathered together a
special group of twelve disciples (the Twelve **Apostles**) to be his constant
companions. He gave particular training to the apostle Simon, a special
friend who fulfilled a role similar to that of Joshua for Moses and Ananda
for the Buddha. (Simon, whom Jesus surnamed Peter, went on to become
a "pillar" in the Christian community after Jesus' departure from visible
accessibility in this world; the Petrine Office defines the function of the
pope in Catholic Christianity.)

Jesus spent entire nights in prayerful communion with God. On one
occasion, he climbed a high mountain to pray, and he heard the voice of
his Father again claiming him as God's "Beloved Son." Three of Jesus'
disciples, Peter, James, and John, witnessed the Jewish prophets Moses
and Elijah (who had also encountered God on a high mountain) discussing with Jesus his approaching passage through death to resurrection. Just as Moses was transfigured after encountering God and as
the Buddha gave off a mysterious aura after his enlightenment, so Jesus
became immersed in blinding light. His face shone as bright as the sun
and his garments became whiter than snow. Once again we are dealing
with a theophany, a supernatural experience to which only mythic language can point. Ecstatic joy flooded the consciousness of Jesus' friends
as they witnessed this remarkable event. Time stood still for them, and
they wanted to remain there forever. Jesus seems at this juncture to have

made a new commitment to his messianic vocation, even though his role as humble preacher would now lead to an unimaginably torturous death on a cross. From that moment forward, Jesus set his face steadfastly toward Jerusalem, where he would suffer, die, and rise back to life in glory.

Jesus met his final and most severe trial early in the morning after a final meal with his disciples, as he was praying in the Garden of Gethsemane outside of Jerusalem. He recoiled in terror from the horrors that were to befall him later that day, overcame his terror, and went willingly to his crucifixion. Jesus in some sense foresaw how men would mock him, beat him, spit upon him, scourge him at a pillar, crown him with thorns, force him to carry a heavy cross, and finally nail his hands and feet to that cross. Jesus' victorious resurrection from the dead after his crucifixion constitutes the very core of the Christian faith commitment and the foundation of Christian hope. Jesus revealed himself to his disciples on the first Easter Sunday as the Christ, as the glorified Lord and Savior who fills the universe with his ruling presence.

The Spirituality of Jesus

Vocation   Jesus' spirituality took shape, developed, and flowered as he progressively realized his vocation to be God's Messiah, "the Suffering Servant of the LORD" (Isa. 42.1ff). We may distinguish two poles in this calling: Jesus' filial love of God as his Father and his fraternal love for humankind. First, Jesus was uncompromisingly a man of God, completely dedicated to God, totally at God's disposal. As we have seen, Jesus experienced an even more personal relationship to God as Abba. Such intimacy with the all-holy One was revolutionary in the Jewish tradition that had nourished Jesus' early years. Yet Jesus gave himself unreservedly to prayerful communion with his Abba and embraced God's fatherly will for him by his every thought, word, and action. Second, Jesus was selflessly and vulnerably a man for all others without exception, relating to every man as his brother and to every woman as his sister. His love for others was embodied in his humble service to others, especially in the extreme act of laying down his life for them.

This vocation involved Jesus in a series of paradoxes. He was the messianic king of Israel, but he had no earthly resources of power as the world understands power. Jesus entered into his kingdom through assuming the role of a lowly servant. He possessed his strength through weakness, his authority through obedience, his wisdom through foolishness, and his glorification through self-renunciation. Jesus endured the shame of crucifixion, but he passed over from death to resurrection. His painful service became redemptive love for all who believe in him, a victory of cosmic consequences, and a triumph over Satan, sin, and death.

Vision   Jesus' vision was the way of the **gospel.** Since Jesus began his work more or less consciously as a reformer of Judaism, his basic frame of reference was thoroughly Jewish, the Torah that Moses had delivered to God's holy people from Mount Sinai. For example, Jesus regularly attended synagogue services on the Sabbath, observed the seasonal festivals, and defended the holiness of God's Temple in Jerusalem. He frequently quoted the Torah and commented upon its implications for the human mind and heart. Through meditation, however, Jesus was able to break through to a deeper appreciation of the Torah, a richer and more internalized understanding that he called his gospel: God the Father's wondrous design for the salvation of all humankind. Jesus' vision opened up to a future world in which the Father would re-create all things gloriously. The Father, Jesus announced, willed to establish his reign over his adoptive children within a transfigured universe.

Jesus enthusiastically proclaimed the generous love and mercy of his Father. Jesus himself was filled with happiness upon contemplating this divine benevolence, and he knew that it was the greatest news that people could ever possibly hear. Jesus compared his gospel to a priceless pearl more valuable than any price and to a buried treasure more costly than any plot of land; he expected his hearers universally to respond with joyful gratitude. Instead, Jesus was often disappointed to find only the sick-at-heart, the *anawim* ("poor and lowly in spirit"), and the marginalized accepting his gospel. The end result of his ministry, in fact, was not simply a renewed Jewish tradition but a whole new community for Jews and Gentiles alike, the **Church** (assembled community in Christ) that would eventually be known as the congregation of "the Christians."

Jesus' transformation unfolded through his passage from mortal humanity to Father-centered fulfillment. On the very feast of the Jewish Passover, Jesus suffered death by crucifixion, but he rose from the dead on the following Sunday. Jesus, by dying and rising from the dead, broke through all the barriers that alienated humankind from the Father. God's Holy Spirit filled Jesus' humanity and established him as the Christ (the Anointed One) and the Lord. Jesus' disciples came to believe in him as their risen Savior, the first born from the dead and the first fruits of a new heaven and a new earth.

Values   For Jesus, the sacred foundation of every meaningful value and priority had to be the person of God the Father. He spontaneously revered the awesome expression of the Father's steadfast love and fidelity in the Torah. Jesus also was certain from the Torah that human beings must love God above all things with their whole heart, mind, soul, and strength, seeking God's reign before all things. Jesus surrendered to God as his absolute Value and unrivaled Priority. He taught people to pray by hallowing God's name, accepting God's will, trusting in God for their daily bread, and seeking God's forgiveness for their sins.

Jesus valued human beings before legalisms and material things. That is why Jesus gave first place to the spirit of the Torah over the letter, to purity of intention over ritually perfect performance, and to interior sincerity over exterior exactitude. He was convinced that what mattered were not legal ties but loving relationships between human beings and God and among themselves. Jesus' priorities provoked conflict with the religious authorities when he argued that the Torah was for human beings rather than human beings for the Torah. That is why he taught people to pray by forgiving those who have offended them and seeking God's protection from temptation and all harm.

Jesus valued every human being as a beloved child of his Father. Because of his confidence in the Father's unconditional love for God's children, he was able to mediate the Father's forgiveness to repentant sinners and fill their hearts with the joy of reconciliation. Because of Jesus' conviction that the Father truly cared for people much more than they could possibly imagine, Jesus was able to channel the Father's healing power to those impaired and debilitated by disease.

Jesus also exulted in the beautiful world of nature, from the birds of the air to the animals of the fields, from the trees, bushes, vineyards, and wild flowers to the mountains, valleys, and waters, from the warm sun to the refreshing rain. Jesus treasured all the beauties of creation as the Father's gifts to all human beings indiscriminately. He saw creation as a glorious mirror that reflects the Father's truth and goodness for the edification of all those with eyes to see and ears to hear. Jesus himself discovered the powerful but gentle presence of his Father encircling him from right to left and cradling him every side in the splendid world about him. That is why he was able to draw from everyday life homely parables that spoke powerfully to the human heart.

Virtues   Jesus' disciples were in awe of him as a man of intense prayer who, with an unearthly wisdom, could discern the innermost dispositions and intentions of the people about him. They honored Jesus as a man of integrity who had attained a rare wholeness through self-discipline, fixed purpose, innocent conscience, and a prophet's fiery courage. They admired Jesus as a man of kindness, gentleness, and a peace not of this world that he claimed as "my peace." Indeed, the disciples lived daily with Jesus, walked with him in his travels, heard him speak as nobody had ever spoken before, and witnessed his extraordinary tenderness for the multitudes.

In the end, however, it was still Jesus' supreme virtue, his **agape** (an unconditional love that seeks no return), that attracted the disciples beyond all other considerations. That is why they grew from their initial awe of Jesus through the ever more confident stages of admiration and devotion. The disciples finally came to know that Jesus was a man of love: Jesus' agape reflected his Father's agape. The Father's agape is essentially a love that is boundless, incessant, and absolute; the Father pours out agape boundlessly, incessantly, and absolutely in every act. God's agape is a universal love that reaches out indiscriminately to the just and the unjust alike as pure grace, undeserved and unmerited. God's agape is a creative and redemptive love that offers healing, elevation, and transformation to all who accept it. It is not that the Father loves human beings because they are lovable, since, in fact, human beings are sinful; rather, it is that people become lovable because the Father loves them.

Jesus revealed his own agape throughout his life of selfless service to the needy of every age and station. Indeed, Jesus personified the very **beatitudes** (declarations of blessedness or happiness) that he announced in his Sermon on the Mount (Matt. 5.2–10). In Christian faith, no human being was ever more gentle, more merciful, or more pure in heart than Jesus was. No individual ever worked harder to create peace on earth. Jesus hungered and thirsted for justice, and he endured persecution for his efforts. Jesus proved his agape definitively when he submitted to a cruel death on the cross, dying with a prayer on his lips for the forgiveness of his enemies.

MUHAMMAD, THE MESSENGER: THE GREAT TEACHER OF ISLAM

The Life of Muhammad

Muhammad was born in Mecca on the Arabian Peninsula. Our information about his early years is sketchy, but we know that he became an orphan during early childhood and grew up in the home of his uncle, Abu Taleb, and his cousin, 'Ali. Muhammad matured to manhood in the midst of poverty and illiteracy, a poor relative of the **Quraysh** clan. It was while he was working as a caravan manager for a wealthy widow named Khadija that he acquired his reputation for sterling integrity. People looked up to Muhammad as an honest man and called him al-Amin, "the trustworthy one." They knew that he was a man of justice and honor who would not cheat or steal, a faithful friend who would not lie or break his word.

Some time after his marriage to Khadija at the age of twenty-five, Muhammad began the practice of withdrawing from Mecca to a cave on Mount Hira in order to spend long periods alone in meditation. On one unforgettable day in 610, as he reflected upon the one God of Ibrihim (Abraham), whom the Jews and the Christians worshipped, he suddenly beheld a vision of the angel Jibril (Gabriel), who informed him that Allah ("the God") had chosen him to be his *rasul* ("messenger"). Thereupon Muhammad began to receive from Allah some verses of the Quran, the pure Word of God as recorded in heaven. Muhammad would continue to channel the incomparably beautiful Quran through his mind and heart and voice, a few verses at a time throughout the rest of his life.

Muhammad became aware of the awful reality of Allah's presence, and he could never be the same again: he would gradually become God's possession, God's servant, and even God's friend. We cannot adequately analyze the psychology of prophetic experience, of course, but Muhammad grew into the conviction that he was in intimate contact with Allah, the all-holy One, **al-Rahman** ("the merciful"), **al-Rahim** ("the compassionate"). The all-powerful God had called him to *rasuliyyah* ("messengerhood").

Muhammad's first trial was to suffer an overwhelming fear and confusion at the thought that Allah, the almighty Creator of the universe, had actually intervened in his life and spoken within him. Muhammad heard deep within himself Allah speaking his Word in sacred verses, and the divine Word must have caused his throat to burn as it flamed upward and blazed outward. Like Musa (Moses), 'Isa (Jesus), and all the holy prophets of Allah before him, Muhammad felt himself constrained to declare a holy message not his own. He could not but cry out with all the strength within him.

Yet Muhammad's natural humility provoked a sense of profound unworthiness and even terror in his heart. How could he be called to be a *rasul* of God? He feared that perhaps he was bewitched. After he recounted his experience to his wife, Khadija, however, he received her assurance that he was not deceived. Moreover, 'Ali, Muhammad's cousin and future son-in-law, also believed in Muhammad's *rasuliyyah*. Muhammad then surrendered in total submission to God's call, and he began to preach. Despite the many persecutions and sufferings that were to follow him throughout the rest of his life, Muhammad courageously fulfilled his prophetic mission to the last. Muhammad became the ultimate messenger of Allah in Islam, God's perfect and final religion.

Between 610 and 632, Muhammad gradually transmitted to the Arabs Allah's Quran, and scribes committed the verses to writing in a variety of ways. When Muhammad had rendered Allah's Quran completely, the book contained 114 suras (chapters), and it revealed God's plan for all human beings to offer submission (Islam) to God. Despite the fact that Muhammad could neither read nor write, he was able to channel without adulteration Allah's Quran in Arabic verses of unequaled eloquence and inimitable beauty. Muhammad was not an author but simply a messenger; he contributed to the Quran neither letter nor word, neither grammatical quality nor literary style.

Muhammad proclaimed to the people of Mecca the absolute oneness of Allah and the terrible evil of idolatry—that is, "associating partners" with God. Furthermore, Muhammad insisted, if God is one, then God's human creatures must relate justly to one another as members of a single family, and the strong must not oppress the weak. With all the zeal and courage of Israel's ancient prophets, Muhammad challenged the affluent merchants of Mecca to practice social justice toward the poor, the widows, and the orphans. Muhammad warned that the world would end with a fearful judgment: Those who embraced Islam and became faithful Muslims would rise from death to the happiness of Paradise, but those who rejected Islam would be condemned to the eternal fires of hell. It is not surprising that Muhammad gradually provoked the Meccans' opposition, and eventually he aroused their murderous hatred.

When Muhammad's enemies decided to kill him in 622 C.E., Muhammad and Abu Bakr, his companion, emigrated to Yathrib, a city that received him enthusiastically and accepted his message. The inhabitants of Yathrib became the first Islamic **umma** (community), and the year 622 became the point of departure for the new Islamic calendar. Yathrib itself acquired the name of **Medina al-Nabi** ("city of the Prophet"), or Medina for short. An intermittent war broke out between Medina and Mecca, with shifting fortunes, but in 630, Muhammad and the Muslims were able to enter Mecca and claim the city for God. Muhammad himself personally destroyed the idols that had desecrated Mecca's holy Kaba, the sacred sanctuary that Ibrihim and Ismail (Ishmael) had built, and he rededicated it to the worship of God alone.

During the last ten years of Muhammad's life, he served as the first **imam** (leader of prayer) at his humble Medina home, which functioned as the first *masjid,* or mosque ("place of prostration"). Muhammad became a noble model of Muslim piety and religious practices, as summarized in the Five Pillars of Islam: *shahadah* (witness), *salat* (prayers), *zakat* (alms-giving), *sawm* (fasting), and hajj (pilgrimage).

Muhammad felt God's presence within him. Muhammad came to the unshakable conviction that Allah was speaking his all-powerful words through Muhammad's mind, heart, and voice. Muhammad felt he possessed no option; he had to utter these words authoritatively, fearlessly, and confidently. He progressed from seeking God to finding God, from persecution to vindication, from unreserved submission to Allah to becoming Allah's noble messenger. Muhammad even received the unique experience of "ascending" on a magnificent animal to each of the seven heavens, where he conversed with prophets of bygone ages.

It was not Muhammad but God who founded Islam. Allah called Muhammad to serve as his *rasul.* Muhammad was, indeed, an extraordinary man among men, a religious hero who changed the whole course of history, a rare kind of prophet, who during his own lifetime saw the vindication of his *rasuliyyah* and the acceptance of Islam by all the tribes of Arabia. Yet Muhammad was no more than a mortal human being, and Islam has made a concerted (and largely successful) effort to avoid deifying him. Muhammad's role in Islam was analogous not to that of Jesus in Christianity but to that of Moses in Judaism. Muhammad was neither a divine person nor a mediating priest between God and men, neither a ruling lord nor a saving redeemer. Muhammad was simply an instrument of the merciful God who alone is the agent of all wonders and the giver of all blessings. Therefore, Muslims have offered their submission and worship never to Muhammad but always to God alone.

Muhammad was "the Seal of the Prophets," which means that he was the last in a long line of prophets that stretches back to Adam. Muslims await no new prophet after Muhammad, since Muhammad sealed all prophecy; indeed, Muslims expect no further revelation beyond the Quran, since God has disclosed in the Quran all that human beings will ever need to know.

Muhammad's historical role has been that of an unrivaled exemplar of righteous Muslim behavior and devout Muslim piety. For that reason, Muslims are acutely interested in Muhammad's **sunna** ("customary practice"), as recounted in the **hadith** (a collection of words and events from the life of Muhammad), a second source after the Quran itself for shariah. Muslims revere Muhammad as the greatest Muslim, pray for Allah's peace (*salam*) upon him, recount stories about him, and try to imitate his example.

The Spirituality of Muhammad

Vocation   Muhammad was a man of rare and outstanding gifts. In the course of his life, he excelled as a charismatic leader, a religious genius, a **mystic,** a preacher, a reformer, a diplomat, a legislator, and even a military strategist. Muhammad's divine calling to the *rasuliyyah* in 610 C.E., however, was the central event in his life, and this very rare vocation (God has also called a few others, such as Moses and Jesus, to the *rasuliyyah*) defined his radical identity and became the distinguishing mark of his spirituality. From that point forward, Muhammad lived utterly at God's disposal. The call to *rasuliyyah* altered the deepest recesses of his consciousness, informed his self-image, inspired his mission, energized his purpose, and fortified his resolve. Muhammad devoted all his time, mental acumen, practical skill, and physical stamina to delivering the Quran, proclaiming God's oneness and mercy, opposing all rival gods, promoting justice for the wronged, and gathering the Arabs together into one umma. Like Moses and Jesus before him, Muhammad became God's special possession, and he lived out the details of his life accordingly.

Vision   Muhammad's vision was the straight path of surrender to Allah, and its framework was Quranic in its every dimension. Allah, the one and only God, who is the merciful and compassionate Lord of the Worlds, creates, conserves, and rules all things with infinite wisdom, irresistible power, and immeasurable mercy. God's holy will is absolute and beyond human questioning. Allah created angels as well as people, but the pinnacle of God's earthly creation is humankind. God has revealed in the Quran an all-embracing and practical way of life for the ennobling of God's beloved human creatures, a straight path that human beings must struggle faithfully to follow. Above all, people are to accept Islam and realize their human fulfillment through submission to God's holy will. Men and women must believe in God, observe the laws of the true religion, destroy all idols, and promote justice for the poor and needy.

Muhammad's pursuit of personal transformation unfolded through a submission to Allah's will that centered Muhammad's being undividedly upon God. Muhammad himself perfectly adhered to Islam, and he modeled that religion for the whole Islamic tradition, with nobility, boldness, devotion, self-discipline, and fortitude. Muslims have remembered how Muhammad observed the Five Pillars of Islam. In his personal life, Muhammad confessed his faith continuously: "There is no god but Allah, and Muhammad is the messenger of Allah." Muhammad led the Muslim community in prayers five times a day. Muhammad gave alms to the poor and needy. Muhammad fasted during the holy month of Ramadan. Muhammad made his own pilgrimage to the holy city of Mecca more than once as leader of the Muslim people. Muhammad also practiced the **jihad** (struggle; sometimes called a sixth pillar) in his pursuit of the straight path. He not only struggled against internal temptations and every external obstacle; he also personally led the Muslim troops in the defense of Islam against the violent opposition of the Meccans.

Values   Muhammad was a man of passionate commitment, brilliant awareness, and pervasive convictions. Just like Moses and Jesus before him, he must have wondered why nobody else seemed to take God as seriously as he did. He could never allow the overwhelming realities that constituted the priorities of his life to become peripheral or occasional concerns. Muhammad's first priority, of course, was the infinitely mysterious God, the unrivaled value of all values. In Muhammad's consciousness, God held primacy of place, front and center, with absolute precedence before all others, because Muhammad's faith in the one God was decisive and unambiguous: *Allahu akbar* ("God is greater"). Consequently, Muhammad also treasured the Quran as the very Word of God, the incomparably beautiful articulation of Allah's will in Arabic, exquisite in every letter and superb in every phrase. God's will and its Quranic expression alone gave form and meaning to all other concerns. Other values were Muhammad's *rasuliyyah* and the religion of Islam itself. Muhammad especially esteemed human dignity, because he knew that God prized people and was intimately available to them.

Virtues   Muhammad was the quintessential Muslim, the man of total submission who surrendered to God as an obedient servant and went on to enjoy intimacy with God as a beloved friend. Muhammad became a man of practical wisdom, habitual prayer, persuasive speech, indomitable courage, ethical conduct, and rare leadership skills. He united all his gifts and directed them with all his energy toward accomplishing the will of God. Muhammad's supreme virtue was his *taqwa* ("righteousness"), a rich enhancement of his character that founded his actions towards others in justice but also oriented them toward God as expressions of his intensely personal piety. Therefore, Muhammad could enjoy the great fruit that Islam promises to those who submit: peace.

Muhammad's fellow Muslims found him to be an extremely attractive human being, and they loved him as a hero preeminent before all others, a man of tact and generosity, an individual of faithfulness and valor. Muhammad was indeed a person of warm charisma and multiple blessings, yet he maintained a remarkable humility and sincerity through it all. Muhammad proved himself to be a willing instrument in the hands of Allah: He lived for God, organized for God, fought for God, suffered for God, and was ready, if need be, to die for God. Muhammad fastened his gaze upon Allah as the ultimate meaning of all that he lived for and all that he did.

MATERIAL FOR DISCUSSION

1. What do you think is Moses' most significant teaching for your understanding of religious spirituality?

2. The Buddha has been dead for 2,500 years. What do you think is the core reason for his fascination among people today?

3. What do you think is Jesus' most important contribution to religious spirituality?

4. Do you find anything in the teaching and example of Muhammad that is universally applicable to human spirituality, apart from particular religious worldviews?

SUGGESTIONS FOR FURTHER READING

Buber, Martin. *Moses: The Revelation and the Covenant.* New York: Harper Torchbooks, 1958. This work is a classic in religious biography by one of the great Jewish thinkers of the twentieth century it presents a most readable portrait of Moses.

Coomaraswamy, Ananda K. *Buddha and the Gospel of Buddhism.* New York: Harper and Row, 1964. This remarkable study presents a summary of the Buddhist tradition both by narrating the life of Gotama and by comparing his essential proclamation with the mystical experience of Hindus and Christians.

Haight, Roger. *Jesus, Symbol of God.* Maryknoll, N.Y.: Orbis Books, 1999. This volume by a Christian theologian presents an excellent and straightforward summary of contemporary reflection on Jesus of Nazareth.

Watt, W. Montgomery. *Muhammad: Prophet and Statesman.* London: Oxford University Press, 1961. This investigation by an eminent scholar of Islam presents a valuable account of the life of Muhammad, arranged chronologically and presented from a neutral perspective.

4

Jewish Spirituality

The LORD said, "Shall I hide from Abraham what I am about to do, seeing that Abraham shall become a great and mighty nation, and all the nations of the earth shall bless themselves by him? No, for I have chosen him, that he may charge his children and his household after him to keep the way of the LORD by doing righteousness and justice; so that the LORD may bring to Abraham what he has promised him."

—Gen. 18.17–19

He has told you, O mortal, what is good; and what does the LORD require of you but to do justice, and to love kindness, and to walk humbly with your God?

—Mic. 6.8

My heart is steadfast, O God, my heart is steadfast; I will sing and make melody. Awake, my soul! Awake, O harp and lyre! I will awake the dawn. I will give thanks to you, O LORD, among the peoples, and I will sing praises to you among the nations. For your steadfast love is higher than the heavens, and your faithfulness reaches to the clouds.

—Ps. 108.1–4

Wisdom has built her house, she has hewn her seven pillars. She has slaughtered her animals, she has mixed her wine, she has also set her table. She has sent out her servant-girls, she calls from the highest places in the town. "You that are simple, turn in here!" To those without sense she says, "Come, eat of my bread and drink of the wine I have mixed. Lay aside immaturity, and live, and walk in the way of insight."

—Prov. 9.1–6

In Chapter 2, we worked out a practical and general understanding of religious spirituality as follows: *Religious spirituality* is the inner meaning of human experience as people pursue transformation under the impact of a sacred worldview. Applying this description to Judaism, we may understand Jewish spirituality within the following broad framework: **Jewish spirituality** *is the inner meaning of human experience as people pursue transformation under the impact of the way of the Torah.*

In order to understand Jewish spirituality as fully as possible, we shall approach our subject from a four-pronged perspective. First, we shall try to adopt the "insider" stance of religious Jews in the centrist mainstream. By the same token, we shall refer to the Jewish Scriptures as the "Hebrew Bible," and not as the "Old Testament," a term that we shall reserve for our discussion (in Chapter 5) of these same writings from a Christian point of view. We shall also adopt the more generic division of time into B.C.E. ("before common era," or before the era common to all) and C.E. ("common era," or the era common to all). This usage avoids the ideological bias of our ordinary calendar that distinguishes between B.C. ("before Christ") and A.D. (*anno Domini*, "in the year of the Lord"). Second, we shall concentrate upon Jewish spirituality in terms of its optimum potential as a living tradition, wholly accessible to mainstream Jews who actively draw upon its sources. Third, we shall, as far as possible, pass over the significant differences that characterize the three principal forms of Judaism (Orthodoxy, Conservatism, and Reform). We shall concentrate instead upon the shared spirituality of most religious Jews in their unity as **K'lal Yisrael** ("catholic Israel"). We shall use the term *Jews* without modifiers in order broadly to designate those Jews who believe in Judaism as a sacred worldview and who observe some level of Jewish prayer, practice, and ceremonial. Fourth, we shall approach our subject comparatively, with an eye especially to Christianity and Islam, the two other religions that trace themselves back to the monotheism of Abraham.

We shall focus our attention initially upon the central fountain from which all Jewish spirituality proceeds: the way of the Torah. We shall then explore four subsidiary streams that flow from the way of the Torah into Jewish consciousness: (1) Jewish experience of the ultimately sacred Reality; (2) Jewish growth through community; (3) Jewish formation through sacred literature; and (4) Jewish response to God through prayer and worship.

THE WAY OF THE TORAH

All the great world religions have an essential core of meaning around which all their other values cluster. For example, Christian spirituality flows from the the way of the gospel through discipleship of Jesus, while Islamic spirituality results from the straight path of submission to Allah. Hindu spirituality, on the other hand, is consequent upon the ways of **Sanatana Dharma,** while Buddhist spirituality proceeds from the middle way of the Buddha's Dhamma. All these religions offer peace to those who faithfully follow their central paradigm. The Jewish tradition promises God's shalom to Jews who sanctify their lives according to the way of the Torah.

Jews pursue God's shalom according to the admonition of the Psalmist: "Depart from evil, and do good; seek peace, and pursue it" (Ps. 34.14). The Jewish theme of God's shalom emerges from the Bible's formula for invoking God's blessing: "Thus you shall bless the Israelites: You shall say to them, The LORD bless you and keep you; the LORD make his face to shine upon you, and be gracious to you: The LORD lift up his countenance upon you, and give you peace." (Num. 6.23b–26).

Jews use the metaphor of covenant in order to speak of God's abiding, indwelling presence, not only in dazzling power but also in personal, familiar friendship. God is wondrously available to the Jews, because God has chosen the Jews to be God's own people, God's special possession bound to God by sealed contract. God "chose" the Jews not to be superior over other peoples but to fulfill unique obligations that other nations do not bear. Indeed, the Torah teaches the Jews that all peoples descend from the same two parents (Adam and Eve) and, therefore, that all peoples are equal members of one and the same human family under one and the same God. The Torah reminds the Jews again and again that they themselves once were oppressed strangers in Egypt and that they must always protect the rights of any aliens who may sojourn among them.

God summons the Jews to become consecrated witnesses to God's holiness: "You have seen what I did to the Egyptians, and how I bore you on eagles' wings and brought you to myself. Now therefore, if you obey my voice and keep my covenant, you shall be my treasured possession out of all the peoples. Indeed, the whole earth is mine, and you shall be for me a priestly kingdom and a holy nation" (Exod. 19.4–6a). Jews find in the covenant not only a singular privilege for themselves but also a sobering responsibility with universal implications for others. The Jews must themselves become holy if they are to be God's faithful priests and make God's holiness visible before all the other nations of the earth. The Jews' vocation is straightforward and uncompromising in its challenge: "For I am the LORD your God; sanctify yourselves therefore, and be holy, for I am holy" (Lev. 11.44a). The Jews must become holy through the sanctification of their lives.

Consequently, Jews identify themselves as God's holy people. To put it another way, a Jewish man knows himself to be God's holy man, while a Jewish woman acknowledges that she is God's holy woman. God remains constantly and personally present with the Jews in order that they may live out their vocation. God especially wills that God's holy people should enjoy the surpassing gift of shalom so that they may be authentically whole throughout every dimension of their lives in body, soul, and spirit. That is why the Jews often pray to God for shalom and exchange the greeting "Shalom" with one another upon meeting and upon taking leave.

God has delivered the Torah to God's holy people in forms both written and oral in order that the Torah may penetrate deeply into the very fabric of their life. By the gift of the Torah, God has once and for all determined the fundamental form and orientation of Jewish spirituality. If the Sinai covenant is the bond of the Jews with their God, then the Torah is the vital expression of that bond. The Torah is the charter of Judaism, the sacred summary of what being a religious Jew is all about, and we cannot overestimate its powerful impact upon Jewish consciousness.

The God of holiness has communicated the Torah as a unique legacy to God's beloved people, not because they are particularly worthy, but solely because of God's steadfast love and fidelity. Moses, God's mediating prophet and Israel's greatest teacher, reminded the Jews: "It was not because you were more numerous than any other people that the LORD set his heart upon you and chose you—for you were the fewest of all peoples. It was because the LORD loved you . . ." (Deut. 7.7). God gives the Torah to the Jews, although God has not been so generous to any other nation.

The Torah reveals to the Jews their corporate identity and their collective vocation as God's holy people, and it has served for over 3,000 years as their very lifeblood. The Torah has been the foundation of Jewish values and the inextinguishable light of Jewish vision, encircling the totality of Jewish life with God's expressed will. The Torah guides the Jews in their faith commitment, nourishes their interior freedom, and sustains their hope for survival, despite horrendous oppression and almost incessant persecution. The Torah even provides the Jews with God's blueprint for their individual lives, as they pursue the personal integration and social harmony of God's shalom.

We must be careful to avoid the common error of misinterpreting the word *Torah* as "law," an unhappy rendering that connotes legalism and denigrates Judaism. The term *Torah* more properly refers to "teaching" or "instruction." Non-Jewish observers must realize that Jews do not go through the motions of the Torah as though it were some empty and onerous formalism, nor do Jews chafe against the Torah as though it were some oppressive constraint on their liberty. On the contrary, Jews delight in the Torah as a precious inheritance that elevates them, liberates them from evil, and leads them to God's fulfilling shalom. The Torah enhances the worship of Jews with transcendent significance and expands their life with communal connectedness. The Torah energizes the intellectual activity of Jews and motivates their moral endeavors. The Torah is the leitmotif that resonates with a thousand sacred overtones within Jewish consciousness.

The very sound of the word *Torah* upon Jewish ears evokes religious sentiments within Jewish hearts. The mellifluent syllables of the term *Torah* cause nostalgic feelings from childhood to re-echo in the recesses of Jewish memory. Jews who reflect upon the Torah may recall the image of a devout mother cleansing every nook and cranny of her home in preparation for **Pesah** (Festival of Passover) or of a pious grandfather gently rocking back and forth as he poured forth his prayers. Jews who review the pages of the Torah may savor a sweetness according to the Psalmist's promise: "How sweet are your words to my taste, sweeter than honey to my mouth!" (Ps. 119.103). Jews who recall verses from the Torah may revisit annual festivals of gladness such as **Sukkot** (Festival of Booths), **Chanukah** (Festival of Dedication), and **Purim** (Festival of Lots), with their unique customs that so delight the children. It is not surprising that the heavy aroma of a burning candle, the biting flavor of bitter herbs, or the haunting tones of music in a minor key can cause the forgotten past to revive and flood Jewish hearts with tender recollections.

God's Torah is in the first place a dynamic tradition, whose principal repository is the fervent heart of living and breathing Jewish people as they give themselves to prayer, service, and completion of God's creative process in the world. No human words or verbal formulas can contain the breadth of the Torah or express its wealth. Jews, nevertheless, have entrusted the essential core of the Torah to written form and have utilized the word *Torah* to categorize an ever expanding number of literary collections. By the term *Torah,* Jews often refer to the first five books (the **Pentateuch**) of the Hebrew Bible: Genesis, Exodus, Leviticus, Numbers, and Deuteronomy. By the word *Torah,* Jews may also indicate the Hebrew Bible in its entire thirty-nine books. By expanding the contents of Torah still further, Jews quite commonly mean the whole Hebrew Bible plus the **Talmud,** which is a vast compendium of authoritative commentary on the Bible. Finally, by *Torah,* Jews may denote the complete Bible, plus the Talmud, plus the ongoing rabbinical tradition of scholarly discourse about its detailed ramifications and applications to life.

Psalm 119 abounds in 176 verses of praise of the Torah and its divine wisdom. Jews commonly value the Torah as God's inestimable revelation to God's people, the overwhelming proof of God's providential care from the past even to the present, and the precious token of God's redemptive promises for the future. Jews esteem the Torah above all possessions and before all earthly treasures. Some Jews go to extraordinary lengths to memorize the statutes of the Torah and explore its ever deeper meanings.

Over the course of time, Jews have enveloped the Torah in an aura of mystery. Some Jews have related to the Torah by mystical communion, and they have exalted in its sublime splendor with lyrical praise. Jews at prayer have hungered for the nourishment of the Torah and thirsted for its refreshment. Jews have extolled the Torah under provocative metaphors drawn from the necessities of everyday life: fire and water, wine and oil, milk and honey. They have even revered the Torah as "the sun of the universe" and God's "daughter." After all, traditional Jews suggest, didn't God consult the preexistent Torah before he created the world, making the universe through the Torah and for sake of the Torah? Doesn't God also study the Torah? If only the Jews would universally observe Torah in its entirety, traditional Jews insist, pagan rule would cease in the world.

JEWISH EXPERIENCE OF
THE GOD OF ABRAHAM

Jews believe that the LORD God of Abraham, Isaac, and Jacob exists. Jewish faith in the creative existence of the LORD God is a fundamental source of spirituality that the Jews share with Christians and Muslims: the LORD

God, "God, the Father of Jesus Christ," and "Allah" are the same God. Jews know that the LORD God not only exists but is providentially present to the Jews in order to enter into personal dialogue with them. Jews realize that God exists and is present in covenant in order to bless the Jews in steadfast love and to possess them in faithfulness. Jews acknowledge that God exists and is present to his people in order to shine upon them, to be gracious to them, and to favor them. Jews rejoice that God exists and is present to them in order to grant them the well-being of his shalom.

Jews know that the LORD God is personal—personal not in a human way, of course, but personal in a transcendently divine way. It is obvious from the Jewish Scriptures that the initial understanding of God's personality was **anthropomorphic** ("in the form of a human being"), insofar as they ascribed to God human passions such as jealousy and wrath and even human limbs such as eyes, mouth, and hands. Jews have progressively refined their concept of God over the centuries, and they have stripped away such human limitations as emotions and corporeality. Yet Jews insist that their primal insight into God's personal Reality remains valid, and this truth bears a saving significance.

Jews believe that the LORD God is personal and, therefore, consciously aware of human beings, whom God has created in knowledge and love. The LORD God is personal and, therefore, able providentially to care for his people, forgive them their sins, and restore them to his redemptive embrace. The LORD God is personal and, therefore, is open and available for binding relationships with God's people.

When Jews reflect upon God's personal presence, they recognize that the heavens and the earth cannot contain the one God; rather, God contains the universe and exceeds its every boundary. Yet this majestic God of power and might is immediately present throughout the world in its most minute particles, sustaining their every dimension and encompassing their total mass. God has demonstrated by saving actions that he is close and not distant; he remains among his people in compassionate accessibility. God has become manifest as near and not remote; he responds to his people according to their need.

We must try to appreciate the Jewish focus upon the LORD God in its full depth, extension, and power. The Jewish religion is not just a tribal tradition or even an enhancement of a civilized people—such as political organization and social conventions. Jews know that the LORD God can be neither ignored nor mocked, neither used nor manipulated, neither appeased by ritualism nor controlled by magic. Jews do not take God nonchalantly for granted, as though he were merely one concern among many; Jews worship God as the unrivaled Priority in their lives. Jews question the LORD God and argue with him as they wrestle with the most challenging questions of human meaning—issues such as the mystery of evil, suffering, and death. Jews commit themselves to the LORD God as they hope in his promises. Jews believe in the LORD God profoundly, and they offer their lives in service to him as the supreme Reality in the cosmos. The LORD God exists: For human beings to compromise this belief in practice is to behave blasphemously and idolatrously. The LORD God exists: For people to deny this truth is the height of foolishness: "Fools say in their hearts, 'There is no God'" (Ps. 14.1a).

Jews believe in the LORD God as uniquely *One*, precluding all rivals. Even when the Jews lived within the ancient Roman Empire, they resolutely abstained from the official state religion and worshipped the LORD God exclusively. Julius Caesar allowed the Jews alone among Rome's subject nations to enjoy this liberty. Jews give their hearts undividedly to the LORD God, in accordance with the greatest **mitzvah** ("commandment") of the 613 commandments in the Torah: "You shall love the LORD your God with all your heart, and with all your soul, and with all your might" (Deut. 6.4b–5). This all-consuming love is the thrust that energizes Jewish devotional life and practice: "Keep these words that I am commanding you today in your heart. Recite them to your children and talk about them when you are at home and when you are away, when you lie down and when you rise" (Deut. 6.6–7).

Jews claim as their own the monotheistic faith commitment of the ancient patriarchs from whom they have descended—Abraham, Isaac, and Jacob. For centuries the Jews have boldly proclaimed with their lips the treasured faith of their hearts known as the **Shema:** "Hear, O Israel: The LORD is our God, the LORD alone." The LORD God is one, and Jews find the ultimate reason for their life, faith, worship, and ethics in their exclusive engagement with God according to the Torah.

Jews reinforce their faith through visible symbols, according to Moses' admonition of old. "Bind them as a sign on your hand, fix them as an emblem on your forehead" (Deut. 6.8). When traditional Jewish men pray, they bind leather straps with boxes (**tefillin**) to their foreheads and left arms. The boxes contain tiny inscriptions that are taken from the four places where the Torah commands this religious practice (Exod. 13.1–10 and 11.16, Deut. 6.8 and 11.13–21). Many Jewish families still attach a **mezuzah** (small scroll receptacle) to their front doorposts according to the mandate of the Torah: "And you shall write them on the doorposts of your house and on your gates" (Deut. 6.9). The forthright prominence of this token informs visitors that they are entering a Jewish home.

Jews acknowledge that the LORD God is a God of wisdom who discerns the secrets of the human heart and requires that people live according to sublime moral ideals. Jews trace their collective origin not to their own initiative but to God's direct intervention. Jews have written their history not to praise themselves but to glorify their all-holy LORD for God's mighty works of salvation. David was the ancient "king after the LORD's own heart" who extended Israel's territorial boundaries to their farthest limits. Yet Jews tell David's story not for the exaltation of David but for the glory of God, who forgave David's sins of adultery and murder.

Jewish knowledge of God is markedly practical rather than speculative; it is close to everyday life. Jewish scholarship has always been more devoted to studying the requirements of God's will in the Torah than to developing a systematic theology of God's mysterious being. Consequently, the religious thought of the Jews has retained its close links with the pressing questions of real people. Jews regard any attempt to analyze God's inscrutable attributes while neglecting the performance of his will as no more than a "practical atheism."

Jews fasten confidently upon the LORD God's steadfast love and faithfulness. Jews remember that Moses, their prophet and teacher, received the gift of God's momentous self-disclosure upon Mount Sinai: "The LORD passed before him, and proclaimed, 'The LORD, the LORD, a God merciful and gracious, slow to anger, and abounding in steadfast love and faithfulness, keeping steadfast love for the thousandth generation, forgiving iniquity and transgression and sin . . .'" (Exod. 34.6–7). This revolutionary insight into the "heart" of God provides every generation of Jews with an approach to interpreting the meaning of God's mysterious ways. However challenging it may be to understand God's disposition of things in the midst of pain and suffering, Jews still trust that God governs all things sweetly, with a wise providence informed by steadfast love and faithfulness. Jews firmly hope that God will stand by them always to protect them, offer them reconciliation, and completely restore them to favor when they repent of their sins.

Most important of all, Jews know that God is intimately available to them. Although Jews usually speak of God as "Father" of all humankind, they sometimes use the feminine Hebrew noun **Shekhinah** ("presence of God") to reflect a maternal aspect of God's providence, as God nurtures and comforts God's people. While the Jews were wandering in the desert, God's Shekhinah led them visibly as a pillar of cloud by day and as a pillar of fire by night. After the Jews entered the Promised Land, God's Shekhinah continued to abide among them, dwelling first in a tent and then in the Holy of Holies at the Temple of Jerusalem. Jews know that God's Shekhinah remains among them still, and they draw comforting support from God's availability.

As Jews walk the way of the Torah, they become more sensitive to God's Shekhinah, because the Torah reminds them constantly that they are immersed from head to toe within this invisible Reality. As Jews follow the way of the Torah, they focus upon God, become God-oriented, act for God, and strive to please God by their every act. Indeed, many Jews apply themselves earnestly to the task of remembering God's personal presence in their lives; they wish to remain vividly aware, because they know the dangers of forgetfulness and neglect.

God cannot be depicted in any way on stone or canvas, because the LORD God is completely incorporeal, without face or bodily parts. This prohibition does not imply, however, that God is simply an abstraction, a skillful but distant watchmaker or a detached architect of disinterested force. The LORD God is a living God who has initiated an enduring dialogue with his beloved people. God invites the Jews to be his partners in a reciprocal relationship with him. God bestows upon the Jews the privilege of responding to him in worship, prayer, and service. God empowers the Jews to call upon God, and God hears them. God recognizes the needs of his people, and God demonstrates mercy toward their aspirations.

As Jews mature in their spirituality, many develop a surprisingly personal relationship with God that is reciprocal and dialogical like their human relationships of kinship and friendship. Jews believe that God provides for them as solicitously as a father cares for his family, as tenderly as a mother has compassion on her infant, and as passionately as a husband cherishes his spouse. Jews know that God cares deeply about the best interests of his people, protects them jealously as his own possession when they are in danger, seeks them out patiently when they sin, and heals them when they repent.

Jews acknowledge the LORD God as the Creator of the universe, because they recognize his creative exploits in their history. Their faith breaks forth in joyful thanksgiving: "O give thanks to the LORD, for he is good; for his steadfast love endures for ever!" (Ps. 118.29). God created the Jews as his holy people when they were not a nation but only a horde of runaway slaves. Jews subsequently realized that time had a beginning when God produced the world in the past and that time will have an ending when God transforms the world in the future. Linear historical consciousness causes Jews to enter as fully as possible into each unique and unrepeatable moment of the present. Each day Jews can pray with the Psalmist, "This is the day that the LORD has made; let us rejoice and be glad in it" (Ps. 118.24).

Jews come to know that God has made not only Israel but also the whole world and everything that is in it both to exist and to be good. Jews are given eyes to see the artistry of God in the colors of the natural world and ears to hear the music of God in its sounds. Jews then may enjoy the gentleness of God in the coolness of a breeze upon their faces and the warmth of sunshine upon their necks: a daily bombardment of divine miracles. Jews then may recognize the beauty of God in the innocence of newborn lambs among their flocks, in the purity of the spring rain upon their fields, and in the radiance of golden wheat ripened for their harvests: beauteous marvels abounding.

Many Jews praise the LORD for his continuous creativity from moment to moment, as the LORD pours existence into all things and concurs in their ongoing activity. For all the inanimate creatures glorify their Creator just by being what they are. From the plants and the trees to the fish, the birds, and the beasts of the field, all living creatures praise the one God, their Creator, just by doing what they do. Jews who ponder deeply upon God's creative power are awestruck by the grandeur of lofty mountains, vitalized by the freshness of running waters, and humbled by the raw force of lightning storms. Jews do not feel the need to negate or escape nature in order to commune with their God. On the contrary, many Jews spontaneously enter into their natural environment as through a window that opens outward and up to a higher domain, wherein they can unite with the glorious Creator of all things good.

The world would remain incomplete and deficient were it not for human beings, the special creatures whom God calls creatively to cultivate the world and perfect it. God has made people uniquely in his image and likeness—male and female—as the pinnacle of the material universe so that they may responsibly take charge of governing the world. God has made human beings freely to collaborate as accountable stewards in his magnificent enterprises. The Psalmist cried out with astonishment, "When I look at your heavens, the work of your fingers, the moon and the stars which you have established; what are human beings that you are mindful of them, mortals that you care for them? Yet you have made them a little lower than God, and crowned them with glory and honor. You have given them dominion over the works of your hands; you have put all things under their feet, all sheep and oxen, and also the beasts of the field, the birds of the air, and the fish of the sea, whatever passes along the paths of the seas" (Ps. 8.3–8). Every human life is unique; each individual possesses an inalienable dignity and makes an irreplaceable contribution to the world. Not one human being is expendable. That is why Jewish tradition teaches that saving a single human person is equivalent to saving the whole world.

Thus Jews hold the dignity of human work in high esteem. God provides the raw material, and Jews labor to complete it with finished form—not brutishly and slavishly as animals of burden but intelligently and freely as holy men and women. Farmers bring plants from the soil so that expert craftswomen may fashion them into linens and homemakers may prepare meals to refresh God's priestly people. Shepherds shear their sheep so that tailors may produce fine clothes to vest God's royal people. Miners bring minerals from the earth so that master craftsmen may cut, shape, and polish them into jewelry to adorn God's world with beauty. Jews contribute to the restoration of the world (*tikkun haolam*) according to their talent, education, and opportunity.

Jews commemorate God's creative power once a week, on **Shabbat** (the Sabbath, or Saturday), when the LORD God "rested" from the work of creating the universe. The observance of rest on Shabbat from sundown on Friday until sundown on Saturday is a remarkably rich dimension of Jewish spirituality, since it promotes physical health and psychic integration. On Shabbat, Jews abstain from work and commerce in order to rest from their labors. On Shabbat, Jews make time to abide in God's presence, relieved of stress and pressure as free men and free women, with leisure for refreshment, study, prayer, and family joys at home. On Shabbat, Jews enter into sacred time, since Shabbat is a bridge from this world into God's shalom, where there is only sunlight and no sunset. On Shabbat, Jews experience a healing rhythm within life that they feel deeply but cannot describe in words. Jews bless God for the gift of Shabbat—their opportunity for regaining balanced perspectives, restoring proper priorities, and becoming more fully themselves, renewed and refreshed.

Jews are well aware, of course, that Christians gather in churches to celebrate their faith on Sundays and that Muslims assemble specially for communal prayer on Fridays at noon. Jews feel certain in their hearts, however, that no weekly observance could possibly surpass their Shabbat. Jewish dependence upon familial society for fully Jewish life explains why pivotal celebrations in Jewish worship such as the Shabbat meal take place within the home. At such times the parents, the children, and any special guests gather to enjoy God's gift of wholeness and shalom, symbolized by sharing the same food and drink at the same table under the same roof, as in a restored Garden of Eden.

In order to celebrate Shabbat as a special day, Jews bathe and clothe themselves in their best attire. For the illumination of the home in the early darkness of Shabbat, Jewish women solemnly pronounce the blessing for lighting the Shabbat candles. For the sustenance of Shabbat, Jewish families eat their food on fresh table linens adorned with prized china and silverware; they bite into the crusty bread, taste the sweet red wine, and consume the best meal of the week. For the consummate joy of Shabbat, Jewish families clear the table after dinner and linger on to sing their Shabbat hymns with enthusiasm. Shabbat morning is an opportunity for communal readings and prayers in the synagogue or temple. Saturday evening is an occasion for the Jews to delay as much as possible the departure of the Shabbat and to draw further strength to meet the labors and vicissitudes of the coming week. Traditional Jews add that on Shabbat every Jew has a second soul; moreover, they insist, the Messiah would surely come if only God's holy people were universally and faultlessly to observe Shabbat.

Jews also relate to God as Revealer since God works powerfully in their lives. Jews recognize that the LORD God is almighty because God set them free from slavery in Egypt when they were helpless to liberate themselves. They encounter the LORD as the God of strong, "outstretched arm" who unexpectedly spoke to them when they lived as slaves in Egypt. The Jews could scarcely have foreseen in the beginning all that God would be for them through the Sinai covenant. Little by little, however, the LORD has unfolded his wondrous plan for them and for the world. Jews approach their revealing God above all through his supreme revelatory gift, the holy Torah, and they meet God as actively speaking to them now in the present moment. A God who simply addressed them in the past but speaks no longer would not be a living God. In this sense, God's revealing action is not a once-and-for-all event of the past but an ongoing nourishment of Jewish life from day to day. Even as he teaches the Torah to the Jews, the LORD gradually presents them with precious glimpses of the divine holiness. Jews appropriate this revelation through their worship, prayer, and obedience to the Torah.

Jews also relate to God as Redeemer because God has faithfully demonstrated loving-kindness and merciful forgiveness to Israel. It is particularly at this juncture that we begin to confront the depths of Jewish spirituality. Jews recognize that they constantly fall short of their obligations. Jews realize that they, too, are engaged together with other nations in the mystery of moral evil and that they must seek reconciliation. The LORD is always faithful, however, and restores the Jews to integral wholeness again and again. The LORD's liberating action for shalom expresses the enduring pattern of God's redemptive love. As God once freed the aged Abraham from the burden of childlessness, so God always sets the Jews free. Thus God delivered the Jews from crushing oppression in Egypt (circa 1270 B.C.E.). Later God saved the Jews from conquest by the Assyrians (722 B.C.E.). Later still God restored the Jews to Jerusalem after their seventy-year exile in Babylon (586–516 B.C.E.). Some Jews today interpret the establishment of the State of Israel in 1948 as compelling evidence of God's redemptive work in our own times.

Jews believe that what God the Redeemer has done in the past God the Redeemer will accomplish still more mightily in the days to come. Some Jews look forward to the unimaginable restoration of all things in the age of "messianic" regeneration, when God will inaugurate perfect shalom through the agency of his Messiah. The Psalmist paints a glorious portrait of this future age: "Steadfast love and faithfulness will meet; righteousness and peace will kiss each other. Faithfulness will spring up from the ground, and righteousness will look down from the sky. The LORD will give what is good, and our land will yield its increase" (Ps. 85.10–11). The prophet Isaiah describes the messianic peace as an extraordinary nonviolence that reverses the cruel instincts of brute animals. His poetry is so sublime that its images have become proverbial in the Western tradition: "The wolf shall live with the lamb, the leopard shall lie down with the kid, the calf and the lion and the fatling together, and a little child shall lead them" (Isa. 11.6).

God is the rock of salvation who cannot be defeated, the shepherd of Israel who will not abandon them, the divine king of the Jews before whom all earthly sovereigns must tremble. Jews come to know their redeeming God as absolute Goodness and Wisdom beyond all telling, because God provides so generously for their every need. Jews need to praise the LORD for his boundless mercy that endures forever, because the LORD embraces them so often in healing forgiveness. Jews depend not upon themselves but upon God as their mighty savior.

Indeed, some Jews hope against all hope in the very face of the sword. Despite unjust bias and discrimination, humiliation, persecution, pogroms, and brutal calamities such as the Holocaust, these Jews continue to hope. They commend themselves to the LORD of loving-kindness and faithfulness who, they are certain, will finally vindicate them. They are confident that their immediate experience of life in the present will not be their ultimate experience. They believe that the LORD is a living God whose goodness is more powerful than any evil.

JEWISH GROWTH THROUGH
THE K'LAL YISRAEL

The vital bond of community has always provided the context for Jewish experience of God and functioned as an indispensable core value for all Jewish spirituality. Jews realize that they fully live out their lives and effectively relate to their God only insofar as they remain united to the Jewish people in its catholic totality (K'lal Yisrael). This communal dimension is indispensable to being authentically Jewish, and there can be no properly Jewish experience without it.

The Jews first encountered God during their **Exodus** from Egypt. Moses had gathered them in the desert as a "liturgical assembly" that they might offer sacrifice to God. They learned over the next forty years that they were to participate in God's redemptive plan only as a worshipping community. The invariable context of their religious experience was to be through the people, in terms of the people, and together with the people. Isolated survival by one's own resources was simply unthinkable. Indeed, the Jews of the Exodus generation could conceive of no worse fate than to be cut off from the people, since that would have been to perish utterly in solitude. Consequently, Jews even now identify with the collective experience of God's people in order to attain the holiness and the shalom to which God summons them.

There can be no room in Judaism for an individualistic spirituality, since an exclusively one-on-one relation with the God of the covenant is unintelligible. The covenantal relationship with the LORD through the Torah belongs to the people as a whole. It is the Jewish people and not individuals who have lovingly embodied the Jewish tradition, studied it, nurtured it, determined its implications, developed it, and handed it on from generation to generation. It is the leaders of the Jewish people and not private persons who have discerned the canon of their sacred Scriptures, articulated their vision, and codified their human values. If human life is a journey, then Jews walk their pilgrimage together in a joint fellowship under the guidance of their scholars and rabbis. If religious life is a passage to transformation, then Jews pass over in mutual dependence upon one another as God's holy people.

The experience of Jewish community binds all Jews together with millions of kinsmen and kinswomen. This relationship extends back through time over forty centuries to its roots within the original clan of Abraham, with his hope for a progeny more numerous than the stars of the sky and the grains of sand in the desert. In spatial terms, it stretches horizontally around the globe, connecting the **Ashkenazim** (European Jews who have observed the customs of medieval German Jews) with the **Sephardim** (Jews of Mediterranean and Arab countries who have observed the customs of medieval Spanish Jews). The bond of God's covenanted people transcends diversities of social class, livelihood, and material wealth, as well as differences of local language, custom, and culture.

Jews trace their need for community to God's originating purpose for instituting marriage, the most basic community of all. The LORD God declared the human need for company with a helpmate if human life was to be "good." Jewish Scripture recounts the creation story: "Then the LORD God said, 'It is not good that the man should be alone; I will make him a helper as his partner'" (Gen. 2.18). Since God is the author of marriage, Jews enter into their marriage through a sacred rite. The rabbi attends the marriage in order to bless the couple, who meet under the *huppah* (canopy) to declare their intentions with the exchange of a ring and the sharing of cups of wine.

Jews are truly a family of families, and the family is their indispensable social unit. The Jewish family safeguards the Jewish tradition and guarantees Jewish survival. The Jewish mother exerts far-reaching influence upon family life, because it is her responsibility to create a Jewish home, preserve the spirit of the Torah within its walls, and pass it on to her children. People are authentically Jewish (aside from conversion) when they have a Jewish mother. Jews name their children after deceased relatives in order to symbolize the living continuity of Jewish tradition through the ages. Jewish boys enter into the Jewish people through *brit milah* (circumcision) on the eighth day after their birth, a rite that is basically familial, even if it often occurs nowadays in a hospital.

Jewish thanksgiving for all the joys of their family life is proverbial, while the warmth, renewal, and delight of Jewish family gatherings constitute a recurrent theme in Jewish literature and folklore. The enduring bonds of the Jewish family are never more in evidence than at their annual celebration of Pesah. The whole family gathers with honored guests at sundown of the preceding evening in a spirit of wonder and thanksgiving. The father solemnly introduces the ancient rite of the **seder** (Passover service) and passes on the hallowed **Haggadah** ("narrative") that recounts how God intervened with miracles to liberate Israel from the bondage of Egypt. As members of the family consume the **matzah** (unleavened bread), the *maror* (bitter herbs), and the sweet wine, Jews experience God's sacred presence. They sing the hymns, offer the prayers, and listen to the four-point dialogue between the father and the youngest child about why this night is so different from every other night. Jews identify personally with the Exodus generation through the power of liturgical ritual: It was not just their forefathers, but it was also they themselves who gathered in the desert to offer sacrifice at the time of the Exodus from Egypt.

Many Jews attest that their most soul-wrenching experience of community occurs annually during the "High Holy Days," or "Days of Awe," when almost all Jews together devote themselves to penance for their sins. Jews congregate in their synagogue or temple on the first day of the month of **Tishri** (September) for the "holy convocation" of **Rosh Hashanah** ("head of the year," or New Year). For nine days they search their consciences, repent of their sins of the past year, and make reparation for anything that they have done to offend other persons. On the tenth day of Tishri, Jews gather together for long hours in the synagogue or temple in order to observe Yom Kippur, the most solemn of all holy days. This is surely the occasion when many Jews feel most immersed within the centuries-old dialogue of the Jewish people with their God in terms of sin, conversion, and forgiveness. No words can describe the depths of tearful emotion that Jews sense when the cantor intones the first notes of the *Kol Nidrei* ("all vows"), the solemn hymn that introduces Yom Kippur—that holiest of days, when Jews fast absolutely, no food or drink, in reparation for their sins.

Jews require a quorum of ten men (**minyan**) if they are legitimately to constitute a congregation for public prayer or worship. By the same token, the communal dimension of Judaism is one reason why Jews yearn to return to their ancient geographical dwelling place, their "Promised Land." After all, Jews feel, the holy people of God must actually possess the Holy Land that the Lord gave them along with the Torah if they are fully to realize their destiny. A sovereign nation needs at least a small parcel of earthly territory to embody its identity. Jews have fostered a moving mystique about Jerusalem, the ancient capital of the Holy Land, and the site of the God's holy Temple. That is why Jews always "go up" when they make a pilgrimage to Jerusalem, no matter how high the elevation is at their point of departure. That is also why Jews offer one another an enthusiastic toast of wine during the celebration of the Passover feast: "Next year in Jerusalem!"

FORMATION THROUGH
THE HEBREW BIBLE AND TALMUD

Christians instinctively think of the Old Testament when they consider the significance of the Jewish experience for them. Muslims refer respectfully to the Jews as being (like them) one of the "peoples of the Book" to whom God gave Scriptures. In view of the nonliterary dimensions of Judaism, however, we must realize that those Christian and Muslim attitudes are only partially valid from the Jewish point of view. The Jewish tradition is alive and much richer than any book or books—even inspired Scriptures—could summarize or contain exhaustively. It remains true, nevertheless, that Jews have been a particularly "bookish" community, a people who have depended upon the written word and its symbolism for their almost miraculous survival through history. Jews have always focused upon the Hebrew Bible and related literature as the written expression of the Torah—and, therefore, as the fundamental substance of their prayer and worship, piety and study.

Sacred erudition has a prominence in Judaism that knows no parallel in other traditions, because many Jews pursue Torah studies as their noblest occupation. They have placed sacred learning at the very heart of their formation as God's people, not only in synagogues and temples but also in their homes. Consequently, Jews have themselves produced abundant literature and have made education a priority of the first order for their children. The Jewish rabbi is not really like the Christian priest or minister but is, rather, a dedicated scholar of the Torah, who studies and interprets it for the real-life needs of his congregation. Traditional Jews often pray and yearn that their family may be privileged to have a son or a son-in-law who is a scholar or a rabbi. Even on ordinary weekdays, Jews have a preferential option for Torah studies among all leisurely pursuits available to them. Consequently, even their recreation may be educational and spiritual.

For Jews, the Hebrew Bible is the primary book and a priceless heritage—a virtual encyclopedia of literature that gradually emerged from their worship and from their reflection upon their experience of God and with God over a millennium. It represents the heart of the Jewish tradition insofar as it has been reduced to written form. God is the primary and inspiring author of this vast collection of writings, although a multitude of people (mostly anonymous) contributed their own labor and talent as genuine authors on a secondary level. The Hebrew prophets typically prefaced their solemn messages with those awesome words that thunder forth from the sacred page: "Thus says the LORD . . ." (as we find, for example, in Jer. 2.2a).

The Jews combine the first letters of three Hebrew words in order to coin the acronym **Tanakh** as their word for "Bible": the letter *t* from *Torah*, the letter *n* from *Nevi'im* ("prophets"), and the letter *k* from **Ketuvim** ("writings"). The Jews feel an awesome reverence for the Bible as truly God's Word, however extensive and many-layered may be the human process that determined its final form; they know that God has spoken to them and continues to address them through the mediation of its pages. Moreover, the Hebrew Bible exercises its supreme impact upon Jewish spirituality in the course of Jewish liturgy, when Jews gather in sacred assembly to encounter the LORD and hear God speak to them once more. The Bible furnishes the content of the sacred readings in a service of worship, while the entire Torah provides the spirit of the prayers.

Of course, Jews may at any time read their Scriptures privately or in small groups—for example, in search of God's shalom and refreshment on Shabbat. In this way, Jews turn to the Torah for renewal of hope, to the prophets for formation of conscience and comfort of spirit, to the writings for edification and practical wisdom, and to the Psalms for heartfelt prayer. The very utterance of the word *Torah* evokes an immediate response of religious awe in Jewish sensibility.

The Torah scroll is the quintessential embodiment of the sacred among God's people. Professional scribes of consummate skill and devotion dedicate all their talent to creating perfect replicas of the sacred text on parchment and rolling it on two wooden spindles; every synagogue or temple cherishes its precious copy of the scroll. Jews always protect the Torah scroll from profane view, and they do not move it from place to place unless they are using it for sacred worship. Jews wrap the Torah scroll with a richly adorned veil and reserve it within an **ark** (container) that faces Jerusalem from the highest place at the center of the synagogue or temple, while a lamp burns always before it. The rabbi removes the Torah scroll only for solemn recitation as public instruction, cradling it in his arms with reverent love and placing it carefully on the **bimah** (pulpit), while the congregation rises. The reader does not touch the sacred text directly, but only by means of a **yad** (pointer).

Jewish boys become adults within the Jewish people at the age of thirteen through the bar mitzvah ceremony, when, after prolonged and extensive religious training, they receive a call for the first time to come up and read publicly from the Torah. This rite of passage is a moving and joyful occasion in which a large group of relatives and friends are delighted to participate. In modern times, many communities have added a similar ceremony (**bat mitzvah**) for adolescent girls. Jews have designed both rituals in order to make an indelible impression upon their young people, who must now observe the 613 mitzvot in their lives.

Seven weeks after Pesah, Jews celebrate the festival of **Shavuot** ("weeks") to commemorate God's gift of the Torah at Mount Sinai; they stay awake all night and studying the Torah. When the Jews have finished reading Deuteronomy in the autumn on the last day of the festival of Sukkot, they at once return to the first lines of Genesis. Then they celebrate the holiday of **Simhat Torah** ("rejoicing in Torah") by carrying the Torah scroll around the congregation in glad procession.

The Talmud, which is the most important written summary and codification of the accumulated oral commentary on the Torah, stands second only to the Bible in terms of holiness and authority. The Talmud developed gradually over a lengthy period, but its definitive edition (circa 500 C.E.) is composed of the **Mishnah** ("repetition") and the **Gemara** ("completion"). The Talmud provides in written summary a detailed and practical application of the Torah. The ancient rabbis intended through their commentary to "build a fence around the Torah" in order to ensure that the Jewish people would avoid the slightest violation of God's explicit commandments. Thus they extended the boundaries of the commandments into neutral areas in order to provide a broad margin of safety. For example, in order to ensure that Jews rested on Shabbat and abstained from the slightest hint of any labor, rabbis forbade the people even to touch a tool on Shabbat: Jews would not be tempted to work, the rabbis reasoned, if they could not even touch the necessary implements.

Talmudic scholars love to spend hours poring over the texts, dissecting them minutely, and engaging in a vigorous and heated discussion of their meaning through dialectical reasoning. Scholars devote themselves to inferring the most far-reaching implications of the Torah and to commenting on the subtlest ramifications of each mitzvah. A Jew may devote his whole life to mastering all that he can learn about a single text of the Talmud, and then he is known as *squire* ("weapon-bearer") of that text. Groups of Jews may commit themselves jointly to working through the whole Talmud over a seven-year period.

Jews regard Judaism as a complete way of life, the way according to the Torah. Since God has entered into covenant with the Jews, Jewish religion must encompass not only belief and ritual but also the totality of human living. Since Jews are God's holy people, they must do far more than simply follow a code of ethics and live a "good life." Since Jews are God's own possession, they must make their days, their works, their relationships, their every breath and heartbeat holy. Since Jews are a priestly people, they must transform the most ordinary aspects of human existence into acts of worship, from the most lofty to the most mundane. Since Jews are a nation set apart, they must make of their every occupation a prayer that nourishes communion with God and contributes to the coming of God's reign.

The Torah essentially contains the 613 mitzvot, which are the all-encompassing statutes for determining Jewish holiness. Taken together, these mitzvot sanctify every facet of existence from the physical to the social, from the emotional and mental to the spiritual. For the glory of God the 613 mitzvot regulate speech and prayer, diet and hygiene, labor and rest, marital relationships and contractual agreements. They hallow human relationships to God, to other Jews, to sojourners or strangers, and to oneself. The mitzvot contain 248 positive commandments: These order the Jewish people toward ennobling worship of the one true God and toward humanizing behavior in all of their activities. The mitzvot include 365 negative statutes: These protect the Jewish people from the debasing worship of false gods and from all of those acts that would injure them and diminish their humanity.

The most famous among all of the 613 mitzvot are the Ten Commandments (Exod. 20.1–17 and Deut. 5.6–21) that point toward holiness from an ethical point of view. These moral guidelines have had an incalculable effect not only upon the Jewish people but also upon the conscience of the whole Western world. Some people who disavow any affiliation with institutional religion still speak of observing "ethical monotheism," by which they mean acknowledging the one God as Creator and accepting the Jewish Ten Commandments as morally normative. (The precept that requires that the Jews must rest on Shabbat is binding only for the Jews, of course, although the derived notion of abstaining from labor over the weekend has become virtually universal among people of all persuasions.) Indeed, the God of the Jews is a moral divinity who delivers the Ten Commandments to God's chosen people in order to promote morality among all the peoples of his world. The God of justice calls the Jews to bear witness to the LORD by their works of justice in order that all the nations may find their way to God. Non-Jews upon seeing the righteousness of Jews should glorify God and exclaim, "How great must be the LORD, the God of Israel!"

Jews acknowledge that they must respect and safeguard the inherent rights of all human beings, not only on the individual level but also within familial and other social relationships. In particular, they must not injure the bodily life, marriage bond, property, reputation, and integral well-being of others. Jews are obliged to relate to their parents honorably, communicate with one another truthfully, and fulfill their oaths and promises faithfully. Jews must decide upon the right moral choices between their good tendencies (*yetzer ha tov*) and their bad tendencies (*yetzer ha ra*).

The LORD calls Jews to much more than a negative morality of avoiding harm to others, however. They must positively promote and vindicate human rights. God insists through the prophet Amos: "Take away from me the noise of your songs; I will not listen to the melody of your harps. But let justice roll down like waters, and righteousness like an ever-flowing stream" (Amos 5.23–24). The LORD summons the Jews to become holy with his justice and, consequently, to render positive service to others.

The Jewish concept of holiness includes *tzedakah*, the principal moral value and one of the most practical dimensions of Jewish spirituality. Jews must actively do the good and the right. When Jews defy evil and give of themselves to their fellow human beings through works of righteousness, they serve to keep the world on an even keel and preserve it from calamity. *Tzedakah* leads to human welfare and shalom. Jews who lead lives of uncommon righteousness are known as **tzaddikim.** When Jews wish to confer their highest compliment upon non-Jews, they give them the title of "righteous gentiles." When Jews live justly and cause non-Jews to esteem God's holy people, they sanctify God's name.

The meaning of the term *tzedakah* has evolved far beyond "justice" or "righteousness" in any juridical sense. *Tzedakah* now includes the dimensions of love and mercy and is equivalent to "benevolence," "philanthropy," "sharing," or "charity." Jews make *tzedakah* donations on special occasions such as a festival, the birth of a baby, a marriage, or the anniversary of the death of a relative. Jewish parents keep a "*tzedakah* box" in their homes and encourage their children regularly to place coins in it, in order to alleviate the needs of the poor. Synagogues and temples have a *tzedakah* box available for their congregations. For that matter, many Jews sum up the entire Torah as God's mandate that the Jews must not hate but love: "You shall not hate in your heart anyone of your kin; you shall reprove your neighbor, or you will incur guilt yourself. You shall not take vengeance or bear a grudge against any of your people, but you shall love your neighbor as yourself: I am the LORD" (Lev. 19.17–18).

The prophet Isaiah felt the words of the LORD flaming forth from within him: "Is not this the fast that I choose: to loose the bonds of injustice, to undo the thongs of the yoke, to let the oppressed go free, and to break every yoke? Is it not to share your bread with the hungry, and bring the homeless poor into your house; when you see the naked, to cover them, and not to hide yourself from your own kin? Then your light shall break forth like the dawn, and your healing shall spring up quickly . . ." (Isa. 58.6–8a). Jews feel bound by covenant to care for all the poor persons in society without exception, and even strangers or sojourners are the object of their concern. Widows and orphans forcefully symbolize all needy people, since they are the epitome of powerlessness and vulnerability, who depend utterly upon the *tzedakah* of others for their survival.

One poignant aspect of Jewish *tzedakah* is that it treats marginalized persons not merely as the objects of free and optional beneficence but as people who have a claim in justice upon the wealthy and the secure. God grants material riches to certain individuals as he chooses, and there is nothing wrong with possessing property as such. Yet it remains unquestionably true that all things belong to God, who merely entrusts material wealth to those whom he calls to build up and transform the world. Wealthy Jews do not have unqualified title to their possessions, as though they could dispose of them unconscionably according to their whim. On the contrary, Jews must preserve the resources of the world, utilize them, and responsibly share them with others. Jews who have possessions are morally obliged to give a portion of them to those who are less fortunate.

It is at this level that we may particularly appreciate the overflow of Jewish spirituality for the benefit of the whole human community. Jews highly esteem the gift of life, and they praise God for having created them to dwell in this world. Jews are convinced of the importance of making a difference in the lives of others. Jews must make God's earth a more human habitat for Jews having lived upon it. The relationship of Jews with God through Torah enhances their connection with all their fellow human beings.

Jews render concrete expression to their spirituality through espousing the cause of the little ones of the world: the poor, the weak, and the needy. Jews of means feel stung in conscience and moved by compassion when they confront the miserable plight of so many impoverished men, women, and children. Moral formation of Jews in the way of Torah moves them to give food to the hungry, to provide shelter to the homeless, to care for the sick and terminally ill, and to bury the dead. Moreover, the communal connection among Jews inspires them to do what they can to eliminate systemic injustice within social institutions and structures. For example, Jews are renowned for their outstanding schools, hospitals, homes for the elderly, and other projects that they sponsor through Jewish charitable institutions.

Jews are often filled with prophetic passion to protest against whatever assaults human life. Jews oppose all that is oppressive and destructive of human dignity. Jews are in the forefront of movements to improve education, eradicate disease, abolish the exploitation and abuse of children, free women from oppressive conditions, and vindicate the rights of laboring people. When Jews provide their leadership for the alleviation of human misery and the betterment of the world, they bring their spirituality to concrete fruition.

The Torah also includes many mitzvot that are strictly religious rather than "ethical." Precepts that distinguish sacred time, place, and rites of passage or purification fall into this category. Jewish dietary laws of **kosher** ("clean") are religious in this sense, according to **kashrut** (the collection of dietary precepts). Animals that have a cloven hoof and chew the cud, fish with fins and scales, and nonpredatory birds are kosher, providing that a certified Jewish butcher under rabbinical supervision slaughters them as compassionately as possible (with a sharp, smooth-bladed knife) and removes all the blood. Even then, Jews may not eat their meat together with any dairy product such as milk, butter, or cheese. Jews avoid eating all other animals, fish, or birds, because they are **traif** ("unclean," literally "torn"). Jews may eat all vegetables, nuts, and fruits, however, since those foods are **parve** ("neutral").

It is important that we appreciate the Jewish dietary laws in their spiritual significance and not simply as principles of remarkably sound hygiene. There is an obvious connection between bodily nourishment and the interior vitality of human beings. After all, eating and drinking are among the most basic of all human activities, indispensably connected not only with survival but also with the creation of community. As the saying goes, "We are what we eat." Nevertheless, the fundamental reason why the Jews observe a special diet is that the LORD, their God, has commanded them to do so. Jews know that consuming food is a common and universal pastime, but it cannot be "ordinary" for them.

The Jews want always to remember and never to forget the continuous presence of the LORD, their God, and their calling to be his holy people. They want always to remember and never to forget that they must become holy, because the LORD, their God, is holy. Kashrut hallows life, because kashrut sanctifies the most basic process for the sustenance of life. Often enough, kashrut is inconvenient and difficult to observe, especially when Jews visit non-Jews outside of their own homes, eat at a college cafeteria, or dwell in an area far from a kosher butcher. Yet kashrut exerts a powerful impact upon Jewish spirituality by creating Jewish consciousness, reinforcing Jewish identity, and expressing Jewish community. Kashrut, indeed, deepens the internal awareness of Jews on each trip to market for groceries, on every vacation, and at every civic banquet.

JEWISH RESPONSE TO GOD
THROUGH WORSHIP AND PRAYER

We must appreciate the fact that Judaism, for all its institutional structures, precepts, obligations, and customs, is above all a personal relationship of the Jews with their personal God. Without this dimension, Jews would not be able to communicate with God, and Judaism would risk becoming oppressive, a shell of empty ritualism and external forms. With this connectedness (sustained through sacred words and gestures), Jews have enjoyed a dialogue with God for over three millennia. Jewish prayer is basically human conversation with God. If the covenantal relationship of the Jewish people with their LORD through Torah is what Jewish religion is all about, then prayer is a privileged feature of the Jewish spirituality that overflows from that relationship. In fact, the Torah calls the Jews to encompass every aspect of their lives with prayer, and when Jews pray they become most completely themselves.

In ancient times, Jewish worship of the LORD primarily involved sacrificial offerings at the altar of the Temple in Jerusalem. After the destruction of the Second Temple in 70 C.E., however, prayer and study became the primary modes of worship. Christians are supposed to pray "always," while Muslims pray five times a day. Jews transform every act of life into prayer, but they also pray formally, both privately and communally. Jews say prayers three times daily, morning, noon, and evening. Jews also pray frequently throughout each day—before and after meals, in the course of their labors, upon undertaking a journey, and at countless other times. Jews pray communally during Shabbat and major holy days, such as Pesah, Shavuot, Rosh Hashanah, and Sukkot, and during the solemn fast of Yom Kippur. Jews pray at the significant junctures of life, such as births, weddings, and funerals. Jews pray both spontaneously in their own words and, more frequently, in phrases from the **Siddur** (prayer book), claiming the sacred words of their tradition as their own.

It is fascinating to observe the great biblical heroes and heroines at prayer. Men such as Abraham, Moses, and David as well as women such as Miriam, Hannah, and Esther seem to have enjoyed a spontaneous talent for prayer. They conversed familiarly with the LORD God as friend speaks with friend, as wife with husband, or as child with parent. They approached God confidently to bargain for favors, wrestle with problems, or negotiate on behalf of others. They turned to God with candor to proclaim their innocence, but also with repentance to seek God's mercy. They expressed their sentiments to God forthrightly and unabashedly from the heart. They used the surprising and even contradictory language that we might expect in a personal relationship: for example, humble boldness, trusting doubt, or obedient questioning of God's will.

The Book of Psalms in particular contains poems that combine a wide variety of themes with an amazing universality: We find prayers of petition, adoration, praise, hope, love, joy, faith, cursing, complaint, yearning, surrender, sorrow, and even desperation. Jews realize that God reads their hearts, and yet they must speak to God about what they feel. Jews recognize that God knows their difficulties, and yet they must inform God about them and seek his assistance. Jews do not suppose for a moment that God somehow needs their praise and thanksgiving, but Jews must at all times, in every place, and in all situations give thanks to the LORD their God, for God is good.

In our exploration of Jewish spirituality, we return ever again to the twin themes of vivid consciousness and habitual remembrance. Jews want to be ever mindful of all that God is for them and all that God has called them to be. Forgetting leads to calamity, but remembering leads to life. The Jewish Scriptures read, "So you shall remember and do all my commandments, and you shall be holy to your God. I am the LORD your God, who brought you out of the land of Egypt to be your God: I am the LORD your God" (Num. 15.40–41).

Jews know that they cannot possess anything unless the LORD grants it to them in generosity and steadfast love. Thanksgiving, therefore, is surely one of the most prominent features of Jewish prayer as it encircles Jewish life. Jews spontaneously and habitually bless God as soon as they call to mind what God has done for them, is doing, and will do for them: "Blessed art Thou, O Lord, our God, King of the Universe. . . ." Jews then pronounce the specific reason why the LORD God should be blessed and praised in thanksgiving on this particular occasion. When Jews bless the LORD for his gifts, they become mindful of the Creator and express their continual devotion to the King of the Universe. When Jews bless God, they are made to remember the LORD God and their unconditional dependence upon him. When Jews bless God, they also are made to remember how absolutely povery-stricken they are of themselves, because without God they can do nothing.

Jews have a proper blessing for every occasion, because every experience is an opportunity to raise their minds and hearts to God in heightened awareness. Perhaps they have awakened from sleep with the use of their faculties. Perhaps they have savored a pleasure. Perhaps they have experienced a tragedy or enjoyed good fortune. Perhaps they are about to drink a glass of wine or eat a piece of bread. Jews have a proper blessing for every human event from the birth of a child to the marriage of a young couple. Jews also have a proper blessing upon seeing every natural phenomenon from a rainbow to a sunset.

At no time is prayer more significant for Jews than when they gather together for communal worship, since Jewish worship is the privileged occasion for intense "re-collection" of all that being Jewish involves. Jewish worship involves the assembly of God's people, and the miracle of divine dialogue unfolds in its very midst. When Jews worship together, their thought of God moves from the periphery of consciousness to its center point. They hear the Torah proclaimed, and they remember to open their minds to the Light and their hearts to the Fire. When Jews worship together, they become for one another flesh-and-blood symbols of their common faith and hope. They rub shoulders with their brothers and sisters, and they receive bodily assurance about the things that matter most. When Jews hear the rabbi leading them in chanted prayers, they are made to know once again that the LORD is always attentive to God's people, thinking of them, forgiving them, strengthening them, loving them, waiting upon them.

Rabbi Israel ben Eliezer (1700–1760), known as the *Baal Shem Tov* ("master of the good name"), insisted that it was not enough to study God's Torah, follow its statutes, and pray in a formal way. He founded a movement of Jewish enthusiasm known as Hasidism, which is still found among some traditional groups in the United States. The Hasidim ("pious ones") are strictly observant in their practice, yet they express their love for God with spontaneous freedom, fervent devotion, and intense feelings of joy. The Hasidim are convinced that Jews should not have to wait for their God. Jews can and must rejoice in God's presence here and now, experiencing God in ecstatic prayer. The Hasidim sing and dance with boundless joy, because the LORD God is God and it is so very good to be a Jew. They give their leader, the **rebbe,** unhesitating obedience, and they look to him as their mediator with God. Some of the Hasidim follow the teachings of the **Kabbalah,** the medieval movement of esoteric Jewish mysticism.

MATERIAL FOR DISCUSSION

1. What do you think about the Jews' understanding of study as a primary exercise of Jewish piety?

2. How significant do you think it is for the Jews to "remember" communally by celebrating an annual festive dinner such as the seder (Passover meal)?

3. What positive values do you think that people of all persuasions can derive from the study of Jewish spirituality?

4. From your own knowledge, what do you think Jewish spirituality has in common with the spirituality to be discovered in other religious traditions?

SUGGESTIONS FOR FURTHER READING

Dosick, Wayne D. *Living Judaism: The Complete Guide to Jewish Belief, Tradition, and Practice.* San Francisco: HarperSanFrancisco, 1995. In this work, the author delivers what his ambitious title promises. The work presents a most ample description of Jewish spirituality in an interesting and readable way. It is an excellent resource for all who seek to understand Jewish spirituality more fully.

Green, Arthur, ed. *Jewish Spirituality: From the Bible Through the Middle Ages.* Vol. 13 of *World Spirituality: An Encyclopedic History of the Religious Quest.* New York: Crossroad, 1986. In this large compendium, the editor has gathered an extensive anthology of articles on all aspects of Jewish spirituality from its earliest beginnings to its medieval developments.

———. *Jewish Spirituality: From the Sixteenth Century Revival to the Present.* Vol. 14 of *World Spirituality: An Encyclopedic History of the Religious Quest.* New York: Crossroad, 1987. In this companion volume, the editor has gathered articles on various dimensions of Jewish spirituality insofar as it has developed over the past 500 years.

Heschel, Abraham Joshua. *The Earth Is the Lord's* and *The Sabbath.* New York: Harper Torchbooks, 1966. This book combines two remarkably insightful essays by a famous Jewish philosopher, theologian, rabbi, and mystic of the twentieth century. The first essay provides a warm insight into the intimate closeness of God through his creation. The second essay reveals the rich meaning of the Jewish Sabbath as a participation in God's time.

Neusner, Jacob. *The Way of Torah: An Introduction to Judaism.* 5th ed. Belmont, Calif.: Wadsworth, 1993. This textbook is part of a larger series from this publisher, titled "Religious Life in History." It is a splendid introduction to the centrality of the Torah as the sacred pattern or "myth" that informs Jewish life and practice.

Wiesel, Elie. *Souls on Fire: Portraits and Legends of Hasidic Masters.* Trans. Marion Wiesel. New York: Random House, 1972. The author has compiled a thoroughly enjoyable series of short stories about many Hasidic rabbis of old, such as the Baal Shem Tov, who by their words and example kindled the spark of joyful enthusiasm in Jewish spirituality.

5

Christian
Spirituality

*When Jesus saw the crowds, he went up the mountain; and after he sat
down, his disciples came to him. Then he began to speak, and taught them, saying: "Blessed are the poor in spirit, for theirs is the kingdom of heaven. Blessed
are those who mourn, for they will be comforted. Blessed are the meek, for they
will inherit the earth. Blessed are those who hunger and thirst for righteousness, for they will be filled. Blessed are the merciful, for they will receive mercy.
Blessed are the pure in heart, for they will see God. Blessed are the peacemakers,
for they will be called children of God. Blessed are those who are persecuted for
righteousness' sake, for theirs is the kingdom of heaven. Blessed are you when
people revile you and persecute you and utter all kinds of evil against you falsely
on my account. Rejoice and be glad, for your reward is great in heaven, for in the
same way they persecuted the prophets who were before you."*

—Matt. 5.1–11

*Pray then in this way: Our Father in heaven, hallowed be your name.
Your kingdom come, Your will be done, on earth as it is in heaven. Give us this
day our daily bread. And forgive us our debts, as we also have forgiven our
debtors. And do not bring us to the time of trial, but rescue us from the evil one.*

—Matt. 6.9–13

97

*Very truly, I tell you, unless a grain of wheat falls into the earth and dies,
it remains just a single grain; but if it dies, it bears much fruit. Those who love
their life lose it, and those who hate their life in this world will keep it for eternal life.*

—John 12.24–25

*When he was at the table with them, he took bread, blessed and broke it,
and gave it to them. Then their eyes were opened, and they recognized him; and
he vanished from their sight. They said to each other, "Were not our hearts burning within us while he was talking to us on the road, while he was opening the
scriptures to us?"*

—Luke 24.30–32

In this chapter, we shall continue to use Chapter 2's working description
of religious spirituality: *Religious spirituality* is the inner meaning of
human experience as people pursue transformation under the impact of a
sacred worldview. Applying this description to Christianity, we may understand Christian spirituality within the following broad framework:
Christian spirituality *is the inner meaning of human experience as people
pursue transformation under the impact of the way of Jesus' discipleship.* We
must now review the essential factors that enter into the Christian inner
meaning of human experience.

In order to present Christian spirituality as faithfully as possible, we
shall pursue our investigation by taking a threefold approach. First, we
shall try to enter into the perspective not of neutral and detached observers but of engaged Christians who wholeheartedly believe in their
religion and faithfully practice it as God's revealed plan for human salvation. Second, we shall focus upon Christian spirituality in terms of its op-
timal potential, insofar as Christians actually draw upon its sources and
attempt religiously to appropriate them. (Many who call themselves
Christians identify with Christianity only in a nominal or cultural way.)
Third, we shall, as far as possible, overlook the many differences that
characterize the four major Christian families (Catholicism, Eastern
Orthodoxy, Anglicanism, and Protestantism) and concentrate upon
Christian spirituality in its broadest dimensions.

Christianity is a vast tradition with well over a billion adherents,
and, even within the same Christian "family," individuals differ across
a very wide spectrum. We shall, therefore, use the unmodified term
"Christians" rather than the more universal phrase "the Christians" when

we wish to describe the common and usual attitudes of mainstream practitioners, although there may be some exceptions. For example, almost all Christians practice the rites of baptism and the **Holy Eucharist** (the bread-and-wine memorial of the Last Supper), but neither Quakers nor Christian Scientists observe these practices.

On a few salient points, moreover, we must distinguish Christianity's two principal interpretations of the Church: Catholic and Protestant. Within the Catholic category, we include all those Christians who unite with Christ through sacramental incorporation into the Church itself: for example, Catholics in communion with the Bishop of Rome (Roman Catholics), Anglicans, Eastern Orthodox, Copts, Armenians, Old Catholics, and many others. Our Protestant classification comprises all those Christians who understand the Church as an assembly of those who unite with Christ directly and immediately by faith alone: for example, Lutherans, Presbyterians, Congregationalists, Methodists, Baptists, Disciples of Christ, Free Evangelicals, Pentecostals, and many others.

We shall first investigate the central wellspring of all Christian spirituality: *the way of Jesus' discipleship*. We shall next examine this fountain in terms of four streams: (1) Christian experience of the ultimately sacred Reality; (2) Christian growth through community; (3) Christian formation through sacred literature; and (4) Christian response to God through worship and prayer. We shall also present some concrete examples of how these factors affect Christian life, values, and consciousness.

THE WAY OF JESUS' DISCIPLESHIP

There is a close etymological connection between the word *disciple* and the word *discipline*, insofar as a disciple is one who submits to the discipline of a master teacher. Religions often include some form of discipleship within their program of instruction and training. A Hindu sits at the feet of her **guru** (spiritual instructor) as she tries to "see" what her guru has "seen"; a Zen Buddhist practices **zazen** under the guidance of her *roshi* ("aged teacher" or "Zen master") as she seeks enlightenment. By the same token, a Sufi Muslim attends to every utterance of his *shaykh* ("leader") so that he may enjoy God's presence here and now, while a Hasidic Jew gathers at table with his rebbe in order to appropriate the strictest ideals for Jewish life.

The way of Jesus' discipleship is the pattern of Christianity that underlies all its institutional structures and stamps its spirituality with a unique character. Discipleship of Jesus in its mature development is always a two-sided coin. Giving oneself to Jesus involves bonding not only with God as Father but also with a vast multitude of human beings as brothers and sisters. Believers engage themselves with the glorified Jesus, who in himself constitutes their access to God and their communion with one another.

Christian discipleship is both individual and social. It is necessarily personal, because adult believers sustain their union with Jesus only by a free option based upon conscious knowledge. Protestant Christians particularly emphasize this individual or "vertical" bond (without negating the communal aspect). On the other hand, Christian discipleship is also indispensably communal, because believers relate to Jesus in terms of the Church that stems from him. Catholic Christians particularly focus upon this collective or "horizontal" connection (without neglecting the personal factor).

Christians find their overarching worldview in the way of Jesus' discipleship. As disciples of Jesus, Christians share in Jesus' filial life and piety as the natural Son of God, and they claim the dignity of adopted sons and daughters of God. As disciples of Jesus, Christians bond with Jesus as the risen Lord of the cosmos, and they connect with the people and things of that world. As disciples of Jesus, Christians follow Jesus, the perfected human being, and they draw their ethical priorities, values, and ideals from his example.

Christian spirituality always involves the struggle against the internal and external temptations to evil that assail us through the course of our lives. Christians agree with Jews and Muslims that our human predicament is not a self-centeredness that results from intellectual deception by error or ignorance but an egocentricity that flows from the moral evil of sin. Instead of worshipping the God who created us, we commit a kind of idolatry and worship ourselves to the exclusion of God. Instead of orienting our lives toward the God who alone is absolute Life, we turn backward upon ourselves in a collision course toward self-destruction and death. Christians insist that we must look to Jesus as Redeemer for the liberating grace to escape the trap of inflated self-interest and turn toward God.

Christians believe that we not only grow up in a human solidarity of separation and alienation from God, but we aggravate that collective estrangement by our own personal transgressions of God's will for us. Sometimes we abuse our freedom and make bad choices because of disorderly passion, inveterate habit, and volitional weakness. Sometimes we may even violate our conscience and deliberately do with full responsibility and accountability what we know to be seriously wrong. God has provided humankind with moral laws (such as the Ten Commandments of the Jewish Torah, for example) that forbid our harming ourselves. If we could not injure ourselves and if God did not care about us, there would be no such thing as sin. We do offend God and commit sin when we hurt ourselves, because God cares about us. Christians look to Jesus as Savior for the grace to overcome their aversion from God and be converted back to God.

A wide chasm usually separates a great teacher's lofty norms for spiritual fulfillment from the actual practice of his or her disciples, and the division between the ideal and the practical is particularly acute in Christian consciousness. For Christians do try to imitate Jesus, even though they believe that Jesus is the Son of God incarnate. Christians try to follow Jesus as the perfected man of consummate virtue who has already realized in himself their noblest aspirations. At the same time, Christians acknowledge that, despite their most heroic and faithful efforts, they will inevitably fall far short of Jesus' incomparable example. Christians confront their own moral weakness at every juncture of their lives, a sinfulness that compromises their noblest ventures. Christians often follow after their Master confusedly, with faltering steps and divided purpose.

In the end, Christians know themselves to be "unprofitable servants." Christian life involves a cyclic rhythm of sin and repentance. Christian spirituality always requires, therefore, the conversionist rhythm of ever renewed beginnings, followed by repentance once again. Christians must turn themselves ever again from distracted forgetfulness and bad choices. They must chart new strategies in the face of flooded roads and unforeseen detours. That is why, for example, Benedictine monks commit themselves to a daily conversion. That is also why so many Christians practice a periodic examination of conscience, record their insights regularly in a personal journal, or submit their daily regimen to a trusted friend's critique.

Personal and communal discipleship of Jesus requires that Christians divest themselves of their inflated egos. When Christian disciples renounce all egocentricity, they die to themselves and give themselves over to the Master as their new spiritual center of gravity. When they abandon all self-aggrandizement, they discover in the risen Jesus their saving source of human meaning. When Christian disciples empty themselves of selfishness, they make room for the Master to possess them with his redeeming presence. When Christians abandon all self-centeredness, they begin to focus upon Jesus-centeredness.

Early disciples recalled the uncompromising words of Jesus' challenge. In the New Testament, we read his remembered teaching: "Then he said to them all, 'If any want to become my followers, let them deny themselves and take up their cross daily and follow me. For those who want to save their life will lose it, and those who love their life for my sake will save it. What does it profit them if they gain the whole world, but lose or forfeit themselves? Those who are ashamed of me and of my words, of them the Son of Man will be ashamed when he comes in his glory and the glory of the Father and of the holy angels'" (Luke 9.23–27). We shall confront a similar challenge in Chapter 8, when we examine the Buddha's insistence that his disciples must shatter their egos, strip away clinging attachments, and acknowledge their emptiness if they are to enter into Nibbana.

Jesus himself willingly embraced his cross, and he made of his death an act of self-oblation to God. By the obedient love with which Jesus endured the agony of his dying, Jesus transformed human death from a plummet toward oblivion into a bridge to resurrection. At the same time, Jesus exposed the bankruptcy of worldly prudence and turned conventional presumptions upside down.

Jesus demonstrated that self-abnegation achieves genuine completion, servanthood defines authentic leadership, and foolish weakness is wise power in disguise. Men and women must give rather than receive. Guests must retire to the lowest places at table. Last persons will be first persons, while servants will be rulers. Human beings must deliver themselves to conversion and regeneration with the humility, simplicity, and open trust of little children. Indeed, the littlest persons will be the greatest in the **reign** (God's dominion): "At that time the disciples came to Jesus and asked, 'Who is the greatest in the kingdom of heaven?' He called a child, whom he put among them, and said, 'Truly I tell you, unless you change and become like children, you will never enter the kingdom of heaven. Whoever becomes humble like this child is the greatest in the kingdom of heaven'" (Matt. 18.1–4).

Jesus by his words and his works proclaimed what he called his gospel. He announced that a new age had dawned and that God was determined to grant a reign of reconciling love and peace to all human beings. Jesus reached out to the marginalized and vulnerable people, to the outcasts who were diseased, dispossessed, destitute, disenfranchised, and defenseless—and, most especially, to sinners. No longer should men and women be burdened with guilt or be anxious about the future, Jesus assured them, since the reign was already at hand. The reign would blossom infallibly into full fruition, as a seed planted in good soil overcomes every obstacle and grows into golden wheat. Human beings had only to turn to their heavenly Father with the simplicity of children who are utterly convinced that their father loves them with a compassionate and healing love. No sin could be too much for such a love.

Jesus gradually learned to interpret his own uniquely divine connection with God as a filial relationship (as son to father). On one occasion, Jesus openly thanked his Father for the opportunity to reveal God's love for all humankind as God's adopted children: "At that time Jesus said, 'I thank you, Father, Lord of heaven and earth, because you have hidden these things from the wise and the intelligent and have revealed them to infants; yes, Father, for such was your gracious will. All things have been handed over to me by my Father; and no one knows the Son except the Father, and no one knows the Father except the Son and anyone to whom the Son chooses to reveal him'" (Matt. 11.25–27). Jesus invited people generally to model themselves after him: "Come to me, all you that are weary and are carrying heavy burdens, and I will give you rest. Take my yoke upon you, and learn from me; for I am gentle and humble in heart, and you will find rest for your souls. For my yoke is easy, and my burden is light" (Matt. 11.28–30).

Large crowds of men and women throughout Jesus' mortal ministry used to lie on the grass and listen spellbound to his words. Since Jesus proclaimed sublime teachings on his own authority, people gave him titles of respect such as "Master" and "Teacher." Occasionally, individuals such as Mary of Bethany, a Samaritan woman, and Nicodemus would converse with Jesus one-on-one, and their attraction toward him often blossomed into trusting familiarity. Jesus was able to convince people of the Father's incredible generosity and care for them, because Jesus himself loved them so much. Jesus' message of the Father's love was new and exciting, and it dilated their hearts with joyful hope and peace.

Jesus summoned twelve of his followers, whom he called his apostles ("persons sent with a solemn commission"), to proclaim the gospel in his name. Gradually, however, Jesus' apostles realized that God had inaugurated his dominion of love through a world-changing event: the resurrection of Jesus from the dead. The Father had established the risen Jesus as the new man, the embodiment of all that the Father had willed for humankind from the beginning of the world. The Father had manifested the glorified Jesus as the first fruits of a new creation.

When the apostles went forth to preach the gospel in Jesus' name, therefore, they spontaneously presented the risen Jesus as the very heart of their message. They preached not a "religion" in the sense of an organized system of salvation but the person of the Savior himself. The apostles connected Jesus' good news of the Father's reign with the glad tidings of the Father's exaltation of Jesus as **Lord** ("absolute Sovereign") and

Christ. God had established the reign through revealing that Jesus was the powerful Son of God and victor over Satan (the devil), sin, and death. The apostles announced that citizenship in the Father's reign was coextensively one and the same with discipleship to the risen Jesus.

The apostles had been present when Jesus restored at least three persons from death to life: the widow of Naim's son, Jairus's daughter, and Jesus' close friend Lazarus. In those cases, however, Jesus had merely resuscitated dead persons to the same frail life that they had known formerly—they were to die again. Jesus' resurrection from the dead, on the other hand, meant that he had entered into a completely new bodily form. Jesus accepted a torturous death, but the Father received him with a welcoming embrace. Jesus entered into freedom, immortality, and unimaginable glory. Jesus passed over from death to newness of life, from frailty to strength, and from the lowliness of a slave to the majesty of a Lord. The risen Jesus was identically the same human teacher of Nazareth who had dwelled on earth among the apostles, yet they could scarcely describe his glorification. Jesus as the risen Lord utterly dwarfed their fondest expectations, and all their old categories of thought and speech collapsed in inadequacy.

Jesus as risen Lord might easily have created a wall of awestruck fear and even separation between himself and the apostles, had he not already granted them the gift of his friendship as a mortal human being. The night before Jesus died, he had announced to them: "You are my friends if you do what I command you. I do not call you servants any longer, because the servant does not know what the master is doing; but I have called you friends, because I have made known to you everything that I have heard from my Father. You did not choose me, but I chose you" (John 15.14–16a). Now the apostles would retain their familiar relationship with Jesus, their marvelously human friend, although they deepened this bond into a total commitment to Jesus, their divine Lord. Through the centuries, other Christian disciples have felt a special confidence in Jesus' humanity, according to the following admonition: "For we do not have a high priest who is unable to sympathize with our weaknesses, but we have one who in every respect has been tested as we are, yet without sin" (Heb. 4.15).

Christians gradually developed a series of special appellations for Jesus that pointed to his new role and function in their lives. These titles given to Jesus are significant for our investigation of Christian spirituality, because they suggest the actual impact of the risen Jesus upon the inner being of his disciples. Christians depict Jesus with provocative images: Jesus is at once the Lamb of God who offers himself in worship to God and the Good Shepherd who lays down his life for his flock. Jesus is Savior and Redeemer because he has reconciled all humankind with the Father and has made available God's forgiveness of sins. Jesus is Mediator and Son of God in power because he channels to believers the Father's gift of the Holy Spirit. Jesus is High Priest because he intercedes with the Father on his disciples' behalf, offering up their prayer and worship to God. Jesus is Head of the Church because he constitutes one living organism with the Church as his body. Jesus is Bridegroom of the Church because he has consummated an eternal covenant with the Church as his bride. Christians tend to avoid Jesus' preferred name for himself (Son of man) and to use instead the more expansive titles of "Lord" and "Christ." Often believers refer to Jesus as Our Lord, Our Lord Jesus Christ, or Christ the Lord, so that his titles function as though they are surnames.

Christians do try to imitate Jesus' example and obey his teachings by walking faithfully in his footsteps, yet their discipleship to Jesus involves more than the merely external imitation of his virtues. We come here to a salient and distinguishing characteristic of Christian spirituality: devotion to Jesus available within. Christians believe that they receive the risen Lord into their hearts, not only as a beloved memory of the past or as a noble exemplar for the future, but also as a vital and powerful presence in the here and now. For Jesus promised that he would remain with his disciples always and make his home among them. Paul the Apostle, in turn, extolled this mystery: "To them God chose to make known how great among the Gentiles are the riches of the glory of this mystery, which is Christ in you, the hope of glory" (Col. 1.27). Christians believe that the glorified Christ, empowered with unimaginable freedom, is immediately accessible within all his disciples, no matter where they may find themselves in space and time.

Since Christians know that the risen Jesus abides within them, they seek to open themselves ever more fully so that Jesus may deepen and extend his presence. Christians want to "put off" their sinful identity in the "old Adam" in order to "put on" the persona of the "new Adam," Jesus. Since Christians recognize that Jesus is alive, available, and active within them, they regard the risen Christ as their invisible companion who actively accompanies them on their journey to the Father. (Popular Christian hymnody often reflects this conviction.) Jesus walks ahead of believers to lead them when the way is obscure. Jesus encompasses Christians on all sides to protect them when the path is rugged or dangerous. Jesus seeks to intensify his presence within disciples throughout their lives in order to metamorphose them after his own image. Finally, Jesus is present at that critical moment of all moments, when Christians must achieve their own passage into eternity.

The risen Jesus Christ himself is the personal object of Christian faith, and he calls for an individual response from each disciple. For almost 2,000 years, believers have by countless words tried to articulate their experience of Jesus. Christians have written down many of these utterances in Scriptures inspired by God, in creeds proclaimed in liturgical congregations, in dogmas infallibly defined in **ecumenical councils** (universal assemblies of bishops), and in publications of every kind. Christians have borne witness to the risen Lord in sermons, in admonitions, in spontaneous conversations among friends and relatives, and even in bloody martyrdom. Yet disciples do not commit themselves primarily to words or heroic gestures about Jesus, however moving; to texts about Jesus, however inspired; or to pronouncements about Jesus, however infallible. Christians give themselves to Jesus himself, the risen Lord who incarnates the truth.

The risen Jesus is himself the personal foundation of Christian hope. Ever since God raised Jesus from the dead, Christians have hoped in the certain victory of grace over sin, love over hatred, and life over death. For almost two millennia, Christians have cherished the promises of Jesus in regard to their own bodily resurrection to be with their loved ones in heaven. Yet Christians do not hope primarily in the splendid future that Jesus has prepared for those who serve him, however strengthening. Christians hope in Jesus himself, who embodies Resurrection.

The risen Jesus is himself the model and source of Christian love. For almost twenty centuries, many Christians have tried faithfully to observe Jesus' "new commandment": that they love others even as Jesus has loved them—that is, altruistically, selflessly, and seeking no return. Yet Christians do not primarily obey abstract precepts of ethical wisdom, however sublime. Christians want to imitate Jesus himself, the embodiment of divine love.

Christian priests and ministers often provide their audiences with uplifting insights into their tradition and a grasp of the practical morality that flows from those insights. Ordained persons receive their training principally, however, in order that they may communicate the person of Jesus himself—as crucified yet risen. Christian leaders sometimes organize communities of believers into structured congregations with guidelines for worship and communal discipline, but they seek primarily to connect people with the person of Christ himself and sustain that bond. Christian Churches often administer complex institutions, but they all function ultimately for the sake of a personal and communal relationship with the Lord himself. From orphanages, hospitals, and publishing houses to schools, seminaries, and universities, all ecclesiastical enterprises exist in order to nurture the way of personal and communal discipleship to Jesus as the living pathfinder to the Father.

CHRISTIAN EXPERIENCE OF THE
GOD AND FATHER OF JESUS CHRIST

Christians, of course, identify the ultimately sacred Reality with the God and Father of Jesus Christ. We have seen that the Jews believe in a God of boundless *hesed* and *'emet*. We shall see in Chapter 6 that the Muslims believe in a God who is al-Rahman, al-Rahim. Jesus boldly proclaimed the Father's agape ("unconditional love") by announcing the impartial abundance of God's mercy toward the ungrateful and the wicked: "But love your enemies, do good, and lend, expecting nothing in return. Your reward will be great, and you will be children of the Most High; for he is kind to the ungrateful and the wicked. Be merciful, just as your Father is merciful" (Luke 6.35).

Christians believe that God is agape, an unqualified and unlimited gift of self in love for all humankind without exception. In the New Testament, we read, "Beloved, let us love one another, because love is from God; everyone who loves is born of God and knows God. Whoever does not love does not know God, for God is love. God's love was revealed among us in this way: God sent his only Son into the world so that we might live through him. In this is love, not that we love God but that he loved us and sent his Son to be the atoning sacrifice for our sins. Beloved, since God loved us so much, we also ought to love one another" (1 John 4.7–11).

Christians believe that God's very nature is inexhaustible agape, an agape that overflows upon each human being without discrimination or measure. Many Christians rejoice that God is boundless agape—they know that they do not first have to be worthy or perform meritorious actions in order to deserve God's agape. God creates the universe, sustains it, and blesses its goodness, because God is agape. God bestows agape gratuitously—all is grace, all is cause for thanksgiving. God redeemed the human race out of agape through the crucifixion of Jesus, when men and women were still sinners. Paul the Apostle wrote, "For while we were still weak, at the right time Christ died for the ungodly. Indeed, rarely will anyone die for a righteous person—though perhaps for a good person someone might actually dare to die. But God proves his love for us in that while we still were sinners Christ died for us" (Rom. 5.6–8).

If we were to ask Christians what God means to them, many of them would say without a moment's hesitation: "God is love." This means that all of God's attributes have divine love at their determining core, from justice and mercy to power and wisdom. While some Christians do emphasize the divine judgment and some do fear the divine punishment for sin, many other Christians interpret God's plan totally in terms of divine love, from creation and conservation of the universe to redemption of humankind. Believers sometimes identify themselves as those who have been "made to know" that God loves them. Many disciples even venerate Jesus' crucifixion by wearing a cross about their neck or displaying a **crucifix** (a cross with an image of the nailed Jesus upon it) in their home, because they believe that Jesus' death was God's most persuasive demonstration of love.

Christians' confidence in God's agape underscores every aspect of their faith commitment and punctuates every dimension of their spirituality. Christians' belief in divine providence, for example, precludes the image of God as a detached architect who stands back and waits to see what will happen with his creation. On the contrary, God intervenes as "Lord of history" to govern the destinies of all nations. God governs all human beings sweetly, as he attends to their every thought, sustains their every breath, concurs in their every heartbeat, and calls them to eternal happiness. Indeed, God is available to each man and each woman with loving solicitude, because God esteems each individual as beyond any price. Christians believe that God truly cares about them, has their best interests at heart, and—despite those unspeakable tragedies that might suggest the contrary—is working to ensure that all things work out for the best in the end.

Jews and Muslims share Christians' faith in the one God of Abraham, the almighty Creator of heaven and earth. In Jewish and Islamic belief, however, God's unity utterly precludes any plurality of persons. Consequently, many Jews and Muslims view the Christian belief in the **Blessed Trinity** (the doctrine of three equal and co-eternal divine persons in one divine nature) suspiciously as a disguised **tritheism** (belief in three gods). Yet Christians insist that the one God has revealed that God is living agape, not only in his redemptive providence for the salvation of human beings but also within his very nature.

The Gospel of John has played an incalculable role in Christian spirituality, and no verses have made a more significant impact than the verses of its opening chapter: "In the beginning was the Word, and the Word was with God, and the Word was God. He was in the beginning with God. All things came into being through him, and without him not one thing came into being. . . . And the Word became flesh and lived among us, and we have seen his glory, the glory as of a father's only son, full of grace and truth. . . . No one has ever seen God. It is God the only Son, who is close to the Father's heart, who has made him known" (John 1.1–3a, 14, 18). For Christians, God's love is so boundlessly fertile, so vitally active, and so dynamically relational that not only two but even three divine persons possess the divine essence co-equally and co-eternally.

These three divine persons are God the Father, God the Son, and God the Holy Spirit. The three divine persons are truly distinct from one another so that the Father is not the Son, the Son is not the Holy Spirit, and the Holy Spirit is not the Father. Yet the three divine persons are inseparably united in the same divine essence, "substance," or nature. The Father does not make or create the Son, nor is the Father any older or greater than the Son is. The Holy Spirit is not merely an impersonal force; the Holy Spirit is every bit as personal as the Father and the Son are personal. Each person is totally identified with the infinite Truth, Goodness, Beauty, Wisdom, and Power of the one divine Being (or Godhead).

Christians approach the Father and the Son distantly and analogously in terms of their everyday experience of parenthood and sonship. Christians can provide no personal analogue for the Holy Spirit, however. They can only fall back upon inanimate biblical metaphors that appeal to the imagination. Some Christians may open themselves to the Holy Spirit as "the stirring of a wind" or "the gentle whisper of a breeze," "the brilliant light" or "the purifying flames of a fire." Other Christians may meditate upon the Holy Spirit as "the refreshing coolness of water," "the hovering presence of a dove," or "the consecrating and healing anointing with oil." Others still have suggested that the Holy Spirit is like the eternal "embrace" or even "the kiss" that at once unites the Father with the Son and expresses their unity.

Christians insist that God is a community of three equally divine persons in loving relatedness. The life of God courses eternally among the three divine persons. Thus, God's interior life is a family of three equally divine persons who actively connect with one another in knowledge and love—three eternal persons who actively connect with one another even now, as they will actively connect with one another always. We find a distant analogy in the human family, since husband and wife may know and love each other, may speak of "their love" that they possess in common, and may even body forth "their love" in a child. Some Christians reflect upon the Father as "the Person who loves," upon the Son as "the Person who is loved," and upon the Holy Spirit as "the Person who is the love between them."

The Christian doctrine of the Blessed Trinity is not merely some sort of divine conundrum. Neither is the Blessed Trinity merely a riddle to be solved, an irrational contradiction that people must accept out of humility, or some perplexing problem to be pondered. The Blessed Trinity is a transcendent mystery, the inscrutable infinity of the really Real that exceeds all human comprehension, defies all human formulation, and explodes all human categories. The divine mystery makes our minds whirl, and we are bewildered, not because darkness deceives us but because unfathomable light blinds us. The mystery of the Blessed Trinity in itself is the most knowable Truth, the most lovable Goodness, and the most sublime Beauty of all, and uncomprehending believers can only bow their heads before it in profound adoration. The Blessed Trinity is finally not a statement boldly to be affirmed or a proposition rashly to be analyzed but a mystery reverently to be worshipped and contemplated.

Having noted this, Christian theologians have still attempted to articulate the analogous and distant fruits of their worship and contemplation. The trinitarian doctrine of Christians speaks of the dynamic life of three divine persons, who not only relate to one another but also disclose themselves uniquely through Christ, the Second Person incarnate. Human beings may relate as individuals to each of the three divine persons. Disciples relate to God the Father as Creator, to God the Son as Redeemer, and to God the Holy Spirit as Sanctifier. The Holy Spirit comes in order to empower men and women to believe in Jesus as Lord and Savior. The Holy Spirit then incorporates believers into the risen Christ in order that they may live as the Father's adoptive sons and daughters in the Son. It is the Holy Spirit who heals people from their sinfulness by restoring them to the Father. It is the Holy Spirit who binds believers into the Christian community and enables them to hope, to love, to pray, to worship, and to give themselves to others in service. Some Christians regularly seek the guidance of a trusted "spiritual director" who acts as an instrument of the Holy Spirit, but it is always the Holy Spirit who is the chief source of all Christian spirituality.

Jesus insisted that people must trust in God unquestioningly and appreciate how God's love encompasses them night and day, from moment to moment. Indeed, Jesus revealed, God is a kind Father who provides for his children much more solicitously than he feeds the birds of the air or clothes the lilies of the field. Jesus promised his friends that their faithfulness could leave no room for anxiety or fear if only they believed enough. The Holy Spirit constantly renews Jesus' call to this "spiritual childhood," that all disciples may approach God with the simple confidence of little children who know how precious they are to their father.

When disciples respond to the Holy Spirit's direction within them, they begin to enjoy the freedom of God's children. The Holy Spirit overcomes their sinful alienation and estrangement from God. Paul the Apostle offered his Christian converts a remarkable hope, providing that they walk in the Holy Spirit. The Holy Spirit frees believers from the fleshly works of sin: "Live by the Spirit, I say, and do not gratify the desires of the flesh. . . . Now the works of the flesh are obvious: fornication, impurity, licentiousness, idolatry, sorcery, enmities, strife, jealousy, anger, quarrels, dissensions, factions, envy, drunkenness, carousing, and things like these" (Gal. 5.16, 19–21a). Paul went on to list, on the other hand, the marvelous fruits of life in the Holy Spirit: "By contrast, the fruit of the Spirit is love, joy, peace, patience, kindness, generosity, faithfulness, gentleness, and self-control" (Gal. 5.22–23a).

A fuller consideration of the Christians' personal and communal discipleship of the risen Jesus, then, reveals its necessarily trinitarian structure. Divinely redemptive love comes down to human beings from the Father through the incarnate and glorified Son in the Holy Spirit. Christian spirituality, on the other hand, is fundamentally a matter of disciples returning in the Holy Spirit, through the incarnate and glorified Son, to the Father. In the sequence of historical consciousness, Christians first become disciples of Jesus Christ, personally and communally. Next, Christians come through Jesus to know the Father, whom Jesus proclaimed and served so unreservedly. Finally, Christians discover the presence of the Holy Spirit within them, gently calling them to live according to their dignity as God's adoptive children.

CHRISTIAN GROWTH THROUGH THE CHURCH

Religious people tend to band together in communities in order to realize all the communal dimensions of their tradition. We have already noted in Chapter 4, for example, the significance of K'lal Yisrael for the spirituality of Jews, who follow the way of Torah not simply as individuals but as God's holy people, a community that is covenanted both to the LORD God and to one another. In Chapter 6, we shall study the amazing holding power of the worldwide *umma* for the spirituality of Muslims, who walk the straight path of Islam not simply as individuals but as a brotherhood/sisterhood, a community whose members are bound both to Allah and to one another. In Chapter 8, we shall investigate the liberating power of the Samgha for the spirituality of Theravada Buddhists, who follow the middle way of the Buddha's Dhamma as members of a monastic order, a community whose members seek Nibbana together. It is not surprising, therefore, that the Church is a necessary factor in the spirituality of Christians, a community that follows the way of Jesus' discipleship. Indeed, early Christians would have considered discipleship on an exclusively "Jesus-and-me" basis to be deficient and incomplete.

From the beginning of his ministry Jesus sought to provide his followers with a communal life; he led them in common instructions, shared meals, collective retreats, and joint service to others. Eventually, Jesus chose twelve of his disciples to be his apostles, a closely knit group that he called "the Twelve" (probably in symbolic parallel with the Twelve Tribes of Israel). Jesus gave special formation to the Twelve as he founded a new Israel, and he made them the official witnesses of his resurrection. After God glorified Jesus, the Father sent the Holy Spirit to transform the Twelve Apostles and 108 other men and women into the infant Church. Jesus' disciples became the new people of God in Christ's Body, a community united with God and with one another by the New Covenant. The risen Jesus continued to be present among them as he had promised: "Again, truly I tell you, if two of you agree on earth about anything you ask, it will be done for you by my Father in heaven. For where two or three are gathered in my name, I am there among them" (Matt. 18.19–20).

The earliest Jewish Christians naturally interpreted their collective experience in terms of familiar Jewish categories. They believed in Jesus as a "new Moses," who through his "new Exodus" from this world back to the Father had inaugurated a "new Israel" of a "New Covenant." Since early Christians had come to know the risen Jesus while they were still members of God's holy people, they readily identified themselves in terms of their new solidarity as God's holy people in Christ. Beautiful words to this effect are ascribed to the apostle Peter: "But you are a chosen race, a royal priesthood, a holy nation, God's own people, in order that you may proclaim the mighty acts of him who called you out of darkness into his marvelous light" (1 Pet. 2.9).

Christians joyfully congregated in order to celebrate their new corporate identity: "They devoted themselves to the apostles' teaching and fellowship [*koinonia*, "communion"], to the breaking of bread and the prayers" (Acts 2.42). Through their sharing of both goods and burdens, they attempted to fulfill Jesus' ultimate challenge—that they must love one another as Jesus had loved them. Greek-speaking Jewish Christians referred to each worshipping assembly as an *ekklesia kyriake* ("Lordly assembly"). Our Anglo-Saxon noun *church* (like the German word *Kirche* and the Scottish word *kirk*) is derived from *kyriake*, the second term in that phrase. The concept of "Church" primarily characterizes Christians as a called congregation, or gathered people, and refers only by extension to the sacred edifice in which Christians happen to come together.

Indeed, Jesus' reconciling mission was precisely to overcome all estrangement and create solidarity. Jesus by his death and resurrection healed humankind from every division that separates human beings from God and from one another. The Church, therefore, is universally for every individual of every ethnic group in every generation. The Church cannot tolerate any cliques among individuals or factions among various social groups. The Church must reach out especially to the poor in addition to the wealthy, especially to the sick in addition to the healthy, and especially to the vulnerable in addition to the powerful. Christians are bound to love all human beings without exception, whether they feel attracted to them or not, whether they even like them or not. (Loving is a matter of benevolence or freely and responsibly willing good toward others, while liking is merely a matter of spontaneously agreeable feelings toward others.) Disciples must offer their deliberate friendship to all their fellow human beings—not only to the like-minded companions who share their background but also to the people of vastly different lifestyles and cultures. This obligation binds the consciences of Christians categorically and defines their spiritual authenticity. Martin Luther King, Jr. (1929–68), for example, was a Baptist minister who preached the Gospel as he led the Civil Rights movement for the liberation of African Americans. Members of the Salvation Army with their clanging bells provide a loud voice to the weak and the needy during holiday seasons. The Catholic Relief Agency is always there on the spot with food and medicine for the victims of natural or human-made catastrophes. Christians of all persuasions know that they must respond generously whenever other inhabitants of the planet suffer the calamities of war, famine, flood, earthquake, and fire.

Christians hold the vision of Paul the Apostle: "There is one body and one Spirit, just as you were called to the one hope of your calling, one Lord, one faith, one baptism, one God and Father of all, who is above all and through all and in all" (Eph. 4.4–6). Christians around the world pray together, reciting the Lord's Prayer in the first-person plural according to Jesus' own instruction: "Our Father, who art in heaven. . . ." Catholics,

Eastern Orthodox, Anglicans, and many Protestants stand and recite the Nicene Creed (a classical statement of Christian doctrines) on Sunday, often beginning their profession of faith in the first-person plural: "We believe in one God. . . ." Christians especially appreciate the value of genuine community, when peoples of countless nations, languages, regions, etiquettes, and cultural conventions gather together in unity. Christians need not actually assemble in one physical place, of course; even when they are widely dispersed and involved with all the details of their particular lives, they can still count on the silent support of their brothers and sisters in Christ.

Christian spirituality is about disciples opening themselves so that they may be filled with the mind and heart of the risen Jesus. Christians must be men and women of God with and for others. Christians acknowledge that they must bear one another's burdens and always avoid the pitfalls of narrow narcissism. Christians must extend their community by welcoming the strangers, comforting the sick, bringing Holy Communion to the shut-ins, and visiting the imprisoned. Consequently, Christians establish all kinds of institutions for the service of the physically and spiritually needy by way of food, shelter, education, and health care.

Christians pursue their pilgrimage not by themselves as lonely travelers, but in the sustaining companionship of a vast multitude. Their spirituality grows strong and endures, especially within an intricate network of mutual concern and assistance. Christian faith, hope, and agape are communal possessions, which disciples receive, nourish, deepen, and reinforce in the midst of community. Consequently, when Pentecostal Christians (believers who emphasize the experience of baptism in the Holy Spirit) and **born-again Christians** (believers who emphasize the experience of a second birth by faith) assemble for worship, they like to give public testimony to the workings of Christ in their lives. Many Catholic and Protestant **charismatics** (believers who are especially devoted to the Holy Spirit and the Spirit's gifts) belong to prayer groups that assemble regularly for congregational praise and mutual support.

Paul the Apostle described the shared joy of early Christian communities:

As God's chosen ones, holy and beloved, clothe yourselves with compassion, kindness, humility, meekness, and patience. Bear with one another and, if anyone has a complaint against another, forgive each other; just as the Lord has forgiven you, you also must forgive. Above all, clothe yourselves with love, which binds everything together in perfect harmony. And let the peace of Christ rule in your hearts, to which indeed you were called in the one body. And be thankful. Let the word of Christ dwell in you richly; teach and admonish one another in all wisdom; and with gratitude in your hearts sing psalms, hymns, and spiritual songs to God. And whatever you do, in word or deed, do everything in the name of the Lord *Jesus, giving thanks to God the Father through him.*

—Col. 3.12–17

Monasticism (found not only among Catholics, Eastern Orthodox, and Copts but also among some Anglicans and Lutherans) offers to Christian men and women a particularly intense form of structured life known as **cenobitical** ("communal"). Christian men and women draw apart from the enticements and noisy distractions of secular life and join monasteries in order to devote themselves more totally to the pursuit of Christian holiness. For over 1,500 years, Christian monks and nuns have lived in cloistered monasteries according to the rule of a famous abbot such as Basil the Great (330–79) in the Christian East or Benedict (480–550) in the Christian West. Monks and nuns seek a more heightened consciousness and more constant awareness of God's loving presence to their right and to their left, above them and below them, in every place and in every activity. They spend long hours in manual or scholarly labor, punctuated regularly by choral psalmody and public worship. Monks and nuns live their total lives for God, however, and their every heartbeat can be a prayer of personal communion. Not uncommonly, they attain advanced stages of contemplative piety and holiness.

Since the Middle Ages, charismatic men and women have modified the monastic model of common life so that members may be more mobile and free to serve others in urban ministries. For example, Francis of Assisi (1181–1226) founded the Order of Lesser Friars, or Franciscans, Dominic Guzman (1170–1221) instituted the Order of Friars Preachers, or Dominicans, and Ignatius of Loyola (1491–1556) established the Society of Jesus, or Jesuits, while Teresa of Avila (1515–82) inspired the Order of Discalced Carmelites. There have also been many other institutes for dedicated sisters, brothers, priests, and missionaries. In modern times, Brother Roger, a Protestant of the Reformed tradition, founded an ecumenical monastery at Taizé in France and dedicated it as a dynamic center for reform and reconciliation in the contemporary Church.

Members of Christian orders and congregations may give themselves totally to Jesus with vows of poverty, obedience, and celibate chastity. Some groups are more contemplative and quiet in their lifestyle, while others are more active in the service of others as teachers, nurses, or missionaries. Yet their fundamental purpose is always the same: to consecrate their lives undividedly to a regulated common life for the sake of ever deeper communion with the risen Jesus for God in the Holy Spirit.

Catholic, Anglican, and Eastern Orthodox Christians believe that the risen Jesus mediates or **sacramentalizes** (communicates through visible signs) his redemptive presence in and through the Church. They understand their union with Jesus as dependent upon and coextensive with their incorporation into Jesus' community of the redeemed. This belief is a decisive factor in their spirituality, since they regularly experience the risen Jesus in the company of one another. Catholic, Anglican, and Eastern Orthodox Christians especially encounter Jesus as High Priest as they assemble for worship through the ministry of the Church's ordained bishops, priests, and deacons, who, they believe, act in the name and power of Jesus.

The Protestant reformers decided that Catholic emphasis upon a mediational Church granted too great a role in the salvific process to sinful human beings. They called upon each person individually to seek **justification** (the process of being made righteous by God for Jesus' sake) directly by faith alone and not sacramentally through the Christian community. They still insisted, however, that new Christians must go on to join in community with the other believers who know Jesus. The role of Protestant ministers, then, is not to mediate Jesus but to preach the Word of God and stir up faith in Jesus. Despite this critically important disagreement over the proper role and function of the Church, the vast majority of Christians still agree that some degree of ecclesial involvement is indispensable to their spiritual growth. Even the Quakers, who dislike external ceremonies, come together quietly to sit in one another's presence as they await God's stirrings within them.

Catholic Christians make much of their belief in the **communion of saints,** by which they feel a connection not only with all the living members of the Church but also with all those who have been members of the Church before them. Catholic belief in the communion of saints refers preeminently to Mary, who is the virginal and sinless mother of Christ, the foremost member of the community of the redeemed, and the one believer in whom God perfectly realized his plan for all people. Catholics believe that Mary exercises a maternal love for all of Jesus' disciples as for her own spiritual children. Mary's function, of course, is necessarily secondary and subordinate to Christ's role. Yet Mary is a very significant person in the lives of those who love her, draw near to her, and ask her to pray for them to her divine Son. Catholics feel a remarkably tender dimension in their spirituality, because they are confident that Mary is truly their spiritual mother. Eastern Orthodox Christians are particularly devoted to the glorified Mary who dwells with her Son in heaven, and they mention her constantly in their weekly **Divine Liturgy** (Eastern Orthodox celebration of the Holy Eucharist, or Lord's Supper) as the holy Mother of God and ever virgin Mary.

The Christian communion of saints also includes the martyred men and women who shed their blood for their faith, together with all the other heroes and heroines who have practiced extraordinary virtue and are publicly acclaimed as the Church's saints. The communion of saints even involves that much larger number of anonymous persons who persevered in their discipleship and who have gone ahead to receive their eternal reward with Christ in heaven. Catholic, Anglican, and Eastern Orthodox Christians believe that disciples in need of assistance can request the intercessory prayers of these persons before God. Believers study the lives of these people as concrete realizations of God's redemptive plan. Many parents carefully name their children after saints in order that their offspring may have a special patron or patroness in heaven. Catholics often speak with warm affection and familiarity of favorite saints such as St. Thérèse of Lisieux (1873–97) and St. Antony of Padua (1195–1231).

Eastern Christians adorn their churches and homes with sacred **icons** (holy paintings prayerfully created by monks) that portray the risen Jesus, the glorified Mary, and the saints in an idealized state as resurrected in glory. The holy icons are not merely pictures that beautify their surroundings. Eastern Christians revere them as powerful conduits of grace. When Eastern Christians enter their churches, they fervently bow their heads before the holy icons and kiss them as sacramental windows that open out to the heavenly dimension of reality.

FORMATION THROUGH THE CHRISTIAN BIBLE

In Chapter 4, we noted the creative contribution of the Hebrew Bible to Jewish spirituality. In Chapter 6, we shall emphasize the even more critical role of the Quran in Islamic spirituality. At this juncture, we shall explore the incalculable impact of the Christian Bible upon Christian spirituality, an influence that has been continuous and decisive for over 1,900 years. If the Christians' paradigm for spiritual pilgrimage to the Father is the way of Jesus' discipleship, then their Bible has functioned as a beloved *vade mecum* ("handbook") for their journey. The Church, filled with the presence of the risen Jesus, has passed down its developing tradition of collective reflection upon Jesus and his gospel, and the Bible holds an unrivaled position within this legacy as the distilled essence of it all.

When early Christians gathered for worship, they found the inspirational form and content for their prayers in their beloved Hebrew Bible. They read these familiar texts in the light of their new experience of the risen Jesus, however: Christian Jews differed from non-Christian Jews especially in their interpretation of certain texts as messianic (prophetically related to the Jewish Messiah). When the Christians separated definitively from the Jews (about 90 C.E.), they appropriated the Jewish Scriptures as their own.

Christian writers also developed theological portraits of Jesus and commentaries on his significance, including the **Gospels** according to Matthew, Mark, Luke, and John and an extensive body of **Epistles** (letters) attributed to Paul the Apostle and others. Assembled Christians found themselves reading selections from these new works with the same reverence that they had previously reserved for the Jewish Scriptures. In the late fourth century, Church authorities approved twenty-seven of these early writings as a canon for a Christian New Testament, as distinguished from the reinterpreted Jewish Scriptures, or Christian Old Testament. The Christian Bible is the composite result of this long and complicated process.

Christian faith in Jesus parallels Christian beliefs about Scripture. In Jesus, the Son and personal Word of God became truly a man. In Jesus, therefore, the Son and personal Word of God became incarnate in the Jewish culture, with every mental, linguistic, physical, spatial, and temporal limitation that human experience implies, save only sin. In Scripture, the revealing Word of God became truly a book. In Scripture, therefore, the revealing Word of God became written in the Hebrew and Greek languages, with every conceptual, literary, categorical, lexical, and grammatical limitation that human composition implies, save only the teaching of religious error.

Christians believe that God is the principal author of the Bible. This article of belief means not only that the Holy Spirit inspired (gave special guidance to) the authors who produced its pages but also that the Holy Spirit continues internally to direct those who read the Bible in faith. Moreover, Christians encounter the risen Jesus in every chapter of the Old and New Testaments, and they hear him speak to them here and now. We cannot calculate the full extent of this powerful source of growth in Christian spirituality.

Christians have always proclaimed the Scriptures when they have assembled for their **liturgy** (communal and public worship of God the

Father through Christ in the Holy Spirit by words and symbolic gestures). In the liturgical celebration, lectors read the Scriptures solemnly, while the congregation tries attentively to listen and then prayerfully to respond. In private reading, Christians expectantly approach reflective perusal of the Scriptures as a graced opportunity for interpersonal dialogue with their Lord. Disciples open their hearts to the Master as he continues to teach. Monks and nuns refer to the reflective perusal of sacred Scripture as *lectio divina* ("divine reading"), the prerequisite for their prayer life.

Christians read the Bible not only in order to learn the teachings of Jesus, but also in order to know and love Jesus in a communion of mind and heart. Ever since the Protestant Reformation in the sixteenth century, Protestant Christians have especially promoted study and prayerful reflection upon the Bible. Protestant belief in the Bible as the sole rule of faith has been a decisive factor in shaping Protestant vision and piety, and biblical verses and motifs have given Protestant spirituality its special character. Nowadays, Catholics, too, devote themselves to reading the Scriptures in order to grow in faith and nourish their prayer life. Through the sacred page Jesus becomes the supremely significant Reality in the lives of Christians. Jesus possesses his disciples with his healing presence and strengthens them with his counsel.

Conservative, or "Evangelical," Protestants, who base their religion resolutely and exclusively upon the inerrant Word of God as found in the Bible, often describe themselves as "born-again Christians." Frequently enough, born-again Christians are more than willing to narrate the story of their first encounter with Jesus, and their account follows a typical pattern such as the following:

A potential convert first meets some believers, who offer him their own testimony of how Jesus has permanently turned their lives around for the better. The person must study key texts from Scripture so that he too may welcome Jesus into his heart and become a saved person, a Christian. That evening, the potential convert opens a Bible, perhaps to John 3.5–6: "Jesus answered him, 'Very truly, I tell you, no one can see the kingdom of God without being born of water and Spirit. What is born of the flesh is flesh, and what is born of the Spirit is spirit.'" He closes his eyes and reflects upon his options, praying for the grace of conversion. The inquirer begins to feel an interior call, a warm invitation to surrender himself to Jesus. He responds with a saving act of faith, and he gives his life over to Jesus: "I totally commit myself to you, Jesus Christ, as my personal Lord and Savior." Our new convert then feels flooded with the joyful certainty that all his sins have been forgiven and he has been saved: He is amazed, overwhelmed, weeping, and smiling, all at the same time.

Note that the born-again encounter with Christ has been thoroughly experiential. From this point on, a born-again Christian knows Jesus, not merely as a famous teacher of the past but also as a living savior who instructs him in the present. He makes continual reference to Jesus in his everyday life, not merely as to a noble exemplar in a book but as to a real friend who is present here and now actively to reinforce his resolution and encourage him. Our convert always remembers that particular place and moment in time when he began to see everything in a new way. The event was momentous, and it has marked a decisive juncture in his life; he can never be the same again. In due course, our new Christian probably seeks out a community of believers for fellowship and requests sacramental baptism by water.

Pentecostal (or "charismatic") Christians also seek to meet Jesus personally in a special way—in terms of an event known as baptism in the Spirit. Pentecostal spirituality is very experiential and often involves joyful excitement, sweet tears, and a variety of physical phenomena. The process of becoming a Pentecostal Christian follows a regular pattern along lines such as the following:

A potential convert makes the acquaintance of some individuals who invite her to attend a meeting of their prayer group. She agrees to come, and she finds herself together with several dozen other persons, all of whom welcome her with visible happiness and enthusiasm. Smiling people mingle with one another and exchange signs of affection. Our inquirer stays securely close to familiar faces, but she does attend to the unstructured prayer as it develops freely and spontaneously. She enjoys the hymnody, as people joyfully bless Jesus and proclaim his Lordship in song. Our potential convert observes with wonder as people without inhibition raise their arms high and pray in strange languages. She notes phrases such as "lifted up," "slain in the Spirit," and "thank you, Jesus." She listens as individuals **prophesy** (speak on behalf of God) in a strange tongue or interpret someone else's **prophecy** (a message spoken on behalf of God) for the community.

After about two hours of group prayer, the leaders at the front invite anyone who desires special prayers to come forward. Those who seek particular blessings (such as a healing) present themselves, and several people pray over them. Despite her mixed feelings, our potential convert also requests prayers, and she too receives the baptism in the Spirit—she even experiences a variety of charisms such as **glossolalia** (speaking in tongues) or prophecy. The new Pentecostal's principal gift, however, is a dimension of conviction, realism, and depth in her knowledge of Jesus as Lord, a "faith on faith" that she had not experienced before.

CHRISTIAN RESPONSE TO GOD
THROUGH WORSHIP AND PRAYER

Christians from their earliest history have brought to mind the risen Jesus by celebrating their liturgy on Sunday, the Lord's Day. According to the Bible, God created the world in six days, rested on the seventh day, and re-created the universe through Christ on the "eighth" day. (There is no ninth day, since Sunday opens out into the eternal light of the Resurrection.) In Christian liturgy, Easter Sunday is the queen of all festivals, and every other Sunday is an Easter in miniature.

Artists of every generation have devoted their creative talent to enhancing the liturgies of the Christian Church. Poets have composed solemn prayers of enduring eloquence in order to express this worship with sacred words. Architects have designed churches of every size from modest chapels to towering cathedrals in order to envelop this worship within sacred space. Artists have produced stained-glass windows, painted biblical scenes, and sculpted figures of wood and marble in order to enhance this worship with sacred environment. Musicians have composed classical pieces for choir, organ, and ensemble in order to give body to this worship with sacred song.

When Christians gather for their Sunday liturgy, they experience their finest hour of the week and realize their identity most vividly. Most Christians celebrate the Holy Eucharist. It is impossible to overemphasize the central significance of the Holy Eucharist in Christian spirituality. The word *Eucharist* means "thanksgiving" and refers back to the Jewish *berakhah* ("blessing"), upon which it is based for its rhythm and thrust of praise. Eastern Orthodox Christians gather for the Divine Liturgy, Catholics and Anglicans offer the **Mass,** and most Protestants speak of the Lord's Supper, or **Holy Communion.**

Christians differ widely in their beliefs about the Holy Eucharist, but they all agree that it enables them in some sense to meet Christ and commemorate his redemptive death and resurrection. For example, Catholics, Anglicans, Eastern Orthodox, and some Protestants find in the Holy Eucharist both the summit of their life and the fundamental source of all their activity. Other Protestants also consider the Holy Eucharist to be very important, of course, but they tend to emphasize the centrality of the Bible in their lives. Christians also vary in the details of their liturgies, although they all generally structure their celebrations toward encountering Christ both "in word and in sacrament." The opening section of this central liturgical event is the **service of the Word** (a structured series of prayers, scripture readings, and sermon). The concluding and principal section is the **service of the Eucharist** (a thanksgiving that includes an account of Jesus' last supper and concludes with the distribution of Holy Communion).

Jesus himself at the Last Supper commanded that his disciples should do what he was doing as a memorial to himself. He knew well the dangers of forgetfulness. Jesus fully understood how easily his disciples could lose their focus upon him and become immersed in the cares of this world. Consequently, Christians obediently come together in memory of Jesus. They recall their dignity as adoptive children of the Father by Christ's grace, and so they adore and glorify God. They call to mind how much they are indebted to the Father for all that they receive by Christ's intercession, and so they praise and thank God. They remember all the wonders of creation and redemption by Christ's mediation, and so they offer their global supplications to God.

Catholic, Anglican, and Eastern Orthodox Christians especially express their personal relationship with the Lord in the communal context of their liturgy. Above all, they connect with Jesus as he comes to them and deepens his presence within them through Holy Communion. They contact Jesus every time that they receive a sacrament in the Church, and they try to be fully aware of all that is happening to them. The risen Jesus is truly present in the ordained minister, in the proclamation of Jesus' word, in the two or three gathered together in Jesus' name, and in the larger community as they worship the Father.

Catholic, Anglican, and Eastern Orthodox **catechumens** (individuals who are being prepared for entrance into the Church) receive baptism into the community from the risen Jesus through a bishop, priest, or deacon. They sorrowfully confess their sins to a priest in the sacrament of **reconciliation** (also known as penance) as to the risen Jesus, who absolves them of their sins. They receive the **anointing of the sick** (also known as **unction**) from their priest(s) when they become seriously ill, because Christ the divine physician visits them with all his healing power. They experience the Lord also in the other sacraments: It is Jesus himself in person who pours forth the Holy Spirit in **confirmation** (also known as **chrismation**), it is Jesus who binds a couple together in matrimony, and it is Jesus who ordains individuals to the sacred ministry through **holy orders.**

Needless to say, there could scarcely be a monotheistic spirituality that neglected prayer. When Christians pray, they share an experience in common with their fellow monotheists, the Jews and the Muslims, who also pray to a God of compassionate and loving providence. We have learned that the Jews pray three times a day, and we shall see that

Muslims pray five times a day. Christians are told to pray always and not lose heart. For our purposes, we may understand **prayer** as a religious act by which human beings individually or communally commune with the divinely sacred. Christians believe that God knows their identity, loves them uniquely, and is mercifully available to each of them through Christ in his Spirit. They carry on a dialogue with a personal God who is alive, discerns their faintest aspirations, and responds to them.

St. Augustine (354–430) suggested that those who sing pray twice, and many Christians send their prayers heavenward to the accompaniment of solo and choral music. Old Testament psalmody has occupied a position of privilege in this regard, and Christians have progressed over the centuries from *recto tono* (a style of chanting in a single note) to the ethereal melodies of monastic chant. Protestants feel the backbone tingle with joyful enthusiasm when they join in the hymnody of Martin Luther (1483–1546) and Charles Wesley (1707–88). African American Protestants reverberate in body and soul when their gospel-singing choir begins to lead them.

The Father gives the Holy Spirit to Christians in order that they may confidently approach God. Occasionally, Christians pray directly to the Holy Spirit in order to dispose themselves more fully to live by God's grace. Much more frequently, Christians pray immediately to Christ in order to strengthen their relationship with him and be filled with his presence. Most of all, however, Christians structure their prayer life in parallel with the rhythm of their redemption, and they address their prayers to the Father as they journey to the Father through the risen Jesus.

Christians who immerse themselves in prayerful communion with God learn to recognize God's work in their lives as a caring goodness that floods their consciousness and comforts them in their sorrows. They learn to interpret each happenstance in a new way: Whether pleasant or painful, each event becomes a revelation of the Father's kindness and generosity. Passing thoughts disclose heavenly inspirations, accidental meetings become meaningful encounters, and bodily illnesses occasion spiritual growth. Even evil temptations can be challenges toward growth and maturity. Despite all the disappointments, the heartbreaks, and the endless stream of human tragedies that sear the human soul, Christians hope against hope: The Father has truly raised Jesus from the dead, and he will infallibly make everything work out for the best in the end.

When Christians pray, they address God with sentiments of adoration and praise, thanksgiving and love. Sometimes they approach God with heartfelt feelings of contrition for their sins and petition for forgiveness. Often they present corporal and spiritual needs before God—not only their own but also those of others and, indeed, of all humankind. Yet they must at the same time seek to live out their lives according to God's holy will. Christians know that it is always they rather than God who must change, and prayer facilitates the process. Christians by prayer open themselves silently to hear God's response, and they try to appropriate that response into their lives.

Christians sometimes progress through three general stages in their prayer. During their initial stage as beginners, they pray discursively—they verbalize their thoughts spontaneously, or they try sincerely to affirm the words of others. They may call upon an established method of meditation or reflective spiritual reading in order to counter distractions and focus their attention more completely upon God. During their intermediate stage as proficients, they pray affectively and give themselves mentally to successive dispositions toward God, such as faith, surrender, and moral resolution. They learn to be grateful in periods of sensible consolation, but patient and persevering in times of bitter aridity. During their advanced state of intimate union with God, they often pray with utmost simplicity.

Christian prayer is a hungering and thirsting for God, and **fasting** is "prayer of the stomach." Fasting creates a sensation of bodily weakness, the symbol of our absolute dependence upon God's sustaining intervention. Many Christians include fasting, whether voluntary or by traditional precept, among their spiritual exercises. When they fast, they may also do penance in reparation for past sins and discipline themselves in fortification against future temptations. Many Christians fast especially on the weekdays of **Lent** (the forty days of preparation for the solemn feast of **Easter**). Catholic Christians fast before receiving Holy Communion.

Christian prayer is a gift of the self to God, and **almsgiving** is "prayer of the hands." Almsgiving is Christian self-abnegation choreographed, a self-denial with a sting. Christians are bound to love one another as they have been loved. They must show mercy toward others as they have received mercy. They must put the interests of others before their own. Many Protestants regularly **tithe** (donate one tenth of their income), but all Christians are bound by the demands of responsible stewardship. They must even share of their very substance with the Jesus who is present in the destitute.

Christian prayer is a quest for God, and pilgrimage is "prayer of the feet." Christians from the beginning have sought to follow the human example of Jesus Christ, and they have described their spirituality in images of physical movement. They have understood their discipleship as a spiritual pilgrimage, and they have spoken of themselves as wayfarers who walk in Jesus' footsteps. Christians who could afford it have journeyed to sacred sites in the Holy Land (Israel), Santiago de Compostela, Rome, and other places made holy by theophanies or other supernatural events. The poor have trekked labyrinthine paths etched symbolically in the stone thresholds of their local cathedrals. Monks and nuns, who must observe a cloistered stability in one place, have sought their Lord on an inner odyssey, step by step into the deepest recesses of their minds.

Disciples endure temptation, and pilgrims must also withstand the assaults of furious storms and violent banditry. Followers demand community, and pilgrims also require companions (literally, "persons with whom to share bread"), if they are to endure the rejection of unfriendly towns. Believers must discern God's plan for them in the midst of mental fatigue, bodily sickness, and psychic heartbreak, and pilgrims must struggle through hostile forests, ford raging streams, survive arid deserts, and traverse rugged slopes. Above all, disciples experience the Christian life not as an effortless flight to God but as a rough and laborious perseverance through a lifetime.

Protestant Christians often focus individually and communally upon prayer directly to the risen Jesus within them, and their personal devotion to Jesus is clearly a primary element in their spirituality. Many Protestants grow continuously in their personal knowledge and love of Jesus, not only through their reflective reading of Scripture but also through their spontaneous conversations with Jesus as they live out each day, their private meditation, their regular examination of conscience, their journal keeping, and their discussions with Christian friends.

Catholic and Anglican Christians also cultivate a personal relationship with Jesus as the risen Lord in their private prayers and devotions. Catholics, for instance, have a tradition of pouring forth their aspirations to Jesus, whom they believe to be truly present in their churches as the **Blessed Sacrament** (the presence of the risen Christ under the appearances of bread and wine). Catholics reserve this sacramental **Host** in a sacred container known as a **tabernacle** (boxlike receptacle for the reserved presence of the risen Christ under the appearance of bread) in order that they may bring Holy Communion to the sick parishioners. Catholics regularly keep a **sanctuary lamp** (a candle that burns continuously before the presence of the risen Christ under the appearance of bread) in their churches and chapels as a reminder that Jesus is present in the Blessed Sacrament. Catholics often drop by a church in the course of the day and "make a visit" to the risen Jesus, freely addressing him in their own words.

Many Catholics relate to Jesus with deep personal feeling in terms of his genuine humanity. St. Francis of Assisi created the Christmas crèche, which depicts the scene of the stable at Bethlehem, with the infant Jesus, Mary and Joseph, and the animals. St. Margaret Mary Alacoque (1647–90) promoted devotion to the Sacred Heart of Jesus, the fleshly symbol of his love "burning" for them. Private devotions to Jesus through contemplating his image or through meditating upon the **stations of the cross** (fourteen moments along the way between Jesus' condemnation and his final crucifixion) have also proved extremely popular among Catholics over the centuries.

MATERIAL FOR DISCUSSION

1. What are the indispensable factors that identify all Christian spiritualities as Christian?

2. What are the essential differences that distinguish the spirituality of Catholic Christians from the spirituality of Protestant Christians?

3. What is the decisive meaning of the Incarnation for all Christian spirituality?

4. What is the critical significance of Jesus' resurrection for all Christian spirituality?

SUGGESTIONS FOR FURTHER READING

Cunningham, Lawrence S., and Keith J Egan. *Christian Spirituality: Themes from the Tradition.* New York: Paulist Press, 1996. A most helpful introduction to Christian spirituality that expands upon selected themes such as morals, different forms of prayer, asceticism, community, and the eucharistic liturgy.

Downey, Michael. *Understanding Christian Spirituality.* New York: Paulist Press, 1997. A fine summary of current reflections upon the meaning and themes of Christian spirituality, with special attention to theological and historical concerns.

Dupre, Louis, and Don E. Saliers, eds. In collaboration with John Meyendorff. *Christian Spirituality: Post-Reformation and Modern.* Vol. 18 of *World Spirituality: An Encyclopedic History of the Religious Quest.* New York: Crossroad, 1989. The final work in an excellent series of three compendia that analyze major phenomena of Christian spirituality in historical perspective. This volume presents essays that summarize themes of the more recent past, including Roman Catholic schools and movements, various Protestant and Anglican experiences, and Eastern Orthodox developments. It concludes with an exploration of Pentecostal spirituality, Christian feminist spirituality, and ecumenical spirituality.

McGinn, Bernard, and John Meyendorff, eds. In collaboration with Jean Leclercq. *Christian Spirituality: Origins to the Twelfth Century.* Vol. 16 of *World Spirituality: An Encyclopedic History of the Religious Quest.* New York: Crossroad, 1985. A marvelous compendium of nineteen articles that treat distinct subjects such as monasticism, Christology, liturgy, ways of prayer, and icons.

Raitt, Jill, ed. In collaboration with Bernard McGinn and John Meyendorff. *Christian Spirituality: High Middle Ages and Reformation.* Vol. 17 of *World Spirituality: An Encyclopedic History of the Religious Quest.* New York: Crossroad, 1989. A useful anthology of twenty substantial articles by experts on various aspects of Christian spirituality during the High Middle Ages and the Reformation, such as diverse modes of the consecrated life in common, mystical and devotional prayer, the Protestant experiences, and liturgy.

6

Islamic Spirituality

O people of the Book, Our Apostle has come to you, announcing many things of the Scriptures that you have suppressed, passing over some others. To you has come light and a clear Book from God through which God will lead those who follow His pleasure to the path of peace, and guide them out of darkness into light by His will, and to the path that is straight.

—Quran 5.15–16

God is the light of the heavens and the earth. The semblance of His light is that of a niche in which is a lamp, the flame within a glass, the glass a glittering star as it were, lit with the oil of a blessed tree, the olive, neither of the East nor of the West, whose oil appears to light up even though fire touches it not—light upon light. God guides to his light whom He will. So does God advance precepts of wisdom for men, for God has knowledge of every thing.

—Quran 24.34–35

There are three things which, when you possess them, make you taste the sweetness of faith. First, to love God and his messenger more than all other beings. Secondly, to love others solely for God's sake. Finally, to detest the thought of lapsing into unbelief as much as the thought of being thrown into Hell.

—Hadith (Bukhari, *Sahih*), part 1, p. 10, Anas

A man asked the Prophet, "Which Islam is the best?" He said, "Feed and greet with peace those whom you know and those whom you do not know."
                                    —Hadith (Bukhari, *Sahih*), part 8, p. 65, 'Abdallah b. 'Amr

World religions insist that we must achieve union with an ultimate and sacred Reality if we are to enjoy perfect peace. Judaism, Christianity, and Islam agree upon their identification of that ultimate Reality with the God of Abraham, a divine being who is the one and only Creator of the universe; each of these **monotheistic** religions, of course, offers its own distinctive path to God's peace. In Chapter 4, we examined the spirituality of Judaism, which derives its name from *Judah,* the surviving tribe of Israel. In Chapter 5, we traced the spirituality of Christianity, which takes its name from the *Christ,* an important title of Jesus of Nazareth. In this chapter, we shall investigate the spirituality of Islam, which draws its name neither from a tribe nor from a founder's title, but from an obedient disposition of the heart toward God: *Islam,* or "submission."

Allah gave Islam its name when he addressed the Muslims during Muhammad's "farewell pilgrimage" to Mecca, as we read in the Islamic Scriptures: "Today I have perfected your system of belief and bestowed My favours upon you in full, and have chosen Islam as the creed for you" (Quran 5.3b). Muhammad also referred to God's religion as Islam, as we know from the hadith that presents his sunna. For example, Muhammad spoke of Islam when he summed up its Five Pillars: "Islam is built on five pillars: the profession that there is no god but God and that Muhammad is the messenger of God; performance of the ritual prayer; payment of the obligatory charity; the pilgrimage; and the fast of Ramadan" (Hadith [Bukhari, *Sahih*—hereinafter referred to as SB], part 1, p. 9, Ibn 'Umar).

The Arabic term *Islam* designates that religious surrender by which human beings submit to God and devote themselves totally to the fulfillment of God's will. **Muslims** believe that al-Ilah, or Allah, established Islam as the final and complete religion for all of God's human creatures. Accordingly, the person who accepts the religion of Islam and observes its laws and practices is known as a Muslim ("one who submits"). The Muslims' book of scriptures is neither the Hebrew Bible of the Jews nor the Old and New Testaments of the Christians but solely the Quran.

In Chapter 2, we suggested a working understanding of religious spirituality with the following description: *Religious spirituality is the inner meaning of human experience as people pursue transformation under the impact of a sacred worldview.* Applying this description to Islam, we shall approach Islamic spirituality in terms of the following broad frame-work: *Islamic spirituality is the inner meaning of human experience as people pursue transformation under the impact of the straight path of submission to Allah.* Against this horizon we shall now explore the various elements that compose that inner dimension of Islamic experience.

In order to trace these factors of Islamic spirituality as faithfully as possible, however, we shall consider our subject from a threefold perspective. First, we shall try to appreciate Islamic spirituality from the inner perspective of believing Muslims. Second, we shall focus upon Islamic spirituality in terms of all that Islam promises to those Muslims who faithfully practice their religion. Third, we shall overlook the differences that characterize the two principal forms of Islam (**Sunni Islam** and **Shi'ite Islam**) and concentrate upon Islamic spirituality in its most pervasive themes.

Using this threefold perspective, we shall first center our attention upon the wellspring of all Islamic spirituality, the straight path of submission to Allah. We shall next explore four general constituents of Islamic spirituality that flow from this source: (1) Islamic experience of the ultimately sacred Reality; (2) Islamic growth through community; (3) Islamic formation through sacred literature; and (4) Islamic response to God through worship and prayer.

THE STRAIGHT PATH OF SUBMISSION TO ALLAH
Islamic Peace with God

The Arabic root *slm* generates not only the terms *Islam* and *Muslim*, but also the word *salam*, or "peace," a remarkably rich and sonorous word that connotes a cluster of concomitant values. God promises *salam* to those who render Islam to God: "Say: 'God leads whosoever He wills astray, and guides whoever turns to Him in repentance. Those who believe and find peace in their hearts from the contemplation of God: surely there is peace of heart in the contemplation of God!'" (Quran 13.27–28). God has granted the Quran in order that Muslims may follow the straight path of submission to Allah that leads to God's peace.

Islamic peace includes total integration because it heals divided human beings from mental distraction and moral estrangement. Islamic peace conveys safety and security because it protects people from all conflicts, whether individual, internal, and spiritual or social, external, and material. Islamic peace is the pinnacle of human wholeness and the crowning endowment of human well-being. God grants surpassing peace to all those who embrace Islam: Islam and God's gift of peace converge as dynamic correlatives, wondrously intertwined as cause and effect, plant and fruit, fountain and stream.

Muhammad taught the Muslims to wish peace to one another: "A man asked the Prophet, 'Which Islam is the best?' He said, 'Feed and greet with peace those whom you know and those whom you do not know'" (SB 8.65, 'Abdallah b. 'Amr). Consequently, Muslims offer the Arabic salutation *"al-Salamu 'alaykum"* ("peace be upon you") to one another in all situations, both upon coming together and upon taking their leave. In response, Muslims return the greeting *"wa-'alaykum al-Salam"* ("and upon you peace"). Muslims add the blessing *"alayhi 'salam"* ("peace be upon him") whenever they refer to a messenger or prophet of God. Muslims designate all those territories where Islamic law prevails as **Dar al-Islam,** "dwelling place of peace," but they refer to the non-Islamic area of the world as **Dar al-Harb,** "dwelling place of struggle."

Muslims look forward to that moment of unspeakable joy after death when they will hear the gatekeepers of Paradise pronounce the gift of God's peace. God promises them: "Those who were mindful of their duty to their Lord will be driven in groups to Paradise, till they reach it and its gates are opened, and its keepers say to them: 'Peace be on you; you are the joyous. So enter here to live for ever'" (Quran 39.73).

Muhammad as the Exemplar of the Straight Path of Submission to Allah

Prophet Muhammad is the exemplar of Islamic spirituality; he faithfully adhered to the straight path of submission to Allah. God instructs Muslims: "You have indeed a noble paradigm in the Apostle of God for him who fears God and the day of Resurrection, and remembers God frequently" (Quran 33.21). Muslims find in Muhammad the preeminent model of Islamic *taqwa* ("piety") and every admirable ideal for imitation in their own lives. Jews look back to Moses the teacher as "the man of God," while Christians believe in Jesus the Christ as "the Son of God," but Muslims acknowledge Muhammad the Prophet as "the servant of God."

Muhammad responded to his calling with a lifetime of faithful service for God. The Prophet himself rejoiced that he was simply called "God's servant," and he insistently admonished the Muslims against exaggerating his humble stature before God. Muhammad told the Muslims: "Learn the compulsory religious duties and the Qur'an, and teach them to the people for I am mortal" (Hadith [Tabrizi, *Mishkat al-Masabih*—hereinafter referred to as MM] 244, T, Abu Hurayra). Yet God assures the Muslims that Muhammad is God's *rasul* ("messenger") and *nabi* ("prophet"): "Muhammad is not the father of any man among you, but a messenger of God, and the seal of the prophets" (Quran 33.40a).

Prophet Muhammad gave to God all that he was and all that he possessed. Muhammad also referred to God any praise for his charismatic persona, his inspired counsel, and his irrepressible resolve. The Prophet was God's faithful and generous servant in announcing God's messages, enacting God's laws, and uniting the Arabs into a single brotherhood. Muhammad was God's indefatigable and courageous servant in completing his Lord's commission. Muslims cherish their recollections of Prophet Muhammad as their matchless hero who persevered on the straight path of submission to Allah. No other human being has so captured the imagination of Muslims, and no other man has so inspired the conduct of Muslims. Indeed, Muslim parents very often name their male offspring after Muhammad—there is probably no more popular name than Muhammad among boys around the world.

Christian discipleship of Jesus involves not only an imitative following but also a mystical incorporation into Jesus as the risen Lord. Muslims, by way of contrast, bind themselves personally not to Prophet Muhammad but to God alone. The Prophet himself warned the Muslims against praising him in the way that the Christians were accustomed to glorify 'Isa (Jesus), the son of Maryam (Mary), by calling him the Son of God. Muhammad insisted: "Do not extol me as the Christians have extolled the Son of Mary. I am only God's servant. Refer to me as the servant and messenger of God" (SB 4.204, 'Umar).

Being Servants of God and Being Friends of God

Insofar as Muslims imitate Prophet Muhammad, the servant of God, they themselves adhere to the straight path of submission to Allah, and being God's servants is an indispensable factor in their Islamic spirituality. God reveals his absolute power to them: "Creator of the heavens and the earth from nothingness, he has only to say when He wills a thing: 'be,' and it is" (Quran 2.117). Muslims believe that God alone is the absolute Creator of everything that is. Human beings, on the other hand, never even possess themselves, because they must cling always to a dependent and conditioned existence. Men and women are God's created servants and handmaidens, and they continue to exist from moment to moment only because God freely decrees that they should exist. Strictly speaking, God alone has rights, because God alone has made and continues to conserve the universe. Muslims, therefore, recognize that they owe obedient and willing service to God as the Lord of the worlds.

God, after all, has a wondrous design for the completion of the whole universe. God governs the world of desert, rocks, mountains, seas, and heavenly bodies, and all these inanimate creatures obey God's laws for the natural realm. God rules the plants, flowers, and trees, and all these living creatures grow necessarily according to God's biological laws for the vegetative realm. God directs the fish, birds, wild beasts, and domesticated animals, and all these sentient creatures develop instinctively according to God's biological laws for the animal realm. Finally, God has endowed human beings with the dignity of free will, and God summons all these rational creatures freely to fulfill their role as collaborators in God's magnificent plan.

People never confront a more awesome challenge than their vocation to become God's willing servants. God offers people right guidance through the Quran in order that they may adhere to the straight path of submission to Allah and attain true happiness as human beings. God has endowed human beings with the power of making a fundamental choice for the overall direction of their lives. They can devote themselves in service to God for the open-ended future as far as they can control it, or they can withhold themselves from God in a futile quest for autonomy. People can commit themselves to the straight path of submission to Allah, and this decision alone leads to genuine human success in this life and the gift of God's surpassing peace hereafter. Or people can give themselves to idolatrous service of themselves or some false god, and this sinful avenue leads to human failure in this life and eternal frustration in hell hereafter.

Muslims realize, then, that the secret of successful humanity and true fulfillment lies not in winning powerful status, in accumulating material wealth, or in earning earthly prestige, but only in being servants of God. Muslims acknowledge their total dependence upon God for their very being, and they give themselves to God in obedience. Muslims discover their deepest identity and their foremost delight in serving so great a God. We confront here a central theme of Islamic spirituality, and it explains why Muslim parents often bestow upon their sons such names as 'Abdullah ("servant of God") and **'Abd al-Rahman** ("servant of the merciful One").

Muslims can brook no artificial division of their lives into neatly sealed compartments. They understand that they must live a single organic life and that God's will embraces every dimension of their humanity from the physical, the sensual, and the emotional to the intellectual, the volitional, and the spiritual. Therefore, Muslims labor strenuously to ensure that being servants of God characterizes the very fabric of their lives. Muslims practice the religion of Islam pervasively and constantly, not only on Friday (when they congregate at noon for prayer), but also from Saturday through Thursday. Muslims submit to God not only in the *masjid* ("mosque," "prostration place") but also in the home, the university, the laboratory, the workplace, and the political arena. Muslims seek to be Islamic homemakers, Islamic merchants, Islamic professionals, Islamic tradespeople, Islamic farmers, Islamic journalists, Islamic artists, and so on. Muslims can tolerate no division between religion and culture, no false dichotomy between the sacred and the secular. Muslims pursue a fully integrated life in which all their actions disclose the single meaning of being servants of God.

Faithful service to God tends to blossom into an extraordinary friendship with God. Indeed, Muhammad gave himself to *'ubadiyah* ("being the servant of God") with such unreserved fidelity that he also came to enjoy *walayah* ("being the friend of God"). Muslims, then, who submit to God totally throughout every aspect of life can begin to enjoy even now an intimate bond of devotion with God.

Muhammad in a *hadith qudsi* (non-Quranic revelation of God that Muhammad handed on to the Muslims in his own words) announced that God offers this wondrous friendship to his special servants. Muslims recall:

The Messenger of God said, "God Most High has said, 'I shall be at war with anyone who shows hostility to a devoted servant of Mine. Nothing is more pleasing to Me as a means for My servant to draw near to Me than the religious duties which I have imposed on him. My servant continues to draw near to me with additional voluntary acts of devotion so that I love him. When I love him I am the Hearing with which he hears, the Sight with which he sees, the Hand with which he strikes and the Feet with which he walks. Whenever he asks Me for anything I give it to him. Whenever he asks Me for refuge I grant him it.'"
—SB 8.131, Abu Hurayra

Muhammad further disclosed that even the inhabitants of heaven become the friends of God's faithful servants:

The Messenger of God said, "When God loves one of His servants He says to Gabriel, 'God loves so and so. You must love him as well.' So Gabriel loves that person. Then Gabriel calls to the inhabitants of heaven, 'God loves so and so. You must love him as well.' So the inhabitants of heaven love that person. Moreover, as a result of this he prospers on earth."

—SB 4.135, Abu Hurayra

Islamic Right Belief and Right Conduct

Commitment to God in faithful belief is a defining element in Islamic spirituality according to the straight path of submission to Allah. Muslims must accept without doubt or hesitation all that God has revealed through the Quran. God sums up the contents of Islamic faith in terms of five articles: "O believers, believe in God and His messenger and the Book He has revealed to His apostle, and the Books revealed before. But he who believes not in God and His angels and the Books and the prophets and the last Day, has wandered far away" (Quran 4.136).

Muslims are, in fact, well known for their tenacious perseverance in upholding all that they believe. Non-Muslims recognize their remarkable conviction about their faith, their unflinching certitude, and their determined affirmation. Muslims reinforce their commitment by acknowledging God whenever they hear his name pronounced. For God exhorts them: "Only they are true believers whose hearts fill up with awe when the name of God is mentioned; and their faith is further strengthened when His messages are read out to them; and those who place their trust in their Lord, Who are firm in devotion, and spend of what We have given them, are true believers" (Quran 8.2-4a).

It is not sufficient in Islamic spirituality simply to believe, however. The straight path of submission to Allah also demands that worthy Muslims do what is good, and right beliefs without upright works are valueless in the religion of Islam. Allah is the merciful God of righteous judgment, who has linked the right worship of God indissolubly with a just society among humankind.

Muhammad also insisted upon the permanent bond between authentic faith in God and loving service toward other human beings. Prophet Muhammad, therefore, took his place on this burning issue solidly within the prophetic tradition of Jews and Christians. From the Prophet's earliest preaching in the streets of Mecca, he condemned idolatry with no uncertain words, but he also excoriated the powerful rich for their oppression of the enfeebled poor. Muhammad was particularly concerned to protect the most vulnerable persons in his society—the widows, the orphans, and all those pitiable individuals who were incapable of surviving on their own. Obedience to God through the charitable service of one's fellow human beings became an identifying hallmark for all faithful Muslims and the seal of their activities.

God calls human beings to be his vice-regents with divine authorization to govern all other creatures on earth. Muslims, therefore, respond by fulfilling God's will freely and righteously. They devote all their intellectual talents and psychic resources to promoting justice in the world. Muslims energetically promote what is morally good, and they vigilantly resist what is morally evil. They withstand every false god, dethrone every idol, and denounce every blasphemy. Muslims recognize their obligation regularly to minister to their needy brothers and sisters who are hungry, without homes, or sick and dying.

Judaism presents a compendium of the strictly ethical precepts of the Torah in the famous Ten Commandments (Exod. 20.1–17). Christianity offers Jesus' endorsement (Luke 10.15–28) of the Jewish summary of the Jewish Decalogue: "but you shall love your neighbor as yourself: I am the LORD " (Lev. 19.18b). Islam goes further and teaches a detailed program that describes how to love one's neighbor in everyday life on a practical level. Muslims draw their moral guidance for the straight path of submission to Allah primarily from the series of commands and prohibitions in the Quran.

For example, God insists strongly upon the importance of family values in Islamic life. Muslims must honor their parents with gentle respect: "and be good to your parents. If one or both of them grow old in your presence, do not say fie to them, nor reprove them, but say gentle words to them. And look after them with kindness and love, and say: 'O Lord, have mercy on them as they nourished me when I was small'" (Quran 17.22b–24). By the same token, Muslims must care lovingly for their own children and trust in God's providential care for their families. God also prohibits murder, dishonest measurement, fornication, adultery, backbiting, gambling, use of intoxicants, arrogance, infanticide, and the twin extremes of stinginess and extravagance.

Islamic Striving

The spirituality of following the straight path of submission to Allah involves vigorous effort. Muslims recognize that they must strive earnestly and struggle laboriously if they are to remain faithful. God exhorts them: "O you who believe, follow the path shown to you by God, and seek the way of proximity to Him, and struggle in His way: you may have success" (Quran 5.34). The necessity for this jihad ("struggle") emerges from the very fabric of human existence, and it engages the Muslims' energies throughout their lifetime. Some Western journalists have mistakenly reduced jihad to the concept of "holy war," and they have incorrectly equated jihad with terrorism and violent conflict. In point of fact, Muslims follow Prophet Muhammad's guidance on this issue and carefully distinguish between the strictly spiritual struggle of self-discipline, or "greater jihad," and the armed combat of self-defense, or "lesser jihad." Muslims give themselves to the greater jihad every day throughout their lives, but they engage in the lesser jihad, or legitimate holy war, only when the Islamic umma ("community") has become the victim of unjust aggression.

Muslims know that the human condition is problematic, since their daily decisions are fraught with ambiguity. They understand that the human heart is the object of a continual conflict between the *nafs* ("lower self," or "soul"—similar to the Hebrew *nefesh* or the Greek *psyche*) and the *ruh* ("higher self," or "spirit"—similar to the Hebrew *ruach* or the Greek *pneuma*). Therefore, Muslims try to resist the temptations of their *nafs* towards heedlessness of God as they follow the counsels of their *ruh* along the straight path of submission to Allah.

Since the straight way of submission to Allah is in diametrical opposition to the "crooked" road of rebellion against God, Islamic spirituality demands rigorous self-discipline and assiduous self-denial. Muslims must confront acute challenges and overcome severe obstacles in the course of their journey. Muslims must exert themselves resolutely against the allurements of luxury and enticing materialism. They must also resist steadfastly their selfish inclinations toward laziness, lust, covetousness, greed, unbridled anger, pride, and hatred. Muslims must make that considerable effort that is required if they are to utilize their talents, their education, their possessions, and their time in accordance with God's will. Indeed, Muslims must enlist in the most critical contest of all, since they must cross over from self-centeredness to God-centeredness.

In a word, the religion of Islam requires an incessant battle of the spirit, and Paradise is the reward for those who have fought hard and well. God provides the Quran to be the Muslims' indispensable guide for the combat: "This is the Book free of doubt and involution, a guidance for those who preserve themselves from evil and follow the straight path, Who believe in the Unknown and fulfil their devotional obligations, and spend in charity of what We have given them; Who believe in what has been revealed to you and what was revealed to those before you and are certain of the Hereafter. They have found the guidance of their Lord and will be successful" (Quran 2.2–5).

ISLAMIC EXPERIENCE OF ALLAH
Islamic Submission to God, the Lord of the Worlds

Muslims submit to God, the Lord of the worlds, as the ultimately sacred Reality who is the real founder of Islam. Allah is the same God of Abraham whom Jews and Christians serve. God tells the Muslims: "Do not argue with the people of the book unless in a fair way, apart from those who act wrongly, and say to them: 'We believe what has been sent down to us, and we believe what has been sent down to you. Our God and your God is one, and to Him we submit'" (Quran 29.46). Muslims surrender to the God of Abraham as the supreme motivation for their every spiritual disposition and aspiration. In taking this religious stance, Muslims stand firmly within the long prophetic tradition of which Prophet Muhammad was the final representative.

God is the awesome Creator, who made Adam and empowered him to name the animals. God sent down the truth of monotheism upon Abraham. God bestowed the Torah-book upon Moses, the Psalms-book upon David, and the Gospel-book upon Jesus, son of Mary. Finally, God is the one all-merciful and all-compassionate God who has entrusted the Quran to Prophet Muhammad. God is the one all-beneficent God of power and majesty, and the Muslims respond by willingly subordinating themselves to God's will and practicing the religion of Islam.

The religion of Islam embodies the most consistent, straightforward, and uncompromising monotheism. Allah is the only God, who exists uniquely and unconditionally, without possibility of rival. Allah is the one God of boundless power, who brings all things into being and sustains them in their absolute dependence. Allah is the one God of infinite goodness and mercy, who forgives those who repent of their sins. Allah is the one God of infinite justice, who will judge human beings on the Last Day, rewarding the faithful in Paradise and punishing the wicked in hell. Allah is the one God of eternal life, who never tires or sleeps but sees all and knows all. Allah is the one God of unlimited knowledge, whose wisdom is vast and all-inclusive. *Allahu akbar* ("God is greater"), always and simply speaking. Allah suffices.

Muslims obediently resign themselves to God's will, even when they encounter the frustrations and sufferings of life. Muslims believe that God has an explanation for all of their misfortunes, whatever may be their failures, disappointments, and sorrows. They trust in God, who comprehends all things in their entirety as one creation. Muslims possess their souls in peace, since God surely knows what is in their best interests. God's wisdom is inscrutable and unfathomable.

Muslims call upon God by his excellent names according to his explicit injunction: "All the names of God are beautiful, so call Him by them" (Quran 7.180a). Muslims also follow God's further instruction: "Say: 'Call Him Allah or call him Ar-Rahman; whatever the name you call Him by, all His names are beautiful'" (Quran 17.110). Indeed, Muslims like to count off God's ninety-nine "excellent names" as they devoutly finger three times the thirty-three beads of their rosaries. (God's hundredth name is completely hidden and grasped by God alone.) Yet God infinitely exceeds any and all names, even as he immeasurably surpasses all things in inaccessible mystery.

Muslims submit to God as the one God of light, who addresses all peoples definitively in the Quran and summons them to being his servants. Muslims believe in God as the one God of knowledge, who grasps all things with perfect understanding. Muslims feel accountable to God as the one Lord of the worlds, who freely enacts his plan for all creation. Muslims trust in God as the one God of graciousness, gentleness, and kindness. Muslims confidently call upon God as the one God of mercy, who lovingly forgives the sinners who repent. Muhammad told the Muslims about God's infinite mercy: "God created clemency and on the day He created it He divided it into a hundred parts. He kept ninety-nine parts in reserve for His own use and endowed all the beings whom He had created with the hundredth part. If the infidel knew how much clemency God had kept in reserve, he would not despair of Paradise. If the believer knew how much punishment God had kept in reserve he would not feel safe from Hell" (SB 8.123, Abu Hurayra).

Muslims' recognition of God's presence is essential to their spirituality, and it makes all the difference in their everyday life. Muslims acknowledge that God is not simply a divine something, however supreme, but the divine Someone who is alive and aware. God is not simply a divine "power," however immense, but the intelligent and free God of compassionate goodness. God is the one God, who is not detached but provides right guidance for all those who strive to follow the straight path of submission to Allah. Allah is the one God, who governs creation by sovereign right, yet most kindly and gently. Allah is the one God, who is not indifferent to human morality but will judge all people according to their actions after He raises them from the dead on the Last Day. Muslims never cease to proclaim God's transcendence, yet they also know that God genuinely cares about them. Muslims call upon God in prayerful dialogue, for God is aware of them and intimately available to them. God reveals: "We created man and surely know what misdoubts arise in their hearts; for We are closer to him than his jugular vein" (Quran 50.16).

Islamic Piety Toward God

God is the majestic Lord of the worlds. Muslims respond to God with reverential fear and righteousness as is appropriate for intelligent creatures before their awesome Creator. Muslims know that they can never take God for granted, as though they could coerce, exploit, or manipulate the powerful God for their own self-interests. Nor do Muslims presume to approach God as though they could outwit, outmaneuver, or elude the all-knowing God for their petty self-aggrandizement. For Muslims realize that God alone is the one incomparable God of ineffable splendor, before whom they must fall down in most humble submission.

Jews nurture *tzedakah* as their ideal in adhering to the way of the Torah, while Christians pursue agape as their supreme moral value in following the way of Jesus' discipleship. Muslims especially cultivate *taqwa* as their crowning Islamic virtue. Muslims recognize that the sole measure of their stature before God is not earthly prestige, material wealth, or social stature but the depth of their piety. Muhammad praised those Muslims who love both God and Muhammad himself. God repeatedly admonishes the Muslims to be diligent in their pursuit of piety, as, for example, in the following words: "So strive towards piety and excel the others: God will bring you all together wheresoever you be" (Quran 2.148).

Muslims offer their service through devotional acts of worship, but all ritual is in vain unless genuine piety inspires their minds and inflames their hearts. Muslims care for the needy among their brothers and sisters, but all external acts of benevolence are futile unless reverence expands their hearts. In Islamic spirituality, faith devoid of works is worthless. God teaches: "Piety does not lie in turning your face to East or West: Piety lies in believing in God, the Last Day and the angels, the Scriptures and the prophets, and disbursing your wealth out of love for God among your kin and the orphans, the wayfarers and mendicants, freeing the slaves, observing your devotional obligations, and in paying the zakat and fulfilling a pledge you have given, and being patient in hardship, adversity, and times of peril" (Quran 2.177). Muhammad exhorted the Muslims to make their piety practical: "Feed the hungry, visit the sick and set captives free" (SB 7.87, Abu Musa al-Ash'ari).

Islamic Remembrance of God

The Islamic virtue of piety toward God further requires the **dhikr** ("remembrance") of God and the recollection of God's will. God requires this of them: "Recite what has been revealed to you of this Book, and be constant in devotion. Surely prayer keeps you away from the obscene and detestable, but the remembrance of God is greater far; and God knows what you do" (Quran 29.45).

Muslims know that they must not fail to remember God, the absolute Priority of their lives. They recognize the dangers of distraction and the perils of forgetfulness. Muslims realize that believing Muslims can ignore the moral implications of their faith in God. For they can lose their focus upon the Creator, not because they decisively repudiate God but because they do not reflect upon God. Muslims, therefore, guard against *ghaflah* ("heedlessness"). Heedless individuals think only of the immediate goods of this world, while they neglect the final judgment and the resurrection. In their disregard for the straight path of submission to Allah, they wander astray on twisted roads of evil. God warns Muslims that those who become oblivious of God will suffer the direst of consequences: "They encourage what is bad and dissuade from the good, and tighten their purses [when it comes to spending in the way of God]. Of God they are oblivious: so He is oblivious of them" (Quran 9.67).

Islamic spirituality, then, involves not only a relentless striving against spiritual torpor and sluggishness but also the concerted effort always to remember and never to forget. Moses required that the Jews should gather annually for the Passover meal that they might commemorate God and their deliverance through the Exodus. Jesus commanded his disciples regularly to celebrate the Holy Eucharist that they might memorialize him and their redemption through the cross. God teaches Muslims that remembrance is a critical hallmark of their spirituality and that forgetfulness is a principal hazard: "O you who believe, remember God a great deal. And sing His praises morning and evening. It is He who sends His blessings on you, as [do] His angels, that He may lead you out of darkness into light, for He is benevolent to the believers" (Quran 33.40b–43).

Muslims struggle to recognize God, to affirm God, to acknowledge God, and ever to be mindful of what God teaches them in the Quran. Muslims want vividly to realize the all-important truths that shape their lives: God is the one Creator, all creatures must serve God, and they themselves have rightly chosen to follow the straight path of submission to Allah. Muslims regularly cultivate their awareness of God as they perform their prayers five times a day. They also deepen their consciousness of God, because they listen reflectively according to God's instruction, when someone recites the Quran aloud.

Human beings possess absolutely nothing apart from God's benefi-cence, but forgetfulness breeds ingratitude. Muslims, therefore, call to mind that God is the Creator of all things that exist and the Giver of all things that are good. Muslims deliberately recall how much they receive from God's largesse, and their recollection generates heightened attention to God's presence and wholehearted intention to fulfill God's will. When Muslims remember their indebtedness to God, they give thanks to God.

Muslims mention God repeatedly throughout every aspect of their lives, and they are particularly fond of the Islamic prayer of praise: *Allahu akbar*. Muslims understand that the mention of God is a beneficent prac-tice, because Muhammad gave them a precious *hadith qudsi:*

The Messenger of God said, "God says, 'I live up to My servant's expectations. I am with him every time that he mentions Me. If he mentions Me to himself, I mention him to Myself. If he mentions Me in company, I mention him in even better company. If he draws near to Me by a span, I draw near to him by a cubit. If he draws near to Me by a cubit, I draw near to him by a fathom and if he walks towards Me, I quicken My pace toward him.'"

—SB 9.148, Abu Hurayra

Islamic Attention to God and Intention Toward God

Attention is an intellectual function, and all religious traditions urge its critical importance. People must be aware of the religious exercises that they are performing. When people become inattentive, selfishness be-guiles the mind, sensuality seduces the heart, and boredom enervates the spirit. Worldly distractions distort vision, weaken conviction, and sedate conscience. Without interior mindfulness, works of piety such as worship and prayer easily degenerate into empty ritualism. Consequently, just be-fore the deacon in Eastern Orthodox Christianity proclaims the gospel during the Divine Liturgy, he commands the congregation: "Be attentive! Be attentive." By the same token, Buddhists cultivate "right mindfulness" as an element in the Noble Eightfold Path toward Nibbana.

Muslims understand that they become vulnerable to temptations if they follow God's path merely out of habit. Muslims might ignore God's imposing accessibility, not because God is unimportant to them but because they are absentminded and heedless of his presence in their lives. Muslims can violate God's commandments, not so much because they want to be sinful or do what is evil, but rather because they do not attend to God's will for them. That is why the religion of Islam forbids the consumption of intoxicants: Such stimulants impede religious focus upon God. Buddhists similarly avoid the use of alcohol and drugs, because those things impair human awareness.

Religious attentiveness is a matter of mental collectedness. Muslims cultivate a vigilant recognition of God's immediate presence. Muslims try to center their minds upon God as the absolute and unrivaled Priority of their lives. Attentiveness in Islamic spirituality leads Muslims to inquire after God, to listen to God, and to fasten their thoughts upon God. Before Muslims offer prayerful worship to God, they attempt to discipline their imagination and memory in order to block out distractions. When Muslims perform their acts of service to God, they try first to center their minds upon God. When Muslims pray together, the women always stand behind the men, not because women are inferior to men but because women can easily distract men's attention. If some person or event interrupts Muslims after they have begun to pray, they start their prayers over again from the beginning. The created world must take second place before God, who alone can command center stage. The state of being servants of God and the reward, perhaps, of becoming friends of God, then, depend upon deepened consciousness.

Intention, on the other hand, is a volitional function of the free will, or *heart,* and all religious traditions insist that intention also is necessary. For example, Catholic priests used to state their explicit intention to offer the Holy Eucharist before they approached the altar, saying, *"Volo celebrare Missam"* ("I wish to celebrate the Mass"). Similarly, as Muslims offer prayers or perform religious exercises to please God, they strive fully to intend what they are doing. Without deliberate intention, such works become mechanical at best and self-serving at worst.

Muslims determine the inner meaning of their experience (that is, their spirituality) insofar as they direct their obedience toward God, move toward God, and act for the sake of God. When Muslims offer prayerful worship to God, they must obviate any dividedness and unworthy purpose. When Muslims perform their acts of service to God, they must maintain their inner resolution, despite many created attractions. Intention is a matter of elevated aspiration and motivation. Muslims go to the mosque not because they wish to visit with their friends but because they intend to worship God. Muslims fast during the month of Ramadan not because they want to lose weight but because they intend to concentrate upon God as their priority. Muslims go on pilgrimage not because they like to travel but because they set their hearts upon meeting God in the holy places. As Muslims begin their pilgrimage to Mecca, they must state their intention aloud: "I intend to make the hajj." Muslims must fasten their interior vision upon God as a servant focuses upon a merciful master and as a friend relates to a beloved friend.

Muslims make their fundamental choice of God, and they struggle to prioritize their other options in accordance with this basic decision. Muslims orient their minds, their talents, their memories, their emotions, and their bodies toward God, their all-powerful Creator. Muslims fashion their lives and order their works primarily in accordance with God's will. Muslims confidently entrust themselves to God's disposal according to God's good pleasure. Even when Muslims make the simplest plan such as setting a luncheon date or planning a short holiday with a friend, they add the brief prayer "if Allah wills." For God reminds them: "Do not say of any thing: 'I will do it tomorrow,' without [adding] 'if God may please'; and think of your Lord in case you forget, and say: 'Perhaps my Lord will show me a nearer way to rectitude'" (Quran 18.23–24).

Islamic spirituality involves purposeful determination, and Muslims must freely dedicate their hearts to God as a handmaiden seeks solely to please her mistress. Muslims recall the words of Muhammad: "The value of an action depends on the intention. Everyone will be rewarded in accordance with the goal which he set himself. If he emigrated for the sake of God and His messenger, his emigration will be counted to him for God and His messenger. If he emigrated in order to gain something in this world or to find himself a wife, his emigration will be counted to him for the goal which he set himself" (SB 7.4, 'Umar b. al-Khattab).

The Five Pillars of Islam

Muslims have the opportunity regularly to reinforce their remembrance of God, as they observe the Five Pillars of Islam: confession, prayers, almsgiving, fasting, and pilgrimage. Prophet Muhammad is the noble model for all authentically Islamic behavior, and he himself fulfilled these obligations with focused attention upon God and deliberate intention toward God's will. Muslims seek to imitate Muhammad's spirit and sterling example when they themselves offer up to God their own confession, their prayers, their almsgiving, their fasting, and their pilgrimage.

First, Muslims concentrate their minds and hearts upon God many times daily through confession in Arabic: "I confess that there is no god but Allah and Muhammad is the messenger of God." Persons become Muslims by sincerely reciting this verbal commitment to the one God and God's messenger. The confession is Muslims' admission not of their sinfulness but of God's unique existence. The confession is Muslims' testimony not that Allah is a god (since the pre-Islamic Arabs already recognized an "Allah" along with other gods and goddesses) but that Allah alone is the one God. The confession is Muslims' protest not merely that God is greater than other gods but that no other gods can possibly exist.

Muslims recite their confession repeatedly not only within themselves but also before the world with loud voice and forceful tongue. By confession, Muslims bear witness not merely to their monotheistic belief but also to the very foundation of their whole life and practice. By confession, Muslims proclaim the faith commitment on which they make their stand, affirm the decisive core of their worldview, and profess the defining dimension of their personal identity. Muslims are uncompromising iconoclasts who reject the slightest suggestion of idolatry—just as Muhammad himself upon conquering Mecca destroyed all the idols in the Kaba.

Second, Muslims withdraw from worldly concerns and raise their spirits to God through prayers. The **muezzin** (one who summons to prayers) from the **minaret** (tower attached to a mosque) summons Muslims to prayers five times daily: at sunrise, noon, 3:00 P.M., sundown, and nighttime. Muhammad took special delight in this practice, as he told the Muslims: "Perfume and women have been made dear to me and for my sheer delight I have been given the ritual prayer" (MM 561, N & IH, Anas).

Muslims seek to involve themselves reverentially and totally as humble servants in their approach to God through prayers. They begin by performing their ritual ablutions in order to purify body and spirit before they meet God. They wash their whole head and face, together with their hands, arms, feet, and ankles. Then they stand in a clean place (preferably within a mosque, often with a prayer rug) and turn toward the holy city of Mecca. As they then recite the set prayers, they try to combine sharpened minds, ardent hearts, and fervent tongues with the total subordination of their bodies. They perform graceful bows and complete prostrations, with forehead touching the ground. Muslims hope for the forgiveness of their sins through prayers according to Muhammad's exhortation: "Abu Hurayra said that the Messenger of God said, 'If one of you had a river right by his door and he bathed in it five times a day, do you think that there would be any dirt left on him?' They said, 'No, not a trace.' He said, 'That is how it is with the five prayers; by means of them God wipes away all sins'" (MM 565, B & M).

Third, Muslims consciously remember God, their bounteous and generous Lord, through almsgiving, when they annually donate at least two and one-half percent of their available wealth to their fellow Muslims who suffer want. Muslims feel literally indebted to the poor and the needy for God's sake. For Muslims bear in mind that God has made them stewards of whatever property they possess, and they always have a grave obligation not just in charity but even in strict justice to share it with others. In almsgiving, Muslims offer prayerful gratitude and true worship to God, even as they donate to the welfare of the community. God lists a variety of specific causes that Muslims must support in almsgiving: "Charities are meant for the indigent and needy, and those who collect and distribute them, and those whom you wish to win over, and for redeeming slaves [and captives] and those who are burdened with debt, and in the cause of God, and the wayfarers: So does God ordain. God is all-knowing and all-wise" (Quran 9.60).

Muslims realize that those who do not fulfill the duty of almsgiving are liable to God's severe punishment, according to his warning: "Let not those who are niggardly of things that God has given them of His largesse think that this is good for them. In fact, it is worse; for what they grudged will be hung around their necks on the Day of Resurrection. To God belong the heavens and the earth, and God is aware of all you do" (Quran 3.180). Muhammad, on the other hand, told the Muslims that they could avoid hell through almsgiving: "Avoid Hell by giving charity, even if it means sharing your last date, and, if you have nothing at all, by speaking a kind word" (SB 8.144, b. Hatim).

Fourth, Muslims acknowledge their direct and constant dependence upon God's creative power through fasting. During the daylight hours of the month of Ramadan, Muslims must abstain strictly from all food and drink as well as from sexual activity. Muslims pray especially during their fast on the twenty-seventh of Ramadan in commemoration of "the night of power," when Muhammad first began to receive the Quran. While Muslims feel the pangs of their bodies' craving for God's sustenance, they make room for God in their thoughts and reflect upon their deepest hunger for God's peace-giving truth and goodness. While Muslims experience the discomfort of fasting, they recognize the ongoing necessity of disciplining their bodily appetites and passions, lest any physical need distract them from embracing God's will. By fasting, Muslims obtain the forgiveness of their past faults.

God gives ample instruction about the role of fasting in Islamic spirituality:

O believers, fasting is enjoined on you as it was on those before you, so that you might become righteous. Fast a [fixed] number of days, but if someone is ill or is

travelling [he should complete] the number of days [he had missed]; and those
who find it hard to fast should expiate by feeding a poor person. For the good
they do with a little hardship is better for men. And if you fast it is good for you,
if you knew. Ramadan is the month in which the Qur'an was revealed as guid-
ance to man and clear proof of the guidance, and criterion [of falsehood and
truth]. So when you see the new moon you should fast the whole month; but a
person who is ill or travelling [and fails to do so] should fast on other days, as
God wishes ease and not hardship for you, so that you complete the [fixed] num-
ber [of fasts], and give glory to God for the guidance, and be grateful.

—Quran 1.183–185

Muhammad passed on to the Muslims a *hadith qudsi,* in which God
stresses the importance of fasting: "God has said, 'To fast for Me is to give
up eating, drinking and satisfying your passions. The fast is for My sake
and I will recompense the person who fasts and repay all his good actions
tenfold'" (SB 3.31, Abu Hurayra).

Fifth, Muslims become especially God-centered through pilgrimage.
Once in a lifetime, Muslims who have the health and means to do so must
(with explicitly stated intention) make pilgrimage to the Kaba at Mecca
during the pilgrimage month of Dhu al-Hijja. (Muslims may also visit
Mecca at other times out of devotion, but this does not fulfill their obligation of pilgrimage.) Muhammad promised rich blessings for those who
faithfully make pilgrimage: "Anyone who performs the pilgrimage in
order to please God, and while accomplishing it, does not have sex with
his wife or behave immorally, will return home as he was on the day of his
birth" (SB 2.164, Abu Hurayra).

The Kaba is God's house, and only those who have made the pilgrimage can fully appreciate how intense is a Muslim's gratification upon
fulfilling this obligation. Pilgrims must purify themselves ritually first
and avoid sexual activity while they are pilgrims. All the pilgrims feel
unified and equal to one another as they discard fine clothes, perfumes,
jewelry, and any other marks of social distinction. The men shave their
heads or at least cut a lock of hair and dress in two seamless white sheets,
while the women don simple dress without fragrances or jewelry. When
the pilgrims arrive at Mecca, they joyfully cry out, "I am here, O Lord, I
am here!"

Muslims' immersion in God's presence is profound and beyond all
telling as they observe the many holy rituals that follow over several
days. For example, pilgrims circumambulate the Kaba seven times coun-
terclockwise and try to touch the sacred black stone that God gave to
Abraham through the angel Gabriel. Pilgrims also run back and forth in

memory of Hagar's desperate search for water, they stone three stone pillars that symbolize the devil in memory of Abraham's resistance of temptation, and they stand all afternoon on the Plain of Arafat in prayer for forgiveness. Through this most holy of journeys, Muslims orient all that they are and have toward God, and they return to their homes transformed for a lifetime. Many Muslims choose further to visit the tomb of Muhammad at Medina.

ISLAMIC GROWTH THROUGH THE UMMA

Jews relate to the LORD God through their membership in the K'lal Yisrael. Christians worship God the Father through their incorporation into the Church. Muslims are notably individualistic to the extent that each of them freely relates to God directly on his or her own initiative, without any mediating priesthood or other hierarchical structure. Muslims certainly emphasize the role of personal piety in Islamic spirituality. Nevertheless, Muslims also insist upon the communal dimension of their spirituality. All Muslims around the world collectively constitute the *umma* of Islam. All Muslims experience a corporate unity according to Muhammad's admonition to them: "Believer is to fellow believer as parts of a building which support each other" (SB 14, Abu Musa).

Prophet Muhammad summoned the Arabs to transcend their old tribal rivalries and blood-feuds to become one new community, a nation united not by blood ties, regional location, or political loyalty but by the universal religion of Islam. Their shared experience in the company of one another is a vital factor of the straight path of submission to Allah. Since Allah is one God, the whole of humankind must also be one community. Muslims, therefore, realize their Islamic identity concretely in terms of belonging to a single transnational society with a single worldview. Indeed, Muslims seek to propagate Islam everywhere in order that all men and women may be unified in justice and enjoy human success under the one God. Muslims' spirituality would be quite unintelligible if they did not regard one another truly as sisters and brothers within the Islamic brotherhood according to the teaching of Muhammad: "The Muslim is the brother of any other Muslim. He should not oppress him or surrender him. If a Muslim comes to the aid of his brother in Islam, God will come to his aid" (SB 9.28, 'Abdallah b. 'Umar).

Muslims date the beginning of their calendar neither from the birth of Prophet Muhammad nor from his call to messengerhood, but from Prophet Muhammad's *hijra* ("emigration") out of Mecca to Yathrib in

622 c.e. The inhabitants of Yathrib, now renamed as Medina al-Nabi ("city of the Prophet"), accepted Allah as their only God and Muhammad as God's messenger. All the Muslims became a theocratic state as the community of Islam. God told them: "We have made you a temperate people [umma] that you act as witness over man, and the Prophet as witness over you" (Quran 2.13). The community has been expanding ever since as a global religion, a true brotherhood/sisterhood that knows no ethnic, linguistic, or geographical boundaries.

All Muslims collectively make the same faith commitment and perform the same acts of piety. Muslims cherish the same family values and enjoy the same group support. Muslims nourish their communal bond first of all through their close home life with spouse and children. Parents conscientiously train all their offspring to be good and faithful members of the community. Families also celebrate their bond with the larger community by serving generous refreshments as they warmly welcome their guests. As Jews acknowledge their membership in K'lal Yisrael whenever they follow the rules of kashrut at their meals, the Muslims express their membership in the one umma whenever they avoid all pork products, blood, and meat from animals that have been strangled, sacrificed to idols, or found dead.

Muslims usually sense a spontaneous friendship and camaraderie whenever they congregate with other Muslims. Muslims thoroughly enjoy the great Islamic festivals such as **Maulid al-Nabi** (Muhammad's birthday), which are opportunities for renewing their mutual solidarity. Muslims enthusiastically observe their holidays with the exchange of gifts and the healing of any grievances or estrangements among them. The Five Pillars of Islam (plus jihad) also function as a principal support for conscious connectedness in Islamic spirituality.

Muslims around the world together proclaim the same confession in the same Arabic tongue as one nation. By confession, Muslims all testify before the world their most significant identity, and it is an identity that they share in common. Converts join the Islamic community by announcing the same confession with heart and lips.

Muslims of every ethnic origin offer the same prayers in the same Arabic tongue as they orient themselves toward Mecca at approximately the same time of day. Muslims praying and worshipping God in common become a vibrant fellowship. During the weekly congregation in the mosque on Fridays at noon, Muslims together turn toward Mecca, carefully and gracefully proceeding through the prescribed series of ritual gestures in shoulder-to-shoulder synchrony with the movements of a single imam (prayer leader). Muhammad assured them: "Prayer performed in company is twenty-seven times better than prayer performed alone" (SB 1.166, 'Abdallah b. 'Umar).

Muslims at every level of material means share by almsgiving with those of the community who are less fortunate. As Muslims remember their obligation of charitable service to the needy, they act as a more caring society that reaches out to the defenseless, the deprived, and the desperate. Muslims recognize their sacred duty to give assistance to one another, not just as a donation out of generosity to strangers but also as the payment of a debt out of justice to their brothers and sisters in the community.

Muslims who observe fasting during Ramadan bind themselves to one another by the physical pangs of hunger. They take this opportunity to reflect upon their brothers and sisters in the community who so often suffer hunger. Muslims then become a more compassionate people, because they have themselves tasted some of the suffering that so routinely wracks the lives of the destitute among them. At the end of Ramadan, they join together wholeheartedly with relatives and friends for the worldwide celebration of **Id al-Fitra** (Festival of the Breaking of the Fast).

Muslims who make pilgrimage once during their lifetime dramatize the steps of their whole personal journey to Allah. As they converge upon Mecca, they encounter members of the Islamic community from every ethnic and racial group of the globe. Muslims undertake this sacred odyssey together as equals before God, and any mark of discriminating bias or social pride would be intolerable. Muslims experience their communal unity with particular intensity when they stand side by side on the Plain of Arafat from noon until sundown. They press densely together in their millions and beseech God for forgiveness, both for themselves and for all Muslims. Muslims around the world join together in the conclusion of pilgrimage days during the month of Dhu al-Hijja by celebrating Id al-Adha (Feast of the Sacrifice), which recalls God's command to Abraham that he sacrifice his son Ishmael. Many Muslims who have made the pilgrimage retain their sense of joyful fulfillment long after they have returned home. They seem never to tire of recounting their transforming experience to their relatives and friends. Some Muslims even make the pilgrimage year after year precisely in order to recapture this wondrous sense of the community.

Special Islamic practices also serve to remind Muslims of their common engagement with one another. Muslims together bear a corporate obligation to engage in the lesser jihad for the defense of Islam as a transnational community. Muslims must not gamble away their resources, because this would be to waste what they need for their family and the poverty-stricken of the community. Muslims must not charge interest for a loan, because this would be to take advantage of another's need in the community. Muslims must not engage in unethical conduct, because this would be to injure the community and deprive other Muslims of the good example to which they are entitled. Muslims regard *ijma* ("communal consensus") as a guide for living a good Islamic life for the very good reason that the community as such cannot for long agree on an erroneous teaching.

FORMATION THROUGH THE QURAN
The Quran

Jews, Christians, and Muslims all agree that the one God and Creator of the universe has communicated divine Revelation to the human beings for whom God cares so much. Jews are convinced that the LORD God has given them the Torah and that the Hebrew Bible summarizes God's teaching. Jews are, therefore, devoted to the way of Torah as the central paradigm of their spirituality. Christians are persuaded that God has graced all humankind with the person of Jesus Christ, and the Christian Bible represents a written distillation of Jesus' gospel message. Christians give themselves in discipleship not to the Bible but to Jesus as the living source of their spirituality. Muslims, on the other hand, are certain that God's primary gifts to the Jews have not been a teaching (Torah), but the Torah-book, and to the Christians, not a person (Jesus), but the Gospel-book. Finally, Muslims believe, God has given the complete Quran through Prophet Muhammad to the Arabs but for all humankind.

The Quran is **Kitab al-Allah** ("book of God"), Islamic scriptures in 114 suras that together approximate in length four-fifths of the Christian New Testament. God has sent down the Quran as an earthly replica of the heavenly Quran that has preexisted on a tablet with God. God dictated the Quran through the angel Gabriel gradually to Prophet Muhammad, from the time of his call to messengerhood in 610 until his death in 632. 'Uthman (d. 656), the third *khalifa* ("successor to Muhammad"), authorized the canonical text of the Quran. God declares the role of the Quran in Islamic spirituality: "This is the Book free of doubt and involution, a guidance for those who preserve themselves from evil and follow the straight path, Who believe in the Unknown and fulfill their devotional obligations, and spend in charity of what We have given them; Who believe in what has been revealed to you and what was revealed to those before you, and are certain of their Lord and will be successful" (Quran 2.2–5).

The Arabic Quran is literally the uncreated and eternal **Kalam Allah** ("Word of God"). Muhammad contributed nothing to the Quran, however, by way of content, verbal expression, syntax, or literary style, but faithfully handed on what he received. Consequently, Muslims revere the Quran with the greatest devotion. Muslims look to the Quran as the supreme authority for regulating Islamic belief and behavior, and they could never allow any later writings to supplement it or to supplant it. They know that the Quran is God's perfect, definitive, and ultimate Revelation. Muslims believe without question everything that the Quran teaches, and they try to obey without hesitation every pre-cept that the Quran enjoins. Muslims find in the Quran an inimitable grandeur and a matchless eloquence. Muslims readily grant that Prophet Muhammad himself performed no miracles, but they point to the splendor of God's Arabic in the Quran as Islam's unique and all-sufficient miracle. Muslims confidently assure all inquirers that any persons who read the Quran in its original form will also be persuaded of its divine origin.

We can scarcely overestimate the importance of the Quran in the life of Muslims. If the straight path of submission to Allah is the paradigm for Islamic spirituality and if piety is its crowning virtue, then the Quran is its compass and chart. The Quran maps out every step of the straight path of submission, clearly delineating the proper relationship that unites human beings to their God and binds them among themselves. Muslim children frequently learn how to read by studying the Quran at school. Muslims revere the Quran as God's most wondrous gift to humankind, draw upon it for their devotion, and spend their lives in trying to appropriate its verses into their hearts. Muslims delight in hearing accomplished readers and chanters recite the Quran aloud. God urges Muslims to listen to the Quran: "When the Qur'an is recited listen to it in silence. You may perhaps be blessed. Meditate on your Lord inwardly with humility and trepidation, reciting His Book softly, morning and evening, and be not negligent" (Quran 7.204–205). Muhammad instructed the Muslims: "The worthiest of you is the one who learns the Qur'an and then teaches it" (SB 56.236, 'Uthman b. 'Affan).

In a word, Muslims cherish the Quran as Jews revere the Torah and as Christians gravitate toward Jesus. Muslims are from every perspective "the people of the Book" par excellence, who draw upon the Quran for their primary identity and their comprehensive worldview. Muslims treat the Quran with religious awe as a book inherently divine and beyond all criticism, and they draw the inspired content of their prayers and worship from its verses.

Muslims seek to appropriate the Quran into their very being as the dominant nourishment for their consciousness. They study the Quran avidly, hear its words repeatedly, and reflect upon its inexhaustible meaning from their earliest childhood until the end of their lives. Muslims seek to become saturated with the Quran, so that God's Revelation may overflow their minds and hearts to flood their imaginations, their memories, and their emotions. It is not uncommon for some Muslims to memorize the Quran in its entirety from beginning to end. Muhammad taught them: "A person who has an excellent knowledge of the Qur'an is with the noble pious scribes. A person who recites the Qur'an and keeps trying to pronounce the difficult passages where he gets tongue-tied, will have a double reward" (MM 2112, B & M, 'A'isha).

The Shariah

Muslims also consult the Quran as the highest authority and source of the shariah, which summarizes all the sacred laws and obligations for the right guidance of Muslims. If God has handed down a clear mandate in the Quran, all Muslims must observe it dutifully. Some of God's commandments concern ethics, as, for example, when God declares that fornication is morally wrong: "And do not go near fornication, as it is immoral and an evil way" (Quran 17.32). Others of God's precepts center upon worship, as, for example, when God requires the weekly assembly: "O you who believe, when the call to prayer is made on the day of congregation, hasten to remember God, putting aside your business" (Quran 62.10a).

In determining the laws of shariah, many Muslims look to four authoritative sources: Quran, sunna in the hadith, *qiyas* ("analogy"), and *ijma*. If people cannot find a definitive answer on proper Islamic practice in the Quran, they next consult the sunna as contained in the hadith. By studying the hadith, Muslims can reflect upon Prophet Muhammad's typical behavior in various situations, his answers to particular questions, and his solutions to special problems. Since Prophet Muhammad is the noble model of Islamic behavior, the hadith takes second place only to the Quran as a source for the shariah. If Muslims cannot resolve a difficulty from the teachings of the Quran and the sunna, many will look in the third instance to *qiyas* and in the fourth instance to *ijma*.

ISLAMIC RESPONSE TO GOD THROUGH WORSHIP AND PRAYER

Personal Encounter with Allah

Muslims express their piety through their every thought, word, and deed as they struggle to follow the straight path of submission to Allah. Muslims dedicate themselves as servants of God most dramatically, however, during their peak moments of formal worship and prayer, when they prostrate themselves bodily before God in adoration and touch their foreheads to the ground. By worship and prayer with attentive minds and intentional hearts, Muslims approach God with confident reverence. God assures them: "When my devotees enquire of you about Me, I am near, and listen to the call of every supplicant the moment he calls. It behoves them to hearken to Me and believe in Me that they may follow the right path" (Quran 2.185).

When Muslims worship and pray to God, they vindicate their Islamic privilege of direct access to God. Without the mediation of any sacral minister or priest, Muslims acclaim Allah as the one and sovereign God, who is greater absolutely than any other reality. Muslims believe that God rules all things and protects them as they walk the straight path of submission to Allah. Muslims realize that God grasps them exhaustively, and they deliver themselves to God with all that they are in body, soul, and spirit. Muslims gratefully acknowledge that Allah is the good God, who cares about them and forgives them their sins. Muslims boldly proclaim their trust in God, the merciful, the compassionate, who reveals his bounteous blessings: "The blessing of God is at hand for those who do good. Indeed it is He who sends the winds as harbingers of auspicious news announcing His beneficence, bringing heavy clouds which We drive towards a region lying dead, and send down rain, and raise all kinds of fruits. So shall We raise the dead that you may think and reflect" (Quran 7.56b–57).

When Muslims worship and pray to the one true God, they first make sure that all is clean and pure, including their mind, their heart, their body, and the place where they stand and will lie face down. Muslims also make considerable effort to drive all worldly distractions from their mind and focus their consciousness upon God, and they formulate an explicit intention to address God for his sake alone. The ceremonial rituals and formulas of Islamic worship and prayer are amazingly uniform across the various cultures around the world.

All Muslims are trained at a young age to recite the same memorized prayers aloud on the same occasions in the same Arabic. All

Muslims also learn how to accompany their invocations with precisely the same movements of bows, prostrations, and other prescribed movements. As Christians take the Lord's Prayer from the New Testament, Muslims derive their most expressive prayer, the Fatihah, from the opening chapter of the Quran: "All praise be to Allah, Lord of all the worlds, Most beneficent, ever-merciful, King of the Day of Judgement. You alone we worship, and to You alone we turn for help. Guide us (O Lord) to the path that is straight, the path of those You have blessed, Not of those who have earned Your anger, nor those who have gone astray" (Quran 1.1–7).

Islamic Sufism

The religion of Islam has been enriched over the centuries by an emotional, even mystical dimension. The Jewish Hasids developed warm devotion to God in their spirituality, because they felt that mainstream Judaism had become too dryly intellectual. The Christian charismatics cultivated the felt response to the Holy Spirit in their spirituality, because they believed that mainstream Christianity had become too coldly structured and institutionalized. The early Muslim Sufis (derived from *suf*, their traditional woolen garment) sought the most intensely affective involvement of the heart in their piety, because they judged that mainstream Islam, now a vast empire, had become too worldly in its spirit and too mechanical in its practice. Sufis are intent upon the utmost internalization of their religion.

The Sufis are devout laymen and laywomen who unite under a charismatic leader (*shaykh*) in a particular brotherhood (*tariqa*) that resembles a vowed congregation of Christianity, except that a Sufi order is more loosely structured and does not require celibacy. Sufi brotherhoods promote strict ascetic practices such as fasting and vigils, but they especially seek to be transported in union with God. In order to realize an all-enveloping remembrance of God, Sufis follow esoteric methods of prayer such as repeating over and over the name of God and composing tender poems of the love for God.

All Muslims practice Islam in the pursuit of God's peace, but the Sufis want to possess God's awesome presence immediately, here and now, in a transforming communion of love. All Muslims observe the Five Pillars, but Sufis go far beyond these ordinary demands in their generosity and zestful ardor. Sufis give themselves to prolonged meditative prayer together with vigils and supererogatory fasting, and sometimes even to music and dancing or whirling. Sufis are "God-intoxicated" Muslims who have fallen passionately in love with God.

Sufis strive to achieve the most self-effacing—even self-annihilating—abandonment to God. Sufis hunger for an intuitive, non-intellectual encounter with God that transcends all conceptual knowing and verbal description. Like moths irresistibly fascinated by a candle's flame, they yearn to immerse themselves in the self-extinction of ecstatic union with God. Sufis are Muslims who delight in discovering God everywhere throughout the world and savoring the sweetness of God's presence in all things. Sufis joyfully affirm that God is the fullness of being, the sole Reality that truly exists, while they and the world are but nothing. Sufis insist that God is not only infinitely transcendent beyond all things but also wondrously immanent within all things. God is all in all, and material things are but symbols that point to God's immanence within them.

MATERIAL FOR DISCUSSION

1. What are the principal themes in Islamic spirituality?

2. In what ways can the person of no religious persuasion benefit from the study of Islamic spirituality?

3. In what ways can the Jew or the Christian profit from the study of Islamic spirituality?

4. What is the significance of Prophet Muhammad for Islamic spirituality?

SUGGESTIONS FOR FURTHER READING

Esposito, John L. *Islam: The Straight Path*. 3rd ed. New York: Oxford University Press, 1998. A superb study of the religion of Islam in all its various dimensions, presented in a well-organized and readable way. The present author is indebted to this book for many profitable consultations in the preparation of his manuscript.

Nasr, Seyyed Hossein. *Islamic Art and Spirituality*. Albany: State University of New York Press, 1987. This world-renowned authority on Islam paints a horizon for his insightful book with an opening quotation: "God has inscribed beauty upon all things." He then proceeds to analyze calligraphy, architecture, literature, and painting along with Sufi poetry and music as manifestations of Islamic spirituality.

———, ed. *Islamic Spirituality: Foundations.* Vol. 19 of *World Spirituality: An Encyclopedic History of the Religious Quest.* New York: Crossroad, 1987. This first of two anthologies presents Islamic spirituality in terms of its basic roots and sources. The editor has gathered essays that reflect upon the Five Pillars, the Quran, and the hadith but also open up to the study of Sufi mysticism.

———, ed. *Islamic Spirituality: Manifestations.* Vol. 20 of *World Spirituality: An Encyclopedic History of the Religious Quest.* New York: Crossroad, 1991. This companion anthology presents essays on Islamic spirituality as reflected in Sufism, ethnic literatures, theology, philosophy, science, and the arts.

Renard, John. *Seven Doors to Islam: Spirituality and the Religious Life of Muslims.* Berkeley, Calif.: University of California Press, 1996. This accomplished author shares his insights into Islamic spirituality with noteworthy expertise and interesting originality.

Schimmel, Annemarie. *Mystical Dimensions of Islam.* Chapel Hill, N.C.: University of North Carolina Press, 1975. This ample volume presents a thoroughgoing exploration of Sufism in terms of its substantial meaning, history, fraternal orders, psychology, theology, and poetic expression.

7

Hindu Spirituality

Brahman, you see, is this whole world. With inner tranquility, one should venerate it as jalan. *Now, then, man is undoubtedly made of resolve. What a man becomes on departing from here after death is in accordance with his resolve in this world. So he should make this resolve: "This self* (atman) *of mind that lies deep within my heart—it is made of mind; the vital functions* (prana) *are its physical form; luminous is its appearance; the real is its intention: space is its essence* (atman); *it contains all actions, all desires, all smells, and all tastes; it has captured this whole world; it neither speaks nor pays any heed. This self* (atman) *of mind that lies deep within my heart—it is smaller than a grain of rice or barley, smaller than a mustard seed, smaller even than a millet grain or a millet kernel; but it is larger than the earth, larger than the intermediate region, larger than the sky, larger even than all these worlds put together. This self* (atman) *of mind that lies deep within my heart—it contains all actions, all desires, all smells, and all tastes; it has captured this whole world; it neither speaks nor pays any heed. It is* brahman. *On departing from here after death, I will become that." A man who has this resolve is never beset at all with doubts. This is what Sandilya used to say.*

—Chandogya Upanishad 3.14.1–3

The three kinds of Prajapati's children—gods, humans, and demons—once lived with their father Prajapati as vedic students. After they had completed their studentship, the gods said to him: "Sir, say something to us." So he told them the syllable "Da," and asked; "Did you understand?" They replied: "Yes, we understood. You said to us 'Demonstrate restraint (damyata)!'" "Yes," he said, "you have understood." Then the humans said to him: "Sir, say something to us." So he told them the same syllable "Da," and asked: "Did you understand?" They replied: "Yes, we understood. You said to us 'Demonstrate bounty (datta)!'" "Yes," he said, "you have understood." Then the demons said to him; "Sir, say something to us." So he told them the same syllable "Da," and asked: "Did you understand?" They replied: "Yes, we understood. You said to us 'Demonstrate compassion (dayadhvam)!'" "Yes," he said, "you have understood." Thunder, that divine voice, repeats the very same syllable: "Da! Da! Da!" Demonstrate restraint! Demonstrate bounty! Demonstrate compassion! One should observe the same triad—restraint, bounty, and compassion.

—Brihadaranyaka Upanishad 5.2.1–3

This highest brahman, *however has been extolled thus: There is a triad in it—oneself, the foundation, and the imperishable. When those who know* brahman *have come to know the distinction between them, they become absorbed in and totally intent on* brahman *and are freed from the womb. This whole world is the perishable and the imperishable, the manifest and the unmanifest joined together—and the Lord bears it, while the self* (atman), *who is not the Lord, remains bound, because he is the enjoyer. When he comes to know God, he is freed from all fetters. There are two unborn males—the one knows and the other is ignorant; the one is Lord and the other is not the Lord. There is just one unborn female, who is joined to the enjoyer and the objects of enjoyment. And then there is the self* (atman), *limitless and displaying every form, not engaged in any activity. When someone finds these three, he finds this* brahman. *The primal source is perishable, while Hara is immortal and imperishable. The one God rules over both the perishable and the self* (atman). *By meditating on him, by striving toward him, and, further, in the end by becoming the same reality as him, all illusion disappears. When one has known God, all the fetters fall off; by the*

*eradication of the blemishes, birth and death come to an end; by meditating
on him, one obtains, at the dissolution of the body, a third—sovereignty over
all; and in the absolute one's desires are fulfilled. This can be known, for it
abides always within one's body* (atman). *When the enjoyer discerns the
object of enjoyment and the impeller—everything has been taught. That is
the threefold* brahman.

—Svetasvatara Upanishad 1.7–12

Hinduism is a relatively modern term for the Brahmanical tradition that
has been developing over the past approximately 3,500 years. Contemporary Hindus often refer to their religion as Dharma ("law/duty") or
Sanatana Dharma ("eternal law/duty"), and many of them find in
Hinduism their total way of life. Hinduism is by any estimation a venerable tradition that has led billions of human beings to personal integration
and to *shanti*. Hinduism is also a fascinating tradition that provides insights into the human condition, the ultimate human goal, and effective
ways to attain that fulfillment.

Hinduism often expresses this sacred wisdom not through bold af-
firmations of speculative theology but through provocative narratives
from the mythic past or through probing colloquies between a "realized"
person and a seeker. This storytelling approach does not attempt to settle
the great religious questions with clear and definitive answers, but it does
stimulate further inquiry and deeper reflection. Hinduism's inscrutable
sages share the fruits of their rigorous asceticism and profound meditation with all those who search for saving Truth. Hinduism's sacred literature challenges both religious and nonreligious persons fully to actualize
the spiritual potential that lies dormant within their hearts.

Hinduism is at once the most complex and the most inclusive
among world religions. For that matter, Hinduism is not so much a single
religion as an encyclopedic family of traditions that legitimates the most
widely diverse forms of spiritual experience and claims them all as its
own. We may find within Hinduism's broad embrace a whole spectrum of
sacred beliefs and practices. Hinduism approves activities as varied as
sacrificial rituals, festal celebrations, temple worship, domestic cults,
physical austerities, legal observance, communal pilgrimage, good works,
dietary restrictions, devotional enthusiasm, world-renouncing discipline,
contemplative meditation, and mystical vision. We also meet a unifying
theme that totally pervades this sacred amalgam, however: the passionate
quest for *moksha*.

A notable hallmark of Hindus' spirituality is their attitude of sympathetic tolerance toward all religions, as exemplified by their ancient greeting: "From what sublime tradition have you come, noble sir?" Hindus consider human words to be inadequate for expressing the ultimate Absolute, and, therefore, they respect every religious position as a valid although partial perspective. Indeed, Hindus feel a genuine openness toward those who hold convictions other than their own. Hindus themselves may adopt varying beliefs and practices in the course of their lifetime, since Hinduism requires neither confessional acts such as the Jewish Shema and the Islamic *shahadah* nor dogmatic commitments such as the Christian **Nicene Creed.** Hindus, consequently, prefer to focus more upon orthopraxis than upon orthodoxy.

Hinduism claims neither a historical hero like Gotama the Buddha nor a divinely commissioned prophet like Muhammad as its "founder," yet Hindus do look back to a primordial Revelation that *rishis* (seers) intuited and passed down orally from of old. Hinduism presents no writings as authored by a divine person such as the God of Abraham, yet all Hindus revere the Vedic scriptures as a written expression of what the *rishis* originally "heard." Hinduism usually seeks no converts and sends forth no missionaries as Jesus commissioned his apostles, yet Hindu gurus (masters in spirituality) share what they have "seen" with any inquirers who are willing to gaze deeply within their own hearts and discover for themselves all that they truly are.

In Chapter 2, we worked out a practical and general understanding of religious spirituality: *Religious spirituality* is the inner meaning of human experience as shaped by the pursuit of transformation under the impact of a sacred worldview. Applying our description of religious spirituality in a Hindu context, therefore, we may understand Hindu spirituality within the following broad framework: **Hindu spirituality** *is the inner meaning of human experience as shaped by the pursuit of transformation under the impact of the ways of Sanatana Dharma.* With this interpretive tool we may now explore Hinduism's "inner meaning of human experience."

We shall once again adopt a threefold perspective toward insight and understanding. First, we shall try to enter into the consciousness of involved Hindus who fulfill their sacred duties as active practitioners of their religion. Second, we shall center our attention upon Hindu spirituality in terms of its ideal potential and promise for those who diligently pursue its vision. Third, we shall, as far as possible, overlook the many differences that characterize the principal forms of Hinduism (**Shaivism, Vaishnavism, Shaktism,** and nonsectarian reform movements). In the case of Hinduism, it is virtually impossible to affirm any general or universal belief or practice without noting some exceptions. Nevertheless, we shall concentrate upon Hindu spirituality as we may encounter it among the majority of Hindus most of the time, allowing always for the myriad deviations, aberrations, and syncretistic fusions that exist in the folk religion of countless Indian villagers.

We shall first investigate the ways of Sanatana Dharma insofar as Dharma constitutes the central wellspring of spirituality for all Hindus (excepting the holy men and holy women who renounce all things and even transcend Dharma as they reach the brink of salvation). We shall examine Dharma's sacred origin and purpose, its broad implications and applications, and its profound impact upon Hinduism as a thoroughgoing design for life. We shall then explore the principal dimensions of Hindu spirituality that unfold as practitioners pursue *moksha* along the ways of Sanatana Dharma. These aspects are (1) Hindu experience of Brahman; (2) Hindu growth through community; (3) Hindu formation through the Vedic scriptures; and (4) Hindu response to the Godhead through worship/meditation and prayer.

THE WAYS OF SANATANA DHARMA

In order to appreciate the significance of the ways of Sanatana Dharma as vital sources of Hindu spirituality, we must become familiar with some extremely important Sanskrit terms that occur repeatedly within this context and yet elude any exact English translation. Six key terms that designate Hinduism's fundamental concepts, structure its framework, and inform all of its significant practices are the following: *atman, karma,* **samsara,** *Dharma, moksha,* and *Brahman.* We shall explore **yoga,** a seventh key term, in our concluding section, "Hindu Response to the Godhead Through Worship/Meditation and Prayer."

Atman

Hindus insist that we must distinguish two levels of selfhood if we are to realize our true identity in this transient world. Hindus adhere to religious ways that prioritize the needs of our higher self. If we erroneously prefer our inferior, physical self to our superior, metaphysical self, we set ourselves on a collision course toward pain, disillusionment, and human failure.

We human beings have a lower self, the empirical, or "phenomenal," self, which is the center of consciousness within our ever changing corporeality. Our inferior self endures constant modification as our instinctive, sensory, emotional, and mental processes interact with one another. We conventionally refer to our physical self as the "ego" behind our psychological and social experience. We habitually use pronouns, adjectives, reflexives, and intensives of the first-person singular, such as "I" and "me," "my" and "mine," "myself" and "I my very self."

We men and women, nevertheless, are not merely bodies that gradually decay with disease, age, and death. We also have a higher self, the transcendental, or "noumenal," self, which is an innermost identity that is permanent. Our superior self continues imperishably through all our mutations, unaffected by life's ebb and flow. Hindus call our metaphysical self the atman, the permanent reality without beginning or end that remains invulnerable and impervious to change. Since our atman is formless and inaccessible to the senses, we cannot conceptualize or analyze our atman intellectually. Since our atman is deathless and eternal, it remains ever incorrupt and indestructible despite the ravages of time. Yet our most authentic identity is our highest selfhood, our atman.

Karma

Karma means "action," and we may compare the "law of karma" to a system of inherent merit and demerit that governs our moral being. Hindus believe that a free and accountable karma produces a proportionate **phala** ("fruit") for good or ill. In the Upanishads we find the following doctrine:

What a man turns out to be depends on how he acts and on how he conducts himself. If his actions are good, he will turn into something good. If his actions are bad, he will turn into something bad. A man turns into something good by good action and into something bad by bad action. And so people say: "A person here consists simply of desire." A man resolves in accordance with his desire, acts in accordance with his resolve, and turns out to be in accordance with his action.
—Brihadaranyaka Upanishad 4.4.5b

The law of karma, then, operates within us neutrally and without bias. Each of our ethical actions necessarily produces a positive *phala,* and each of our unethical actions inevitably generates a negative *phala.* Our store of karmic consequences, positive or negative, chains us to the relentless wheel of rebirth into this constantly fluctuating universe.

The law of karma does not mean that some supernal judge metes out a reward for righteousness or a punishment for sin. It is more comparable to our feeling of satisfaction when we are kind and generous or the hangover that we suffer if we drink too much. Both the noble deed of selfless service and the ignoble fault of perjured testimony in themselves carry their own karmic indebtedness. The balance of karmic residue from our actions both upright and wicked clings cumulatively to our atman, now and for the future. The karmic fruits of our good actions can project our atman forward and upward to rebirth into some superior status in society, but the karmic fruits of our bad actions can drag our atman backward and downward to rebirth at some inferior level of being.

Samsara

The next term in our basic cluster of Hindu concepts is *samsara* ("impermanence of the universe," or, on the human level, "cycle of rebirth"). Hindus affirm that the physical cosmos is subject to incessant mutation. Old beginnings induce new endings, and old endings induce new beginnings. Despite the seeming solidity of so many material things, they are all constantly in transition to new forms, fluctuating as a rapid stream that rushes on endlessly. Despite the apparent substantiality of so many sentient beings, they are all trapped on a perpetual wheel of birth, death, and rebirth. Although our atman is permanent and changeless, the law of karma holds our atman captive and binds it to samsara, the cycle of rebirth without beginning or end. Hindus sometimes call our karmic entrapment on the wheel of rebirth "the process of reincarnation" or "transmigration of souls." Unless our atman somehow escapes from samsara, it will be reborn ever again to this impermanent world of suffering and tragedy.

Dharma

In Hindu discourse, no term is more varied in its meanings or more rich in its implications than *Dharma*. Hindus rely upon Dharma for the fundamental intelligibility of their lives. Hindus find in Dharma their underlying rationale not only for interpreting the cosmos but also for understanding themselves and how they fit into the cosmos. Hindus look to Dharma in order to make sense out of their progressive interaction with others. Hindus nourish and deepen their spirituality to the extent that they follow Dharma. Hindus reach the fulfillment of their inmost being to the extent that they allow Dharma to encompass and transform them.

Hindus recapitulate and unify their total worldview through the all-embracing concept of Dharma. Dharma itself is an immanent law/duty that is not the volitional ordinance of any personal god but is rather an intrinsic principle that emanates from the impersonal Godhead. Dharma regulates the harmonious order of all beings, both among themselves and in relation to the ultimate Being that is Dharma's source. Therefore, Hindus respond to Dharma as the Absolute Divinity's design for their journey to successful humanity. Hindus faithfully follow Dharma without question because they find Dharma's foundation in Truth to be self-evident.

Dharma is a comprehensive law/duty that governs both the physical and the spiritual orders of the universe. That is why Dharma applies to all sentient beings, including not only animals and human persons, but also the gods and goddesses of the Hindu pantheon (who also are contingent realities bound to samsara and not absolute beings like the God of Western monotheisms). Insofar as Hindus follow Dharma, then, they are privileged to collaborate with the ultimate Reality in sustaining the stability of the cosmos.

For Dharma is a practical law/duty that prescribes not only those norms that Hindus are ethically obliged to observe but also those duties that Hindus must fulfill in their struggle to wear down their karmic bonds and escape samsara. When Hindus view their everyday lives from the perspective of Dharma, they are able to appreciate even their most "secular" dimensions as numinous and their most "profane" events as sacred. In the light of Sanatana Dharma, all their activities become religiously significant. Hindus draw upon Dharma in order to realize themselves as individual manifestations of the Godhead. Through Dharma, Hindus gain insight into their overall progress as they journey toward final salvation. Through Dharma, Hindus receive practical instructions in order to meet the requirements of each stage of their growth within the specific lifetime at hand. In fact, Hindus have woven Dharma tightly into the very fabric of their culture, so that Dharma's values and customs saturate their everyday milieu. Hindus assert the primacy of the spiritual order within the universe, and Dharma provides the detailed framework for that spiritual order.

Moksha

If Hindus must follow Dharma, however, they must also pursue *moksha.* Dharma and *moksha* constitute two poles that are sometimes conflicting and sometimes supplementary in Hindu spirituality. Hindus must realize the "inner meaning of their experience" within a creative tension. Hindus must fulfill their law/duty and support this world, but Hindus must also achieve salvation and escape from this world. Hindu spirituality involves both affirmation of and denial of the same cosmos.

The term *moksha* expresses the Hindus' concept of deliverance from samsara. We all carry individually our own unique karma-laden history of countless rebirths. We must overcome the karmic force that fastens our atman to the samsaric realm, the world of incessant becoming and passing away. *Moksha* is liberation of our atman not from sins that alienate us from God but from the chains that fasten our atman to rebirth. *Moksha* is redemption of our atman not from moral estrangement but from the karmic bonds that shackle our atman to the revolving cycle of death and regeneration. *Moksha* is fulfillment of our atman not in our vision of God but in our release of our atman from endless reincarnation. We must somehow seek *moksha* from this world even as we fulfill the Dharma that tends to enmesh us within it.

Brahman

As Hindus follow Dharma and pursue *moksha* from samsara, they fasten their gaze ultimately on Brahman. Hindus acknowledge Brahman as the Absolute Being that is the foundation of reality in all its diversity. Brahman is the one still point in a revolving world of incessant flux and instability. Brahman is the sole Being that exists unconditionally and simply in a conditioned cosmos of endless complexity. Brahman is the inscrutable and ineffable mystery that underlies the universe and makes it meaningful. Brahman is "that One thing" among things multiple, that absolute Entity among entities dependent, that ultimate Being among beings preliminary, that supremely real Reality among realities less than real. For many Hindus, Brahman is, indeed, the sole existent, the totality that is or can be, the incomparable first without a second.

Hindus acknowledge the presence of Brahman within all things, especially within animals and people. In contrast to Abraham's personal God, however, who remains always radically distinct from creatures, Brahman is the constitutive principle of existence within all things. In the later Vedic scriptures, we find the words:

He sees, but he can't be seen; he hears, but he can't be heard; he thinks, but he can't be thought of; he perceives, but he can't be perceived. Besides him, there is no one who sees, no one who hears, no one who thinks, and no one who perceives. It is this self of yours who is the inner controller, the immortal. All besides this is grief.

—Brihadaranyaka Upanishad 3.7.23b

In further dissimilarity to Abraham's God, the uncreated one who creates everything else out of nothing, Brahman is the uncreated one thing that makes everything as an emanation and manifested form of itself. Brahman is the principle of being that infinitely surpasses personality and all other attributes. Brahman exists immanently at the core of all things and pervasively throughout all things, yet Brahman also exists transcendentally beyond their boundaries.

We cannot conceive a commensurate idea of Brahman in its expansive intelligibility. Indeed, Hindus insist that Brahman in itself necessarily exceeds all comprehension or notional definition, and our finite minds cannot grasp the depth of Brahman's positive meaning. All of these conceptual and verbal difficulties notwithstanding, we must still seek some limited understanding of Brahman if we are to appreciate Hindu spirituality at all. Brahman, after all, is not only the Ultimate divinity that transcends all things in their limitation, but Brahman is also the immediate divinity that exists immanently within all things in their fullness. Even Hindus distinguish between **Nirguna Brahman** ("Brahman-without-qualities") and **Saguna Brahman** ("Brahman-with-qualities").

Nirguna Brahman has no attributes. Nirguna Brahman is fully real, formless, unknowable, unmanifest, and impersonal, because Brahman exceeds all things and shatters all categories of thought. Nirguna Brahman is the divine "It," the impersonal Godhead. About Nirguna Brahman, Hindus can speak but negatively, saying, *"neti, neti"* ("not this, not that").

Saguna Brahman, on the other hand, has attributes. Saguna Brahman is less than real, formed, knowable, manifest, and personal, because Brahman exists immanently in all things as their subtle essence. Saguna Brahman is the divine "He" or "She" rather than the divine "It." Hindus do speak in positive language about Saguna Brahman as "God," and Hindus do attempt to communicate with Saguna Brahman through worship, prayer, and meditation.

HINDU EXPERIENCE OF BRAHMAN

Since Hindus encounter the immediate presence of Brahman in every area of their lives, their awareness takes shape naturally and spontaneously in religious response. By a kind of spiritual instinct, Hindus want to fulfill the duties in Dharma that Brahman's divine presence imposes upon them. Hindus strive to appreciate all that they themselves really are and all that everyone else really is in Brahman. Hindus possess all their being in Brahman and experience all their multiple lives within Brahman.

Hindus follow Dharma throughout every aspect of life in order to become God-realized beings in the "cave" of their hearts. Hindus want to break through their dark ignorance and deceptive illusions in order to unite with Brahman. Hindus want to ground their lives in Brahman as towering trees sink their roots on the mountain slopes and gentle flowers find bedding in the valleys. Since Hindus abide in Brahman, by Brahman, and for Brahman, they derive the full significance of their humanity from the Godhead.

Many Hindus identify Brahman with the universal atman—pure self-consciousness, self-awareness, and spirit. They further insist that their own individual atman with all its feelings, thought, and conscious-ness is, in fact, a portion of the universal atman. They are confident that if they fully realize that their atman is one with Brahman, they will attain *moksha* from the wheel of rebirth. Many gurus invite people to "look within" with heightened awareness in order to realize their own divinity. When spiritually advanced Hindus finally know that God's mindfulness is their own consciousness, they call that transforming experience *sacci-dananda,* an extraordinarily rich term composed of *sat* ("actualized exis-tence"), *chit* ("pure consciousness"), and *ananda* ("unmitigated bliss"). They then are aware that the *sat, chit,* and *ananda* of God's life are one and the same with the *sat, chit,* and *ananda* of their own life.

Hindus follow Dharma precisely because of their immersion within the ocean of Brahman that engulfs them from every side and drenches them at every level. Hindus adhere to Dharma in order to unite insepara-bly with Brahman. Hindus regard no aspect of their lives as utterly neu-tral or devoid of Brahman. At the same time, Hindus acknowledge that their share in Brahman is but a tiny portion of the Godhead's potential for emanation. They recognize that they overflow with Brahman totally, but they also realize that they cannot contain Brahman exhaustively. Therefore, Hindus strive lovingly to perceive the Brahman that resides within all people and endows them too with Brahman's divine dignity.

Hindus enjoy offering *puja* at the temple of their favorite god or goddess during a special festival, but their fulfillment of Dharma enables them to encounter Brahman routinely and everywhere, at the most ordinary times and in the most commonplace circumstances. Hindus wor-ship Brahman not only at shrines and pilgrimage sites, but also in their homes and in their workplaces. Hindus perceive Brahman's numinous power not only at the altars and the statues of their gods, but also in dank caves, verdant forests, lofty peaks, and rushing rivers. Hindus discover Brahman not only in other people but also in all living beings, from the trees, plants, and flowers to the animals, birds, and fish. Hindus delight in making pilgrimages to special sites that are adorned with splendid sculpture, but they also know that their observance of Dharma plunges them into Brahman's presence even within the most modest of homes.

Hindus cultivate their mindfulness of Brahman in the most striking ways. For example, they frequently pronounce the primordial syllable that symbolizes God: **Om.** "*Om*" is the sacred sound through which Brahman brought the cosmos into being. Hindus vocalize "*Om*" as a powerful **mantra** (sacred word or phrase) in order to focus their minds for concentrated meditation. Hindus also utter "*Om*" as an introduction or conclusion to their prayers and Vedic readings: By so doing, they acknowledge Brahman as the source of the cosmos.

Another example is the Hindus' special reverence for the cows that are ubiquitous in the villages of India. Just as Christians resonate to the lamb as an innocent symbol of the nonviolent Jesus sacrificing his life for humankind, so Hindus respond to the cow as a maternal symbol of the nonviolent Brahman pouring out being upon the universe. At another level, it is not surprising to witness a young woman offering obeisance to the spirit of a tree along a country road. Caught up in interior recollection, she is a devout woman who seeks to heighten her consciousness of Brahman within herself. Nor does anybody pay particular notice to an elderly man who sits in the middle of a bustling sidewalk, half-naked, with arms and legs crossed, himself oblivious to the crowd that streams by him. He is a **sadhu** ("just man" or "saint"), who has given himself over to *samadhi* ("deep meditation") in order to realize Brahman within himself.

Brahman did not intervene in history to hand over Dharma to the Hindus the way the God of Moses delivered the Torah to the Jews and the God of Muhammad handed over the Quran to the Muslims. On the contrary, Brahman discloses Dharma as the law/duty for the world insofar as Brahman manifests itself in and through all things that proceed from it. Brahman is not essentially the same as Dharma, but the divine Brahman does cause Dharma to emanate or flow from itself as the structural ordinance for the universe. Thus Brahman's eternal principle of all order, law, and design inheres within the total cosmos coextensively as Dharma.

Hindu Response to Brahman as Personified

As we might expect, most Hindus find Nirguna Brahman to be too remote and abstract to satisfy their needs for vivid intellectual awareness and fervent emotional feeling. They want to be able to transcend themselves through knowing and loving God personally. The majority of Hindus, therefore, prefer to connect with some theistic personification of the unfathomable Brahman. For these Hindus, the cultivation of a relationship with Brahman personified becomes a salient characteristic of their Hindu spirituality.

In this Hindu perspective, there are countless deities, names, aspects, or manifestations that partially represent the supremely one Brahman in terms of a special emphasis. The Hindu tradition, indeed, presents a pantheon of 330 million gods and goddesses from whom Hindus may freely claim the **Ishtadeva** ("God of choice") that best meets their individual needs and dispositions. When Hindus approach Brahman in this personified form, they are able to relate with the Godhead through fascinating myths that appeal to their imagination and through an awe-inspiring iconography that touches their hearts. Hindus can then carry on a dialogue with their God or Goddess through prayers, hymns, and mantras while they share life with their God or Goddess through symbolic rituals.

Hindu spirituality by and large, however, takes shape in three principal forms of devotional commitment: Shaivism (the worship of Shiva the Destroyer), Vaishnavism (the worship of **Vishnu** the Preserver or one of his incarnations), and Shaktism (the worship of **Shakti** the Feminine Dynamic Energy). Hindus often adore Shiva or Vishnu (or one of his incarnations) as a **Mahadeva** ("supreme God") or Shakti (or one of her manifestations) as a **Mahadevi** ("supreme Goddess"). This religious attitude may be either a genuine monotheism (the recognition of but one God or one Goddess) or a **henotheism** (the recognition of one God or Goddess that is the greatest deity among many gods and goddesses).

Shiva   Millions of **Shaivas** (devotees of Shiva) claim some aspect of Shiva the Destroyer or his Shakti as the magnetic focus of their worship. Shaivas worship Shiva as their one Mahadeva, while they consider Vishnu and **Brahma** to be inferior to Shiva. Shaivism constitutes a very large collection of traditions that contribute to Hindu spirituality. Shiva is an awesome God of complex and paradoxical character in whom opposites strangely converge. Shiva is the Mahadeva who is the God of generation, yet Shiva is also the terrifying God of corruption. Shiva is the **Mahayogi** ("great ascetic") who smears his face with ashes as he fasts and stores up his sexual energy in celibate solitude. The masculine Shiva rests passively with cool detachment, yet Shiva also claims as his Goddess consort the feminine Shakti, who actively creates with heated involvement.

Shaiva iconography reflects Shiva's complexity. Shiva is the bisexual God of universality, and Shaiva sculptors mold his body as at once partly male and partly female. Shiva is also the life-giving God of sexual reproduction, and Shaiva sculptors portray Shiva with a stylized **linga** (phallic symbol) in his hand, while **Nandi** (the white bull that is Shiva's vehicle) gazes intently upon him. Shiva is the God of life and death who dances out the recurrent rhythms of living and dying; by way of fascinating contrast, Shaiva sculptors also present Shiva as the graceful **Nataraja** (Lord of the Dance).

In the light of the immense diversity within Shaiva theology, it is not surprising that Shaiva practices should also cover a broad spectrum. Shaivas may, for example, observe rigorous self-denial in the wilderness with the matted hair and disciplined regimen of Shiva the master ascetic. Shaivas may also visit temples of Shakti in terms of a particular manifestation (such as *Chinnamastra, Chandi, Uma,* **Kali,** or **Durga**) in order to express their emotional feelings of devotional attachment to her as Goddess consort of Shiva.

Vishnu and His Avatars   **Vaishnavas** (devotees of Vishnu) adore Vishnu as their one Mahadeva, while they place Shiva and Brahma in second rank after Vishnu. Vaishnavism is another popular source of Hindu spirituality. Vishnu, the almighty preserver and omnipresent protector of all things, is the most popular and benign of all Hindu gods. Vishnu possesses every gentle attribute, from benevolent kindness and fidelity to overflowing compassion and sublime wisdom. Above all, Vishnu is a warm and loving God who cares deeply about the welfare of human beings. Vishnu abides constantly within the hearts of his devotees, and he may even manifest himself to them in visions.

Vaishnavas, therefore, give themselves to Vishnu with devout confidence. Vaishnavas are particularly noted for their ceaseless praise of Lord Vishnu for the unfathomable depths of his love. Vishnu graciously discloses himself to the devotees who long for his embrace. Vishnu embodies his divine presence not only in sacred images and temples but also in animals and human beings. Vishnu is the Savior who comes among us to protect the Dharma whenever its values are in danger. Vishnu is the merciful Lord who intervenes to rescue all those who call upon him.

Hindu iconographers often portray the handsome Vishnu as standing side by side with the strikingly beautiful **Lakshmi** (Vishnu's Goddess consort and chief queen), whom Vishnu embraces affectionately with one arm. Vishnu and Lakshmi represent the ideal couple, unreservedly devoted to each other in marital love. Vaishnava sculptors also present

Vishnu in four-armed human form together with **Garuda** (Vishnu's eagle vehicle).

Most of all, Vishnu is the loving God among us who has already entered the human domain through nine saving **avatars** ("descents") and will return in a tenth avatar in the future. For Vaishnavas, it makes perfect sense that God should come among them in human form—not just once and for all, but repeatedly and everywhere. It is the inescapable logic of divine love. If God really cares for people and they cannot reach out to him, why should he not reach out to them? It would be impossible to calculate the impact of this solid conviction upon Hindu spirituality in terms of spiritual comfort, hope, joy, and devotion.

One of Vishnu's avatars is **Rama,** the ideal warrior-king who rules his people with self-sacrificing love, steadfast courage, and faithful justice for all. Vaishnavas revere Rama as the exemplary man and heroic husband who rescued his beloved wife, **Sita** (an avatar of Lakshmi, Goddess consort of Vishnu), from the evil king Ravana. Hindus have even extended the name Rama to universal use as a nonsectarian synonym for *God.*

A second and the most popular avatar of Vishnu is Krishna, whose consort is the lovely **Radha** (another avatar of Lakshmi). Sometimes Vaishnavas celebrate Krishna as the darling little boy who plays mischievous pranks on his elders. In this guise, Krishna embodies Vishnu with a special focus upon his irresistible charm and his *lila* (whimsical and purposeless play). More often, Vaishnavas rejoice in Krishna as the dancing and flute-playing *gopala* (cowherd) who cavorts flirtatiously with the *gopis* (cowherdesses) until, completely smitten, they each in turn consummate their passion. Under this aspect, Krishna incarnates Vishnu with a special focus upon Vishnu's boundless love for human beings.

Shakti   The **Shaktas** (devotees of Shakti) venerate Shakti or one of her manifestations as their one Mahadevi. Shaktism makes an extremely significant impact upon Hindu spirituality for both men and women. Since Shakti appears under different titles and in widely divergent personas, she appeals to people of many distinct circumstances, temperaments, and tastes.

Shakti may take on a humane and gentle form, such as that of the lovely Parvati, to whom women pray for assistance in their marriages; Parvati gave birth to the popular **Ganesha** (the elephant-headed God), who removes obstacles. Or Shakti may manifest herself as **Kamakshi** (the Great Mother), whose aid women beseech on behalf of their children. At other times Shakti may assume horrendous identities such as those of the blood-drinking Kali or the deadly Durga.

HINDU GROWTH THROUGH COMMUNITY

As we have seen, Hinduism is really a whole cluster of religions and sub-religions that accept the sacred authority of the Vedic scriptures and follow Sanatana Dharma in the most general sense. Hinduism is an ancient tradition that unites all its practitioners in the pursuit of one and the same *moksha* from samsara as they fulfill Dharma in this world. At the same time, Hinduism is an evolving tradition with an inclusive pluralism, insofar as its practitioners follow widely diverse belief systems, techniques, and paths. No individual within a single life span could possibly participate in all that Hinduism validates as authentically Hindu.

Hinduism, therefore, is by no means a single institution binding about a billion individuals together as one people with the same collective identity, organized community, and universal structures. Hindu experience of Hindu community life is different from Jewish experience of K'lal Yisrael and Muslim experience of the one umma of the Muslims, and it is vastly different from Christian experience of the universal Church. For example, a multitude of Hindus may offer their individual worship simultaneously and at the same temple without necessarily feeling the communal bond that Christians experience when they gather for the Holy Eucharist. All the same, Hindus may enjoy a profound sense of bonded togetherness insofar as they participate in their favorite pilgrimage or festival.

Pilgrimages

Hindus know that they must dwell in India, the sacred center of the cosmos, if they are to reap the fruits of their religion as fully as possible. Brahman pervades this country in a special way through and through, sanctifying India as a vast sacrament or conduit of transforming power. Brahman's presence is universally accessible throughout the world, of course, and the Godhead embraces all creatures from all sides as the ocean encompasses the fish that swim in it. Yet Brahman overflows from within this subcontinent as from the world's fountainhead. India is, then, the ideal venue for attaining *moksha,* and just to live in India is to soak in a flood of blessings. Yet Hindus are not content to follow a static existence in the place where they happen to be born. Hindus discern within their hearts an imperious restlessness that impels them to move from place to place. Hindus must journey ever again to those privileged sites where Brahman is superabundantly available. For Hindus are basically a "people on pilgrimage" in search of that final union with Brahman from which there will be no return.

Hindus refer to a pilgrimage as a *tirthayatra* (literally, "tour to a ford"), because their most popular pilgrimage sites involve holy rivers. These external *tirthayatras* represent Hindus' internal faith odyssey choreographed—their gradual movement toward *moksha*. *Tirthayatras* are arduous metaphors-in-action that dramatize the pilgrims' quest to win purification from negative karmic fruits, grace (both for themselves and for their ancestors), and positive merit. Through a kind of religious procession to geographical centers, Hindus are able to present to God the critical needs of their lives, appropriate the divine favor, and, perhaps, participate in the re-presentation of divine activity. Hindu pilgrims especially look forward to an awesome event known as *darshan* ("view"), the sublime joy of beholding God in a sacred image.

Tirthayatras have, indeed, captured the Hindu imagination, and there is no occasion in India when a multitude of pilgrims is not on the move over thousands of roads from one holy place to the next. Countless *tirthas* (pilgrimage sites) adorn the Indian landscape as so many wells within a spiritual oasis. Hindus yield first place to none in their enthusiasm for this privileged enterprise of the human spirit.

Pilgrimage is a communal phenomenon in Hinduism, insofar as Hindus of diverse regions, castes, and sectarian persuasions universally delight together in its collective observance. Hindus usually embrace a *tirthayatra* as a group endeavor from that first moment when they explicitly affirm their intention of becoming pilgrims. Often Hindu pilgrims make a solemn vow to make a particular pilgrimage, and the irresistible thrust of this commitment serves as a sacred incentive to persevere until they have fulfilled it. Hindu pilgrims separate themselves from profane society and enlist in a sacred community until they have been filled with power at the sacred site. Only then may they return home and resume their ordinary lives. Hindu pilgrims typically die to their old selves and enter a fellowship set apart, a congregation of elevated consciousness composed solely of "persons on pilgrimage." Pilgrims symbolize their communal identity by cropping their hair, adopting the pilgrim's special garb, fasting, abstaining from sexual activity, and jointly singing joyful hymns of praise to their Ishtadeva.

Hindu pilgrims set out to visit the ancient localities where the sacred Reality offers itself in bountiful accessibility, but these sites are often distant and the journey fraught with peril. *Tirthayatras* are inherently demanding, but Hindu pilgrims draw strength for their resolve from their reciprocal reinforcement. As pilgrims encourage one another over the passing days, their hopes and labors lead to a shared joy in fulfillment. The common experiences of pilgrims engender a mutual bond of friendship as they traverse the miles of India together from north to south and from east to west. Pilgrims' physical encampments for food and rest along the way become catalysts of spiritual community in hopeful faith and reciprocal love.

Hindus are especially devoted to making pilgrimage to the Ganges River ("Mother Ganga"). It is highly meritorious for Hindus just to utter the name of this holiest of all rivers. The Ganges presents to pilgrims five principal *tirthas:* Gangotri, Hardwar, Gahr-Mukteswar, Prayaga, and that unrivaled city of joyful bliss beyond even Jerusalem or Mecca, Varanasi (known as Kashi, "city of lights"). Pilgrims devoutly immerse themselves in the wondrous water of the Ganges that, they are confident, remains always free of corruption. Pilgrims wash themselves thoroughly, drink deeply, and fill their bottles for the return home. The bath of pilgrims in the Ganges cleanses away all sins, not only for the pilgrims themselves but also for their ancestors back to seven generations. The elderly and the dying lie by the Ganges's sacred banks in the hope of completing their passage into *moksha.* Families carry the bodies of their departed loved ones in order to cremate them in the ever burning pyres on the **ghats** (steps) that lead down to the water. Then pilgrims sprinkle the ashes of their beloved dead on the Ganges as it rushes by.

The pilgrimage festival of Kumbha Mela is an altogether extraordinary religious fair in which several million persons may participate during a single day. Hindus celebrate Kumbha Mela every twelve years at that precise time when astrological factors harmonize most favorably. Monks and tourists join pilgrims from every walk of life in observing this pilgrimage festival at four renowned river sites. Pilgrims bathe in purifying waters that confer the remission of faults and abundant grace. Pilgrims pray privately, join in congregational hymnody, or enlist the service of priests for their sacrificial rituals. Pilgrims attach themselves to one of the many assemblies where gurus earnestly exhort their audiences to explore the hollow of their hearts. The government provides logistical support to meet the needs of security and hygiene. Indeed, India dramatically displays her soul every twelve years by the celebration of Kumbha Mela.

Festivals

Hindu pilgrimages frequently converge upon a splendid **utsava** (festival), which may extend from a single day to a whole month. Several forms of worship may occur simultaneously during the same festival. The *utsava* is an opportunity for Hindus to seek purification at the same time that they adore their God, and Hindus' delight in festivals is a special dimension of their spirituality. The *utsava* is virtually a daily phenomenon in some shrine or temple among the tens of thousands that adorn the Indian landscape. Despite the frequency of festal observances, however, a festival can be a powerful event that combines the fervent devotion of individuals with the infectious enthusiasm of a multitude unified in mind and heart. Vast throngs of devotees gather in one auspicious spot as this spectacle approaches, all of them intent upon a choice blessing that will surely lead them closer to *moksha,* especially the *darshan* of their divine Beloved.

The *utsava* is an extraordinary stimulus for the outpouring of religious sentiment and growth in Hindu spirituality. It occurs only on that most auspicious date on the calendar when the time is precisely right. People can depend upon their God to be most benevolent and generous when the stars and the planets are in their most favorable alignment. The *utsava* is also a further but no less potent occasion for Hindus to draw upon the communal dimension of their religion. Numbered by the thousands, celebrants readily draw renewed faith and hope from their mutual solidarity in mind and heart. Holy men and pilgrims make camp side by side for days ahead of time, while vendors insistently hawk souvenirs, food, flowers, and all the paraphernalia that pilgrims need for worship. Smiling devotees raise their voices in song as they wander around together, mixing in with the crowds that gather about the many shops and stalls.

The most impressive event of the *utsava* occurs when priests remove the **murti** (image of a god) from its sanctuary and place it on a large wheeled vehicle for solemn procession. Dozens of men then pull the enthroned *murti* slowly through the town on stout ropes. Crowds of people, horses, and elephants follow the *murti*'s chariot, all of them decked out in magnificent festive garb. People on the sidelines offer to the *murti* their sacrificial gifts of flowers, fruits, and coins. Hindus relate to their God more deeply in such processions as they join hearts with one another.

There are countless Hindu *utsavas,* and every one of the thousands of temples has its own. Generally, a temple hosts an *utsava* for several days. Sometimes devotees commemorate some event in the life of a god or goddess. Other festivals are seasonal and connected with agricultural planting and harvesting, while still others celebrate fecundity, love, and marriage. Some *utsavas,* such as **Divali** (Festival of Lights), are of virtually universal observance in India.

FORMATION THROUGH
THE VEDIC SCRIPTURES
The Hindu Scriptures

Scripture plays a pivotal role for the practitioners of all world religions, as they attempt to nourish their spiritual experience and interpret it to themselves. We have already reviewed the significance of the Hebrew Bible for Jews, of the Christian Bible for Christians, and of the Quran for Muslims, as these monotheists respond in their own ways to the personal God of Abraham. The Hindus possess in the Vedas a vast sacred literature upon which they may draw as they follow their various paths to Brahman-atman.

The ancient Vedas are Hindu scriptures in the broad sense of that term. Although the Vedas claim no deity as their inspiring author, they do contain the eternal *sabda* ("sound") that reverberates throughout the universe, and they constitute Hinduism's only source of supernatural and eternal Revelation. The Vedas are **Shruti** ("Revelation that has been heard"), because mystical seers and poets of old passed down by word of mouth what they had "heard" inside themselves through an ineffable encounter with Brahman. Sages committed this Revelation to written form only after centuries of the most vigilant and meticulous memorization for oral tradition.

The Vedas consist of four bodies of Sanskrit literature, each of which is vast. First, there are the **Samhitas** ("collections"), which include the Rig-Veda, with its 1,028 hymns of praise, the Sama-Veda, with its liturgical chants for sacrifices, the Yajur-Veda, with its sacrificial mantras and formulas, and the Atharva-Veda, with its magical spells and incantations. The Samhitas furnish the proper words and rituals to the priests as they celebrate all the various sacrifices that they must offer on behalf of their clients. The Samhitas particularly nourish the spirituality of upper-class Hindus insofar as they regularly celebrate the sacrifice of fire. These texts contain the formulas and rituals that Hindus utilize not only in order to maintain the universe on an even keel with right order (*rita*) but also in order to reap material benefits from the gods. Other Vedic collections include the **Brahmanas,** which present general doctrinal texts for the priests, and the **Aranyakas,** which disclose the mystical treatises of forest-dwelling holy men.

Finally, particularly noteworthy are the **Upanishads,** or **Vedanta** ("end of the Vedas"), which combine metaphysical instructions about ultimate Reality with esoteric dialogues between gurus and their spiritual sons. Some of the Upanishads provide provocative insights into our ultimate human identity in and with Brahman-atman: *Tat tvam asi* ("That thou art"). In this treasure house of spirituality, we read: "Who is without beginning or end, in the midst of disorder; who is the creator of the universe displaying various forms; who, alone, encompasses the universe—when someone recognizes him as God, he is freed from all fetters. Who is to be grasped with one's heart, who is called 'Without-a-Lord,' who brings about existence and nonexistence, who is the Benign One, and who produces both the creation and its constituent parts—those who know him as God have cast aside their bodies" (Svetasvatara Upanishad 5.13–14). Hindu intellectuals traditionally study the Upanishads in order to appropriate its metaphysical insights as religious philosophy. Hindu mystics meditate ever again upon the Upanishads as scriptural Revelation, because they seek to "hear" them as directly personal revelation of Brahman in their deepest consciousness.

Smriti ("what is remembered") is a second literary corpus of major significance in Hindu spirituality, although it is not Vedic in the strict sense, because it derives from human authorship. This collection comprises the Sutras, which present comprehensive instructions for Vedic rites through the Srauta Sutras and directions for domestic rites through the Griya Sutras.

Smriti further contains the Dharmasutras and the Dharmashastras, which provide particular applications of Dharma for individual Hindus. Among these, **The Laws of Manu** is a practical manual that provides Hindus with their specific duties on a daily basis according to their class and stage of life.

Smriti also categorizes a vast corpus of popular old writings. Millions of Hindus draw regularly upon this collection as spiritual reading that enlightens their thoughts and inspires their actions. Thus, Hindus have access to two immense epics that glorify avatars of Vishnu: the Ramayana, which exalts Rama, and the Mahabharata, which promotes the praise of Krishna, especially in a favorite subdivision entitled the **Bhagavad Gita** ("The Song of the Divine Lord"). Popular literature also includes the Puranas (Hindu folklore on every theme) such as the Bhagavata Purana, which acclaims Vishnu together with Krishna, and the Sutra Samhita, which recounts the splendor of Shiva.

The Bhagavad Gita provides a classical synthesis of Hinduism's three major *margas* ("ways") to *moksha: jnana marga* ("way of knowledge"), *karma marga* ("way of action"), and *bhakti marga* ("way of devotion"). Its wisdom has profoundly affected the substance, confidence, and interpretation of Hindu spirituality for almost two millennia. The Bhagavad Gita contains a supernal dialogue in which Lord Krishna (disguised as a charioteer) teaches an Indian prince named Arjuna to follow the way of works while remaining detached from the fruits of his action. Krishna reveals:

Your entitlement is only to the rite, not ever at all its fruits. Be not motivated by the fruits of acts, but also do not purposely seek to avoid acting. Abandon self-interest, Dhanamjaya, and perform the acts while applying this singlemindedness. Remain equable in success and failure—this equableness is called the application; for the act as such is far inferior to the application of singleness of purpose to it, Dhanamjaya. Seek shelter in this singlemindedness—pitiful are those who are motivated by fruits! Armed with this singleness of purpose, a man relinquishes here both good and evil karman.

—Bhagavad Gita 6[63] 24[2] 48–50

Krishna also teaches Arjuna that he may transcend obligatory works through the way of knowledge: "Renouncing without exception all objects of desire that are rooted in intentions, taming the village of his senses all around with his mind, he should little by little *cease,* while he holds his spirit with fortitude, merges his mind in the self, and thinks of nothing at all" (Bhagavad Gita 6[63] 28[6] 24–25). Yet Krishna finally transfixes Prince Arjuna by disclosing to him the inspiring way of devotion:

If one disciplined soul proffers to me with love a leaf, a flower, fruit, or water, I accept this offering of love from him. Whatever you do, or eat, or offer, or give, or mortify, Kaunteya, make it an offering to me, and I shall undo the bonds of karman, the good and evil fruits. . . . Reduced to this passing world of unhappiness, embrace me! May your thoughts be toward me, your love toward me, your sacrifice toward me, your homage toward me, and you shall come to me, having thus yoked yourself to me as your highest goal.

—Bhagavad Gita 6[63] 31[9] 27–28, 34–35

The Four Goals

Most Hindus interpret the meaning of their lives in terms of the four classical goals as disclosed in the Laws of Manu. Consequently, they labor from childhood through old age toward the two preeminent goals: the following of Dharma as their life's design and the pursuit of *moksha* as their final liberation from this samsaric existence. As long as married Hindus are involved during their young adulthood in affairs of the family and the larger community, however, they wholeheartedly pursue the other two goals as well: the enjoyment of *kama* ("pleasure," "happiness") in terms of their affective relationships of familial love and the acquisition of *artha* ("material wealth") in terms of their productive relationships of social responsibility.

The Four *Varnas*

As Hindus target these goals, they follow the Laws of Manu in fulfilling the duties and practicing the livelihoods that are appropriate to their *varna* ("social class," or "caste"). Birth into a particular *varna* results from an individual's relative balance of good and bad karmic store from past lives, and so it may serve as a gauge of an individual's spiritual progress until now. Although Hindus categorize themselves according to thousands of subcastes, Dharma prescribes four major *varnas* of descending dignity. Only boys who belong to the three higher castes may become *dvijas* ("twice-born") through the ritual of *upanayana* (sacramental initiation into Vedic study).

According to Hindu tradition, the **Brahmins** (priestly caste) constitute the first and highest *varna*, which emerged from the mouth of **Purusha**, a divine being that the gods dismembered in a cosmic sacrifice. That is why the Brahmins are supposed to be naturally religious people who enjoy the privilege of chanting the Vedas and reciting the awesome mantras. According to their Dharma, Brahmins worship the gods on behalf of others and celebrate the ritual sacrifices that maintain the universe on an even keel. They are also intellectuals who preserve the Hindu tradition through their scholarship and pass it down through their authoritative teaching of the Vedic texts to others.

Tradition discloses that the **Kshatriyas** (warrior caste) make up the second *varna*, which came forth from the arms of Purusha. That is why Kshatriyas are supposed to be strong, courageous, and valiant people who are endowed with an innate aptitude for leading their fellows and ruling the land. According to their Dharma, Kshatriyas must govern society for the common good and defend its citizens in battle. The Kshatriyas must also apply themselves earnestly to the study of the Vedas.

Hindu tradition teaches that the **Vaishyas** (business and agricultural caste) compose the third *varna*, which developed from the thighs of Purusha. That is why the Vaishyas are supposed to be creative, energetic, and industrious people who have a natural talent for productivity. Vaishyas give themselves to farming, cattle raising, commerce, and skilled craftswork. According to their Dharma, Vaishyas have a duty to produce the material goods and foodstuffs that people need collectively. The Vaishyas also have the obligation of Vedic study.

In Hindu understanding, the **Shudras** (servant caste) are the fourth and lowest *varna*, which emanated from the feet of Purusha, organs that are rather base in their function although they are indispensable for stability. That is why Shudras are supposed to assist the twice-born of the three upper castes in all that they need. Shudras do not themselves, however, become twice-born through *upanayana*. According to their Dharma, Shudras are supposed to provide without bitterness all necessary services, especially the most menial works that the members of the three upper castes would find spiritually polluting—that is, a source of impurity for themselves.

The Four *Ashramas*

Upper-caste Hindus who are seriously intent upon attaining *moksha* exert themselves wholeheartedly through four determined *ashramas* (stages of life) and fulfill the duties that the Laws of Manu assign to each period. The *ashramas* represent the ideal spiritual rhythm of a human being's life span, as a person progresses from early growth and preparation for adulthood to the level of mature productivity and then from the subsequent withdrawal away from worldly concerns to a decisive focus upon final release from this existence. These four unique periods are designated as **brahmacharya** (student stage), **grihasthya** (householder stage), **vanaprasthya** (forest-dweller stage), and **sannyasa** (renunciate stage). This division of the human life span into *ashramas* traditionally applied directly to men and only indirectly to women, but nowadays it has become fairly common for women to fulfill at least three of these *ashramas: brahmacharya, grihasthya,* and *vanaprasthya.*

During early adolescence, an upper-caste Hindu receives the sacrament of thread investiture into *brahmacharya*, the first *ashrama*. The *brahmacharin* wears this holy thread across the body from the left shoulder, learns a secret mantra from a guru, and engages in demanding studies for the mastery of Vedic scriptures and meditative disciplines. The *brahmacharin* must learn all the religious duties, prayers, and sacred rituals that Dharma requires from the twice-born Hindu adult. When *brahmacharins* practice celibacy for the sages, perform manual service for a guru, and diligently pursue Vedic study, they discharge the first among their "four debts."

Young adults who have completed the long years of *brahmacharya* then enter *grihasthya*, the second *ashrama* of life. *Grihasthas* enjoy all the pleasures of worldly life, since bodily gratification is also integral to spirituality during this period of development. *Grihasthas* rejoice wholeheartedly in the sexual love of marriage and the tender affection of parenthood. *Grihasthas* also work hard to produce goods and services, not only in order to accumulate wealth but also to benefit the greater community. During this period, *grihasthas* pay off three other debts: offspring for ancestors, hospitality for fellow human beings, and daily sacrifices for the gods. Most Hindus remain at this *ashrama* throughout their life, faithfully discharging all their responsibilities in the hope of exhausting their negative karmic indebtedness and building up their positive karmic store toward a higher rebirth.

Grihasthas who have attained middle age and have adult children who themselves are parents may choose to enter the third *ashrama* of *vanaprasthya*. Since *vanaprasthas* have dutifully met all their obligations to others, they are now eligible to devote all their energies full time to their inner life. *Vanaprasthas* free themselves from all householder activities and obligations, embrace the ascetic lifestyle of hermits, and retire to the forest. A wife has the option of living with her eldest son or accompanying her husband into the forest, provided that the couple dwell together celibately. *Vanaprasthas* take their household fires with them and continue to offer ritual sacrifices for a while. Eventually, however, *vanaprasthas* abandon all external ceremonies and concentrate upon the fiery sacrifices within themselves. Hindus who rise to the stage of *vanaprasthya* take a major step toward rebirth at a high level within the *varna* of Brahmins. *Vanaprasthas* may then aspire to live so that they finally attain *moksha* itself.

Vanaprasthas of advanced age who are determined to seek liberation once and for all from the wheel of rebirth may opt for the fourth and most revered *ashrama*, that of *sannyasa*. Only male *vanaprasthas* who have realized a high degree of holiness are eligible to embrace this *sannyasa*. (If a wife has accompanied her husband during his stage of *vanaprasthya*, she now returns to her eldest son.) Worthy *vanaprasthas* become sannyasins through an initiatory ritual of spiritual death to every secular concern and to every earthly bond—even to wife, family, and friends. Sannyasins offer their sacred thread to the gods and put aside their sacrificial fires forever. Sannyasins renounce both name and property in order to wander vulnerably; they carry only sandals, a loincloth, an outer garment, a staff, a water jar, and a begging bowl. Sannyasins make the sannyasin vow to observe **ahimsa** ("nonviolence"), truthfulness, and complete continence.

Sannyasins go beyond all rules and responsibilities and even transcend Dharma itself in order to immerse themselves undividedly in *samadhi.* Sannyasins hope in this particular lifetime to attain *moksha* itself. Hindus at other *ashramas* are in awe of *sannyasins* as sadhus; Hindus even store up good karmic treasures by caring for those physical needs about which the sannyasins themselves are unconcerned.

HINDU RESPONSE TO THE GODHEAD
THROUGH WORSHIP AND PRAYER

Most religious people prefer to reach their final goal by adopting one of three major approaches, either singly or in combination: a path of knowledge, or mystical insight into ultimate Reality; a path of action, or works of dutiful ritual and upright morality; or a path of devotion, with faithful surrender and love. Hindu orthopraxis endorses all three of these approaches as secure roads for completing the human journey to *moksha:* (1) *jnana marga,* "way of knowledge"; (2) *karma marga,* "way of action"; and (3) *bhakti marga,* "way of devotion." Hindu women and men may choose one or more paths according to their own personal inclination, temperament, need, or caste.

Jnana Marga

There has been a significant dimension of mystical contemplation in Hindu spirituality ever since the emergence of the Upanishads about 2,500 years ago. Brahmanical priests had previously emphasized their path of action through offering fire sacrifices that sustained the world's resources and pleased the gods. Upanishadic sages, however, "heard" the possibility of attaining *moksha* through *jnana marga,* an alternative path of internalized sacrifice ("spiritual heat") through meditation. These sages came to realize the unity of their own atman with the universal Brahman, and they handed down their wisdom orally by dialogical format.

Lord Krishna recommends *jnana marga* to Arjuna in these words: "Hear from me in brief, Kaunteya, how by reaching perfection one attains to *brahman,* which is the pinnacle of knowledge. Yoked with a pure spirit and subduing himself with fortitude, renouncing the sense objects of sound, etc., and discarding love and hatred, seeking solitude, eating lightly, restraining speech, body, and mind, intent upon the yoga of contemplation, cultivating dispassion, ridding himself of egotism, displays of strength, pride, lust, wrath, and possessions, and being no longer acquisitive but serene, he is able to become *brahman*" (Bhagavad Gita 6[63] 40[18] 50–54).

Only a small minority of Hindus seek salvation through *jnana marga*, since it is a rigorous and esoteric discipline. *Jnana marga* may be, nevertheless, the most readily recognized dimension of Hindu spirituality. Tourists in India are sure to encounter, for instance, sadhus who fix their gaze inwardly upon the cave of their hearts and become quite oblivious to the curious stares of passers-by. Documentaries on public television describe contemplatives who have renounced the seductive entanglement of sensual pleasure and material goods in their pursuit of spiritual bliss. Popular magazines such as *National Geographic* portray holy men who have become impervious to their bodily needs because they are caught up in meditative rapture.

Practitioners of *jnana marga* must escape the dark prison of ignorance and error within which their feelings, outward experiences, and intellectual conceptions have chained them. They must control their bodily functions, gradually subordinate their senses and emotions to the rule of their minds, and then proceed to eliminate even their mental activities such as ideation, judgment, and reasoning. Practitioners of *jnana marga* must transcend all those illusions of individual separateness that lead to an erroneous dichotomy between subject and object. They must break through all those stubborn layers of self-centeredness into the depths of their most radical being, where they and the Godhead are one.

Therefore, devotees often apply the physical exercises of yoga ("discipline") in order to liberate their atman from all the distracting images, passions, memories, and ideas that intrude upon their consciousness. Only then may they enter into that trancelike state of self-realization, with all karmic residues exhausted. The yogic quest for enlightenment consists of eight steps, and those who become adept at these skills are known as **yogis** (practitioners of yoga).

In the first two steps, yogis apply themselves to moral reform and spiritual renewal. Yogis not only conquer any obviously dehumanizing vices, such as lust, greed, gluttony, or anger, but also observe the prohibitions of Dharma, such as those that forbid any acts of violence. Yogis struggle further toward the elimination of all those ethical faults that self-centeredness engenders, such as impatience and unkindness or insensitivity and niggardliness. Yogis become persons of mild composure, self-control, and virtue through a rigorous regimen of intellectual study and physical self-denial.

In the next three steps, yogis subject their bodily functions to the control of their minds. They integrate their bodies into serene organisms that will not trouble their souls' probing reflections within. Yogis begin this as-cetic discipline by proper posture, sitting upright and motionless. Then yogis practice the restraint and reduction of their breathing until it almost ceases altogether. Finally, yogis withdraw their five senses from the color, sound, taste, odor, and texture that excite them and hold them captive.

After yogis have subordinated their bodies to their minds, they may now follow the final three steps toward cessation of all mental activities. They must free their atman of distracting intellectual processes such as simple apprehension, synthetic judgment, and discursive reasoning. They must eliminate all cogitation and attain the tranquility that precedes the superconsciousness of Brahman alone. First, yogis focus their intellects by concentration upon one notion, often fixating upon a particular area of the body such as the forehead or heart. Second, yogis enter by meditation into sustained contemplation of divine union to the exclusion of all other realities. At last, yogis by *samadhi* become unreservedly absorbed into Brahman.

Unimaginable freedom awaits yogis as they unite with Brahman, the still point of being, the pinnacle of consciousness, and the boundless ocean of bliss. Purified, disciplined, emancipated, and enlightened with a wisdom that surpasses all knowledge, yogis then rest in a heightened awareness that weds quintessential calm with ineffable peace. Adherence to *jnana marga* engenders unmediated self-realization, an intuitive flash that consumes all accumulated karma in a transforming unification with Brahman. Yogis hope finally to attain their emancipation so that they may die and never return on the wheel of rebirth.

Karma Marga

Countless individuals among the religious people of the world believe that they must be pro-active and work hard if they are to attain their goal of salvation. They find it self-evident that an authentic faith must lead to worship of the Godhead and acts of service for human beings in need—especially for widows and orphans. Hinduism also validates this per-spective, by endorsing *karma marga* as a principal road for ultimately transcending self-centeredness and becoming absolutely one with Brah-man. The Laws of Manu play a significant role as practical guideposts along this path of activity.

Hindus who adhere to *karma marga* strive faithfully to fulfill every duty that Dharma requires, and their motivation endows their works with supernal value as continuous adoration of the Godhead. Yet devotees must beware of *karma marga*'s clinging aftermath, since all actions (whether good or bad) are subject to the law of karma, and even meritorious consequences will bind a person's atman to the wheel of rebirth. Krishna reveals that one may escape this trap by deliberately renouncing the fruits of one's actions beforehand and acting with selfless altruism. Krishna instructs Arjuna:

If one places all karman *on* brahman *and acts disinterestedly, he is no more stained by evil than a lotus petal by muddy water. Yogins do their acts with body, mind, spirit, and even the senses disengaged, in order to purify the self, without any interest in the acts themselves. The man of yoga, renouncing the fruits of his acts, reaches the peace of the ultimate foundation, while the undisciplined man, who acts on his desires because he is interested in fruits, is fettered by* karman*. Having renounced all* karman *with the mind, the soul dwells, happy and masterful, in its nine-gated fortress, neither doing nor causing acts.*

—Bhagavad Gita 6[63] 27[5] 10–14

Those who follow *karma marga* transform their most mundane actions into spiritual sacrifices. Many of these people engage in physical austerities such as fasting and vigils, which symbolize fiery gifts from the "spiritual heat" within. Nevertheless, they also offer sacrifices of plants and material fire to the gods. Fire is **Agni** ("god of fire"), the divine priest who transforms human gifts into ethereal smoke and transports them to the divine realm. During a festival or pilgrimage, believers may have a priest represent them in offering a solemn and lengthy sacrifice at a shrine or temple. Within their own households, the twice-born themselves offer simpler and less elaborate sacrifices, especially their daily offerings of ritual fire. Sacrifices as such are not ordered toward *moksha* but toward the good pleasure of the gods, who can grant people's worldly needs, such as longevity and children or bountiful crops and abundant herds. When worshippers renounce such self-seeking in their offerings, however, sacrifices lead to liberation and eternal unification with Brahman.

Those who follow *karma marga* are faithful to regular worship of the Godhead. These people delight in all the typical forms of prayer to be found in religious experience: public liturgy and private dialogue, mental reflection and vocal mantras, petition and adoration, congregational chanting or hymnody and night vigils of recited praise. Yet Hindus tend to communicate with their favorite god or goddess individually more often than communally. When Hindus pray, they may attend to an internal picture of this deity; at other times they may fix their gaze intensely upon an external image of their special divinity while they repeat his or her name.

One very popular form of worship in *karma marga* is *puja,* a ritual by which Hindus give signs of praise and affection to a deity and receive some divine blessing in return. They may participate in *puja* at a temple with the elaborate assistance of a priest, but ordinary men and women may also conduct *puja* simply and privately at home. In order to celebrate *puja* on a regular and even daily basis, practitioners consecrate a shrine at a privileged site within their houses and place multiple divine images and statues upon it. Hindus may even include the *murti* of a famous holy man in the midst of the gods and goddesses. They enthrone their principal household god in a preeminent position. In this way, they can readily approach their beloved shrine and welcome all these various gods and goddesses into their family abode.

First, practitioners ask each deity to become present and actually dwell within his or her *murti.* Then they offer their honored guests compelling symbols of warm hospitality, such as bathing, drying, and dressing the divine *murtis.* Next, devotees prayerfully offer the deities select gifts such as lovely flowers, sweet-smelling perfume or incense, and even food. Finally, if the consecrated offering is an edible gift, worshippers symbolically appropriate the hoped-for divine blessings by consuming it.

It is a commonplace for religious people to bridge the chasm between matter and spirit by creating sacred signs that remain rooted in the material realm while they point outward to the spiritual world beyond themselves. Hindu religious experience also abounds in such symbolism, and adherents of *karma marga* may draw deeply human gratification from participating in their sacramental rites.

Hindu sacraments are like sacred thresholds that access the world of Brahman; they are also like translucent windows that channel back divine light upon life's meaning. These sacraments enable people to bring holiness to the critical junctures in their life cycle, from conception through birth and young adulthood to marriage, parenthood, death, and entry into the world beyond. We have already noted the significance of *upanayana,* the Hindu sacrament of thread investiture, for entry into the first *ashrama. Upanayana* effects a second birth, by which an upper-caste lad dies to childhood and is initiated into adulthood with the responsibilities of the *brahmacharin.*

Another very important sacrament is the extended ceremony that seals the death of loved ones with sacred meaning. Hindus ritualize the secure passage of their deceased parents from this world into the abode of the ancestors. It is customary for the eldest son to arrange for a parent's body to be cremated immediately upon death. After the cremation, the family observes about twelve days of funeral rites, all of them ordered toward the deceased person's welfare in the next world. For example, they offer little rice cakes to the dead person so that he or she may receive a new body in which to live among the ancestors.

Hindu enthusiasm for *karma marga* is understandable, because it gives pragmatically inclined people an opportunity to get practically involved with achieving their own salvation by good works. If they sustain their selfless detachment from the rewards of those good works, they can feel confident of genuine progress toward *moksha.* Those who follow *karma marga* in this fashion ultimately go through death never to return on the wheel of rebirth.

Bhakti Marga

We also meet throughout the world vast numbers of people who are unshakably convinced that love is the most creative force for good, the unrivaled glue that binds everything together, and the ultimate ground of the universe. Clearly, these persons feel, the deeper meaning of human life must find expression in love. Religious service of the Godhead must be rooted in a fully free and fundamental option for the Godhead that engenders heartfelt devotion. Hinduism also embraces this point of view approvingly.

The Bhagavad Gita is the source par excellence that promotes this broad highway to transforming union with God. Krishna discloses to Arjuna the glad tidings that loving absorption with himself guarantees salvation: "The wise, who are filled with being, love me in the knowledge that I am the source of everything and that everything comes forth from me. With their thoughts on me, their very lives devoted to me, enlightening one another and always recounting my stories, they are full of contentment and delight. To those who, always yoked, love me joyfully I grant the singleness of mind by which they attain to me" (Bhagavad Gita 6[63] 32[10] 8–10).

Hindu orthopraxis validates *bhakti marga* as a straightforward method by which persons of every caste, talent, and education may achieve liberation. **Bhaktas** (those who follow *bhakti marga*) may find *bhakti marga* accessible and efficacious, but they do not find it necessarily easy, since they must transform their emotions and direct them toward the Godhead. Countless Hindus confidently follow *bhakti marga* on their journey to *moksha.* Practitioners hope to eliminate every fault and dispose of all karmic residue through their adherence to *bhakti marga.*

Bhaktas seek gradually to perfect their devotion until love permeates every aspect of their lives. Some *bhaktas* worship their God or Goddess with the erotic and passionate love that people feel for their sweethearts and spouses. Other *bhaktas* give themselves to their chosen deity with the parental and affectionate love that people bear toward their children. Other *bhaktas* devote themselves to their God or Goddess with the kind and benevolent love that people express toward their friends. Still other *bhaktas* choose to surrender themselves to their chosen divinity with the subservient love that people offer to their masters.

Bhaktas also vary among themselves in their choice of the sole object for their love. Many Shaivas deliver themselves to the unreserved love of Shiva as their Supreme Lord. Millions of Shaktas, on the other hand, are passionately devoted to one of Shiva's consorts as their Supreme Mother. Many Vaishnavas feel deep devotion for Vishnu as their Supreme Lord. The most numerous *bhaktas* of all, however, are certainly those who find the enchanting Krishna, the avatar of Vishnu, to be utterly captivating, and they enthusiastically love Krishna as their Supreme God. They delight in repeating mantras of ecstatic praise for Krishna, dancing and singing in the surpassing joy of total surrender.

For *bhaktas*, Sanatana Dharma is not, in the end, a matter of much knowing, however sublime, nor is it a challenge to perform many good works, however noble. For *bhaktas*, Sanatana Dharma is ultimately a matter of loving God, pure and simple. Sometimes their tears well up irresistibly from their devotional affections, for they realize that those who follow *bhakti marga* pass over through death never to return on the wheel of rebirth.

MATERIAL FOR DISCUSSION

1. What do you think are the principal themes of Hindu spirituality?

2. In what ways can persons of no religious persuasion benefit from the study of Hindu spirituality?

3. In what ways can persons of another religious commitment profit from the study of Hindu spirituality?

4. What do you think of the overarching significance of law/duty in Hindu spirituality?

SUGGESTIONS FOR FURTHER READING

Eck, Diana. *Encountering God: A Spiritual Journey from Bozeman to Banaras.* Boston: Beacon Press, 1993. A fascinating presentation of Professor Eck's critical reflections, as her own Christian faith commitment provides the background for her encounter with the vast religiosity in Hinduism's holiest of cities.

Haberman, David L. *Journey Through the Twelve Forests: An Encounter with Krishna.* New York: Oxford University Press, 1994. An insightful study of a particular pilgrimage in honor of Krishna that exemplifies this aspect of Hindu spirituality with concrete details.

Klostermaier, Klaus K. *A Survey of Hinduism.* 2nd ed. Albany: State University of New York Press, 1994. A systematic study of Hinduism as a whole that has proved most useful to me. This volume contains an extensive glossary of Sanskrit terms and a lengthy bibliography.

Narayan, Kirin. *Storytellers, Saints, and Scoundrels: Folk Narrative in Hindu Religious Teaching.* Philadelphia: University of Pennsylvania Press, 1989. A helpful and vivid account of the concrete role of storytelling within Hindu spirituality.

O'Flaherty, Wendy Doniger, trans. *The Rig Veda, an Anthology: One Hundred and Eight Hymns Selected, Translated, and Annotated.* New York: Penguin, 1981. An accurate and readable translation of the Rig Veda by an outstanding authority on Hinduism.

Olivelle, Patrick, trans. *The Early Upanishads: Annotated Text and Translation.* New York: Oxford University Press, 1998. An excellent rendering of the Sanskrit text. I have used this translation in quotations from the Upanishads.

Sivaraman, Krishna, ed. *Hindu Spirituality: Vedas Through Vedanta.* Vol. 6 of *World Spirituality: An Encyclopedic History of the Religious Quest.* New York: Crossroad, 1989. A large compendium of articles on the historical background and development of early Hinduism.

Sundararajan, K. R., and Mukerji, Bithika, eds. *Hindu Spirituality: Postclassical and Modern.* Vol. 7 of *World Spirituality: An Encyclopedic History of the Religious Quest.* New York: Crossroad, 1991. A substantial anthology of articles on the historical development of later Hinduism.

van Buitenen, J. A. B. *The Bhagavadgita in the Mahabharata: Text and Translation.* Chicago: University of Chicago Press, 1981. An accurate rendering of this very important text in readable modern English. Quotations in this book are from van Buitenen's translation.

8

Buddhist Spirituality

There are two searches, the noble and the ignoble. In the ignoble search a person though himself liable to rebirth seeks out what is liable to old age, to sickness, to death, to grief, and to depravity. All objects of attachment are liable to rebirth, and to these objects a person is tied, with them he is infatuated, and to them he is attached. In the noble search a person sees the wretchedness of rebirth, and seeks for the unborn, the supreme peace, Nirvana.

—Majjhima 1.160

Therefore, O Sariputra, in emptiness there is no form, nor feeling, nor perception, nor impulse, nor consciousness; no eye, ear, nose, tongue, body, mind; no forms, sounds, smells, tastes, touchables or objects of mind; no sight-organ-element, and so forth, until we come to: no mind-consciousness-element; there is no ignorance, no extinction of ignorance, and so forth, until we come to: there is no decay and death, no extinction of decay and death; there is no suffering, no origination, no stopping, no path; there is no cognition, no attainment, and no non-attainment.

—The Heart Sutra (Conze translation, 163)

And if any beings, Ananda, again and again reverently attend to this Tathagata, if they will plant a large and immeasurable root of good, having raised

their hearts to enlightenment, and if they vow to be reborn in that world system,
then, when the hour of their death approaches, that Tathagata Amitabha, the
Arhat, the fully enlightened One, will stand before them, surrounded by hosts of
monks. Then having seen that Lord, and having died with hearts serene, they
will be reborn in just that world-system, Sukhavati. And if there are sons or
daughters of good family, who may desire to see that Tathagata Amitabha in this
very life, they should raise their hearts to the supreme enlightenment, they
should direct their thought with extreme resoluteness and perseverance unto this
Buddha-field and they should dedicate their store of merit to being reborn therein.

—*Description of the Happy Land* (Conze translation, 346)

We must briefly recall the practical and general understanding of religious spirituality that we worked out in Chapter 2: *Religious spirituality* is the inner meaning of human experience as shaped by the pursuit of transformation under the impact of a sacred worldview. Applying this description to Buddhism, we may understand Buddhist spirituality within the following broad framework: ***Buddhist spirituality** is the inner meaning of human experience as shaped by the pursuit of transformation under the impact of the Buddha's Dhamma.* Against this horizon we may now analyze the various elements that enter into this "inner meaning of human experience."

In order to trace these factors in Buddhist spirituality as faithfully as possible, however, we shall adopt the following fourfold approach in our investigation. First, we shall proceed as though the objective validity of the Buddhist worldview is a "given." Second, we shall try to appreciate Buddhist spirituality according to its ideal and optimum potential, insofar as faithful and observant Buddhists actually draw fully upon its sources. Third, we shall refer to key Buddhist terms according to the Pali language, an ancient dialect that Gotama the Buddha himself spoke. Fourth, we shall concentrate for the most part upon Buddhist spirituality in terms of its general and universal motifs. We shall, nonetheless, note some of the significant variations that distinguish the two major branches of Buddhism from each other—Theravada and Mahayana.

Theravada Buddhism is sometimes called "Southern Buddhism," because it predominates in the countries of Southeast Asia: Thailand, Sri Lanka (Ceylon), Myanmar (Burma), Laos, and Kampuchea (Cambodia). More conservative and traditional in their attitude, Theravadins claim that their tradition is the earliest and most authentic form of Buddhism, and they trace it back to the words of the Buddha himself in the Pali language. For this reason, Theravadins preserve the closed Pali Canon of Scriptures and prefer to use Pali in their rituals and scholarly works.

For Theravadins, Gotama Buddha is a unique but mortal human being of history. He cannot give people the grace of salvation but can only exemplify the way for others to follow. Gotama, Theravadins insist, discovered his doctrine from his own natural search, and Buddhism is a way of self-reliant works. Theravadins' ideal Buddhists are the ordained monastics, who apply themselves undividedly to the quest for salvation. It is even customary for many young men who have no intention of becoming permanently committed monks to become monks temporarily as part of their education. Theravadins' foremost virtue is wisdom, which precedes enlightenment and gives birth to compassion. Theravadins teach that Nibbana (in Sanskrit, *Nirvana*) is the diametrical opposite of samsara ("continual change and rebirth").

Theravadins emphasize the saving message of Gotama. Theravadin saints are the arahats, who individually reach the final stage of enlightenment and Nibbana, so that they will not suffer rebirth. Some Theravadins become monks or nuns in order to devote themselves to becoming arahats during their lifetime.

Mahayana Buddhism is sometimes called "Northern Buddhism," because it is the prevailing form of Buddhism in the countries of northern Asia: Vietnam, Nepal, China, Mongolia, Korea, and Japan. Mahayana Buddhism as a category may also include the **Vajrayana** ("diamond vehicle") school of Tibet. Mahayanists have been more expansive, developmental, and adaptive in their attitude. They claim that their tradition goes back to a more profound level of oral teachings that the Buddha entrusted only to the more advanced disciples who could understand such things. The Mahayanists' canon of sacred writings is vast and open-ended.

For many Mahayanists, Gotama is an almost divine being, one of many supernatural Buddhas who have appeared and will appear on earth to represent the absolute Buddha-body that underlies all of reality. Buddhas come into the world at certain times in order to share their saving wisdom with others. The following words are ascribed to Gotama, for example, in *The Lotus Sutra*:

The Buddhas, the World-honored Ones, wish to open the door of Buddha wisdom to all living beings, to allow them to attain purity. That is why they appear in the world. They wish to show the Buddha wisdom to living beings, and therefore they appear in the world. They wish to cause living beings to awaken to the Buddha wisdom, and therefore they appear in the world. They wish to induce living beings to enter the path of Buddha wisdom, and therefore they appear in the world.

Shariputra, this is the one great reason for which the Buddhas appear in the world.
                                    —*The Lotus Sutra,* Watson translation, 31

Mahayanists, therefore, distinguish Gotama as Shakya-muni Buddha, a savior of superhuman dignity; but they may also worship Amitabha Buddha, for instance, or Maitreya Buddha, a Buddha who is still to come. The teachings of all Buddhas are of supernatural origin. Mahayanists emphasize a way of devotion and faith in the gift of merit or grace. Their ideal Buddhists are not monastics but laypersons living a secular lifestyle. The foremost virtue of Mahayanists is compassion, which precedes enlightenment and bears fruit in wisdom. Mahayanists insist that Nibbana is present and available in the very midst of samsara.

Mahayanists stress the selfless generosity of Shakya-muni, who deferred Nibbana for forty-five years after his enlightenment in order to remain on earth and share his saving doctrine with others. Mahayanist saints are the bodhisattvas, who attain enlightenment but willingly postpone their entrance into Nibbana until they have saved all sentient beings from the wheel of rebirth. Bodhisattvas accept rebirth again and again in order to build up superabundant merit for the benefit of others as grace. They take the bodhisattva vow, one version of which we find in the *Diamond Sutra:*

As many beings as there are in the universe of beings, comprehended under the term "beings"—egg-born, born from a womb, moisture-born, or miraculously born; with or without form; with perception, without perception or with neither perception nor no-perception—as far as any conceivable form of beings is conceived: all these I must lead to Nirvana, into that Realm of Nirvana which leaves nothing behind.

                                    —*Diamond Sutra,* Conze translation, 164

Many Mahayanists give themselves fervently to popular bodhisattvas such as Avolokita and Manjusri.

We shall first investigate the overarching theme that pervades all Buddhist experience and stamps all Buddhist spirituality: the middle way of the Buddha's Dhamma (in Sanskrit, *Dharma*). We shall next explore four basic factors that give shape and form to Buddhist spirituality: (1) Buddhist understanding of Nibbana, (2) Buddhist growth through community, (3) Buddhist formation through sacred literature, and (4) Buddhist pursuit of Nibbana through religious practices.

All the great traditions offer their practitioners hope for transcendent fulfillment in exchange for their personal conversion. Moses presented hope for shalom through a new identity as the people of God, if only the Jews would enter into the covenant of Sinai. Jesus offered hope for peace through adoption as children of the Father, if only people would change their minds and open their hearts to God's reign. Muhammad promised hope for *salam* through becoming servant-friends of God, if only people would surrender to God. Upanishadic sages held forth hope for *shanti* through self-realization, if only people would realize their union with Brahman-atman. Gotama the Buddha proclaimed hope for peace (*santi*) through enlightenment, if only people would follow the middle way of his Dhamma.

THE MIDDLE WAY OF THE BUDDHA'S DHAMMA
The Role of Gotama the Buddha

We now turn to the Dhamma that Gotama proclaimed and exemplified after his entrance into **Buddhahood** (the state of being an enlightened one). The Buddha did not understand our human predicament in moral terms of sin and guilt, as did Moses, Jesus, and Muhammad. On the contrary, Gotama identified an intellectual problem of ignorance and error that compromises our innermost view of ourselves and of the cosmos as a whole. Shakya-muni insisted that we acknowledge things for what they truly are: conditioned and insubstantial. We must stop fabricating a pseudo-self within the pervasive impermanence that engulfs us, since this error can only lead to a mass of suffering.

In the Theravadin view, Buddhism is nontheistic (or transtheistic), and the term *Dhamma* refers not to some eternal law divinely revealed, but simply to the religious truth that leads to enlightenment. The Dhamma of Gotama, a mortal, involves a rigorous and pragmatic program that relies upon human effort and personal accountability rather than divine assistance. Although the saving goal of the Buddha's Dhamma transcends our immediate and sensory experience, its inspiration, authority, and promise are simply human. Gotama did not demand faith in the guidance or grace of any higher authority but simply invited interested persons to see for themselves by introspection and concerted discipline. The Buddha offered an analytic tool for self-assessment, and he wanted his followers to accept it only to the extent that they could actually validate its truth for themselves.

In the Mahayanist view, the Dhamma is the doctrinal expression of universal truth, and the historical Buddha was a manifestation of this Dhamma. Moreover, supernatural Buddhas and bodhisattvas are available to grant their assisting grace to those who call upon them. Many

Mahayanists, therefore, give themselves devotionally to a Buddha or a bodhisattva with a fervor analogous to that of Hindus who follow the path of *bhakti*. Mahayanists trust that this compassionate Buddha or bodhisattva will bring about their rebirth into the "pure land" or "western paradise" over which he or she presides. From this place of indescribable blessedness (or state of blissful consciousness), they hope finally to achieve ultimate salvation from the wheel of reincarnation.

The essential quest that underlies all Buddhist spirituality is the passage from self-centeredness to the ego-shattering peace of enlightenment (Nibbana) through the middle way of the Buddha's Dhamma. Gotama the Buddha proclaimed the middle way of his Dhamma as a message of liberation for all human beings, just as Jesus the Christ five centuries later would announce his gospel. Indeed, Buddhists look to the Dhamma of the Buddha for vision, nourishment, and hope very much as Christians turn to the gospel of Jesus. We shall now inquire into these "glad tidings of salvation" that continually produce the riches of Buddhist spirituality.

Gotama announced that he had attained enlightenment by breaking with his past life of self-indulgent luxury and by devoting himself undividedly to the quest for peace. He recounted the story to his disciples: "So while I was yet a youth, black-haired and in my prime, in the first years of manhood, against the wishes of my mother and my father who lamented me with tear-stained faces, I had the hair of my head and face shaved off. I put on saffron robes and went forth from my Home to the Homeless life. I became a wanderer and a searcher for what is good, what cannot be surpassed, and I sought the supreme state of peace" (Majjhima 1.160).

Finally Gotama was able to "open his eyes" to the Truth. He described his "awakening" in the following words: "When I had taken food I sat under the shade of a tree, free from sensual desires and evil thoughts. I entered the first state of meditation arising from seclusion and reasoning. Next I entered the second state beyond reasoning. Then the third state, attentive and conscious. Finally the fourth state, entirely pure and mindful. I remembered all my former existences, I saw all beings arising and passing away, I sought the unborn and undecaying and undying. In the last watch of the night I was released, and I knew that rebirth is destroyed, the religious life has been led, done is what was to be done, there is nothing further in this world" (Majjhima 1.242).

Gotama, now the Buddha, hoped that at least some of his fellow human beings would be able and willing to accept his Dhamma. His Dhamma was "religious" (although nontheistic), since it affirmed Nibbana as the transcendent Reality that exceeds the material realm of sense experience and corruption. The Buddha's Dhamma was truth, because enlightenment is a matter of acknowledging things as they really are through rational knowledge and intuitive perception. Yet the Buddha's Dhamma is preeminently "practical" truth, since it offers an experimentally tested and proved method for reaching enlightenment through pro-active doing.

Buddhist spirituality is not a matter of static being but a process of becoming that blossoms into right action with heightened consciousness. Wise mind and compassionate heart do finally unite in peace, but practitioners reach this level of serenity as the crowning achievement of applied effort or devoted faith. As the Buddha lay dying, he admonished his disciples one last time that they must appropriate the Dhamma into their lives on the most pragmatic level if they wished to attain Nibbana and escape painful rebirth. People must make the pursuit of salvation their first priority. Early Buddhists recounted the story: "Then the Exalted One addressed the brethren and said: Behold I exhort you now: Decay is inherent in all composite things! Work out your salvation with diligence! That was the last word of the Buddha" (Digha 2.156).

The Doctrine of *Anicca* and *Anatta*

Gotama concluded that the whole cosmos is **anicca** ("impermanence"), an endless process of flux and becoming. Everything is void of substance, and only sleepwalking people of ignorance and delusion could suppose anything to be stable. Even we human beings are *anatta* ("no-self"), without stable ego or abiding essence.

The Buddha's doctrine of no-self became a centerpiece within Buddhist spirituality. There can be no legitimate basis for self-orientation, self-aggrandizement, or self-defense, since we have no inner self to serve. Our rash judgment, bias, envy, jealousy, prejudice, and covetousness are not only unreasonable but also foolish. Our pride, greed, and hatred are not only dehumanizing vices but also vain conceits. Selfishness lacks point.

Since all sentient beings are equally no-self, Gotama rejected the superiority of gods and goddesses, the sacred authority of the Vedas, the mediational power of the Brahmanical priesthood, and the whole repertoire of Hindu prayers and devotional usages. The Buddha had no use for worship of the gods in the quest for peace. For that matter, the Buddha regarded Brahmanist practices as worse than irrelevant, because they were a bothersome distraction and a waste of valuable energy. Gotama's attitude toward the gods and goddesses of Brahmanism has induced a practical atheism among Theravadins, so that they typically pursue their own enlightenment without reference to any divinities.

Gotama's doctrine of no-self led to his further repudiation of the Hindu caste system, which differentiates people according to four levels of dignity. He could see no logical foundation for separating one person from others or for classifying people discretely according to hierarchical categories. The Buddha affirmed that the only true leader is the person who practices the Buddha's Dhamma: "Seeing that both bad and good qualities are distributed among each of the four classes, the wise do not admit the claims which the priests [Brahmins] put forward. Whoever among these classes becomes a monk, a worthy one, who has lived the life and done what has to be done and become free; he is declared chief among them because of the Doctrine" (Digha 3.83). All of us human beings share the same impermanence and have equal access to the Buddha's middle way.

The Buddha's doctrine of no-self implies a cosmic process of mutual interaction, a vast network in which everything conditions and is conditioned by everything else. Nothing whatsoever, therefore, can escape the cycle of rising and falling, whether it is persons, communities, nations, traditions, or vast civilizations. Gotama's teaching of no-self is the positive affirmation of our universal togetherness throughout the universe. We all belong to one another, and we interconnect with one another within a constantly flowing process. We are all dynamically interdependent within a network beyond human calculation. In Buddhist spirituality, there is no room for feelings of alienation and loneliness.

The Buddha's teaching of no-self explains why wisdom and compassion go together. People who have been made to know that they are connected with all other people feel responsible for all other people, and those who have learned to care for other people recognize their relationship with them. Indeed, Buddhists do feel accountable to the entire ecosystem in which they participate jointly as equal parts with other equal parts. We must respectfully revere all beings in the world and not seek to dominate or exploit them for our own personal advantage.

The Buddha's doctrine of no-self explains a very important objective in Buddhist spirituality: We must "shatter our ego" and not regard our social persona as any more than a conventional convenience. Since everything is subject to generation and corruption within the endless flow of empty impermanence, we should admit no duality, no distinction between subject and object. All things both internal and external are but passing phenomena, momentary sparkles within a unitary stream. All persons throughout the past, present, and future enjoy an interrelationship with one another in a vast network of mutual interdependence that extends beyond time and space. Mahayanists would say that we share in common the Buddha-nature, which is our *sunnata* ("emptiness," "suchness").

The Law of Kamma

The Buddha accepted the law of **kamma** (in Sanskrit, *karma*, "action"), with its relentless consequences for every moral action, whether good or evil. Gotama agreed that our present fortune results from what we have done in the past, while our present activity will produce what we shall be in the future. He went on to draw a most important conclusion for Buddhist spirituality, however: The root of our karmic bondage is our unfounded and vacuous egotism. Since our illusion of self makes us grasp at fleeting things in the hope of self-gratification, our addictions cause the karmic baggage that binds us to the repetitive cycle of birth, death, and rebirth.

The Buddha taught the law of kamma in words such as the following:

Beings have their own Karma. They are heirs of Karma, their origin is Karma, Karma is their kinsman, it is their resource. Karma distributes beings according to lowness and greatness. A man or woman who takes life, killing with blood-stained hands and without mercy to living things, when his karma is worked out, with the dissolution of the body after death, he is reborn in a state of misery, in an unhappy destiny, or in hell. A man or woman who refrains from taking life, who is full of kindness and compassionate to all living things, when that Karma is worked out, with the dissolution of the body after death, he is reborn in a state of happiness, or is long lived, or is reborn in heaven.

—Majjhima 3.202

We must not, however, suppose that the Buddhist notion of kamma is a pessimistic concept that implies a fatalistic control of our life. The law of kamma is really an innate law of our moral being that offers us a solid hope that we can create our own future. Within the parameters of the law of kamma, we possess the capacity knowingly and freely to achieve our own liberation.

The Human Problem: *Avijja*

We have seen how Jews, Christians, and Muslims understand their predicament in terms of sin, or estrangement from God, a moral problem. We can fail to make good choices; and, as a result, we can turn away from our Creator. As we explore Buddhist spirituality, we find that our basic trouble is *avijja,* or "ignorance," an intellectual problem. We can fail to recognize how transient we are in a completely impermanent world; as a result, we can chain ourselves to the wheel of rebirth.

Our ignorance creates the vain conceit that our unchanging self provides personal continuity within our stream of consciousness. The truth of the matter is that we have manufactured a counterfeit ego that alienates us from the rest of the cosmos. Consequently, we project our needy aspirations and negative aversions across a chasm of our own fantasy. We suppose ourselves to be wholly self-contained subjects, discretely set apart from all other objects by the physical extension of our bodies.

In our ignorance, we presume that we are the hub of the universe, the indispensable center of the world, and we want to be sure to get "ours." We are alert ever to vindicate our rights of privilege and ownership, because we look out for "number one." We are confident that the right place is always our place, the right time is always our time, and the right perspective is always our perspective. We would like to receive first consideration before all others. In the deluding fever of our ego-centeredness, we cannot embrace others for their own sake and apart from what they might do for us. In the addicting heat of our concupiscence, we cannot appreciate the true value of others aside from what they can give us.

Our ignorance can introduce disharmony into our families. We can reduce our friendships to conflictive rivalries by such phrases as "this is mine," "you hurt my feelings," and "that belongs to me." As long as we entertain the illusion that we are integrally somebody, we continue to grasp possessively at things that will nourish our fragile self-esteem. As long as we believe that some things are lasting and self-fulfilling, our lusts continue to act as so many hooked fetters that chain us to the wheel of rebirth. The mere appearances that we find so seductive cannot possibly deliver the happiness that they promise, and our cravings leave us abject and frustrated.

Impermanence, suffering, and no-self, then, affect our human condition in its deepest dimensions, and our ignorance of this truth is the root source of our incessant pain of body and sickness of heart. These characteristics also provide the context within which we produce all the karmic baggage that ensnares us and precipitates our recurring rebirth into this transient world. Our "houses are on fire": Flames engulf us and smoke blinds us, so that self-interest blurs our vision and lustful cravings compromise our devotion. We must crash through the windows of our burning inferno and leap to the cool safety net of the Buddha's Dhamma.

The Goal of the Dhamma: Nibbana

Nibbana is the extinction of all grasping attachments. Upon our entrance into Nibbana, we disengage ourselves from all our attachments and become dispassionate. All our internal and external emotions become extinct and "cool." We can love others consistently with kindness, compassion, sympathetic joy, and equanimity, because we have no desire to control them, exploit them, or otherwise use them for our own satisfaction.

Nibbana implies wisdom, because Nibbana emancipates our minds from illusory egoism with its chains of ignorance and error, and so we may apprehend the unfiltered Truth. Nibbana implies compassion, because Nibbana liberates our hearts from narcissistic infatuation and self-serving works, and so we may then enter into the pain of others as our own. Nibbana implies fearlessness, because Nibbana purifies our passions from vain egocentricity with its defensive mechanisms, and so we may triumph over anxiety and dread. The Buddha taught: "One who has wisdom here, who is devoid of desire and passions, attains to deathlessness, to peace, and to the unchanging state of Nirvana" (Sutta Nipata 204).

The Core Doctrine of the Buddha's Dhamma

Just as the New Testament of the Christian Scriptures contains a synopsis of Jesus' preaching of his gospel in his famous Sermon on the Mount, so the Tipitaka ("three baskets") of the Pali Canon presents Gotama's revelation of his Dhamma in his well-known Sermon in the Deerpark. The Buddha referred to this discourse as The Turning of the Wheel of the Law Sutra, because it was through this first proclamation that he launched his mission.

The Buddha's concise doctrine appears deceptively simple, yet it has changed history profoundly. His Sermon in the Deerpark has pierced the innermost hearts of millions of seekers and made them resonate with the joy of salvation. This discourse summarizes the Buddha's core teaching about the middle way of his Dhamma: the Four Noble Truths that culminate in the Noble Eightfold Path. We should not interpret these Four Noble Truths as successive stages in chronological sequence but as four simultaneous aspects that connect to one another in logical interdependence.

A Middle Way   The Buddha's sermon was an unequivocal summons to conversion, inspired by unearthly wisdom and motivated by boundless compassion. Gotama stood before his former associates with radiant countenance and compelling presence. He challenged his listeners to a radical conversion of attitudes, values, and habits, but he promised an unimaginable peace. The Buddha prescribed a humane balance of gentle discipline, prudent restraint, and common sense as the underlying spirit of his Dhamma. He referred to his Dhamma as a "middle way," because it avoided the two extremes of rash immoderation that had impeded both himself and so many others in their quest for peace.

The story unfolds as follows.

At one time the Buddha dwelt in a Deer Park near Benares. There he addressed his five first disciples: There are two extremes which are not to be practised. What are these two? That which is joined to the passions and luxury, which is low, vulgar, common, ignoble and useless. And that which is joined to self-torture, which is painful, ignoble and useless. Avoiding the extremes of sensuality and self-torture, the knowledge of the Middle Way brings insight, calm, enlightenment and Nirvana. What is the Middle Way, by which the Buddha has gained enlightenment, and which produces insight and knowledge, and which tends to calm, to the higher knowledge and enlightenment and Nirvana? It is the Noble Eightfold Way. This is the Middle Path.

—Samyutta 5.420

The Buddha's middle way prohibits the extreme of pursuing fleshly or intellectual pleasures for their own sake, because such indulgence deadens our awareness, blurs our priorities, and blots out our vision. Instead, we must mobilize our spiritual stamina for life's great journey, and we must cultivate an active self-control. We must integrate our bodily functions, detach our senses from their addictions, and discipline our passions into well-ordered unity. Yet the Buddha's middle way also forbids the opposite extreme of afflicting the body with so much fasting and sleeplessness that we cannot concentrate upon heightened awareness. We must moderate any ill-advised zeal to abuse our bodies or neglect their legitimate needs.

Buddhists often regard Gotama as a spiritual physician who out of immeasurable compassion devoted himself for over forty years to healing men and women at the deepest level of their experience. In the course of his enlightenment, the Buddha had completed exhaustive schooling in the nature of human suffering. Through a kind of scientific experimentation, Gotama had identified both the source of pain and the sure remedy for it. Then the Buddha reached out to all who would listen and carefully explained to them the method that they must follow if they would be healed. Buddhists are obedient patients who strive to pass over from self-centered misery to Nibbana-centered health according to their physician's wise prescription.

THE FOUR NOBLE TRUTHS
This is the noble truth of pain; birth is painful; old age, sickness, death, sorrow, despair are painful. This is the noble truth of the cause of pain: it is craving, which leads to rebirth, combined with pleasure and lust, craving for existence and non-existence. This is the noble truth of the cessation of pain: cessation without remainder of that craving; forsaking, non-attachment. This is the noble truth of the way that leads to the cessation of pain: it is the Noble Eightfold Path, namely: Right views, Right intention, Right speech, Right action, Right livelihood, Right effort, Right mindfulness, Right concentration. This Noble Eightfold Path is to be practised.

—Samyutta 5.420

In announcing the First Noble Truth, Gotama the spiritual physician presented his diagnosis of our human condition. *Dukkha* thoroughly debilitates every dimension of our lives. Misery and dissatisfaction mark every level of our consciousness. In our unenlightened state, we experience radical discontent and anguish. The shadows of dread and foreboding darken our every celebration and vitiate our every triumph. Often we feel vaguely aware that something is wrong deep within us, but we cannot name it or describe it. We somehow do not quite fit into things. We are out of sync with the cosmos.

We may sometimes deaden our pain with fleeting distraction or laughter, but our basal disquiet persists. Even when we possess the objects of our craving, our delight is shallow and frustrating. Momentary satisfactions turn to ashes and leave a bad taste in our mouths. In the last analysis, we cannot retain any happiness totally, completely, and endlessly. Even our most beloved friends disappoint us, and we betray our own ideals. Our every experience of happiness is conditioned, subject to becoming and passing away. Our physical pleasures last but a moment; our mental joys give way to boredom. Sometimes we are far from the people whom we love; at other times, we are briefly together, yet we know that we must separate once again. Failure inevitably undercuts our success, fatigue interrupts our refreshment, anguish displaces our well-being.

For "Dr. Buddha," then, the critical challenge of human life was to escape to Nibbana and realize the only effective cure for suffering. Buddhists adhere to Shakya-muni's Dhamma because they too seek refuge from dissatisfaction. They interpret their spirituality as a passage from ignorant self-orientation to wisdom and compassion—from heartsickness, addiction, and anxiety to health, freedom, and peace. Buddhists recognize how vain and foolish it is for us to harbor the cravings of an illusory ego for the sake of fleeting appearances. Our self-serving ploys and strategies always lack point, since we really possess no self to preserve, no identity to promote, and no ego to defend.

Buddhists through the centuries have reflected exhaustively upon every aspect of the Buddha's middle way, and they have carefully enumerated all the elements that constitute the Dhamma. We meet a typical list of these factors in the Buddhist analysis of suffering according to eight headings. The first four types sum up our physical sufferings as "the four great rivers of suffering." These include the shock of our being born into this world, the disabilities of our old age, the aches and pains of our diseases, and our death. The second four types belong within the category of emotional pain. These four types include our union with the unpleasant, our separation from the pleasant, our disappointment because we do not possess our desires coupled with our fear of losing what we do possess, and our dependent existence.

In the Second Noble Truth, Gotama the spiritual physician revealed the fundamental cause of our condition: our *tanha*. Of course, we must not interpret the concept of "craving" as any and all desires without exception. After all, some aspirations such as our intention to attain enlightenment are good, necessary, and salutary. Craving desire, on the other hand, comprises all the grasping of our fabricated ego. We project our imagined self into the world as the center of gravity for everything else. We inflate our illusory selves by exploiting the objects of our craving as though they were also separately permanent, when, in fact, other things share our instability, and they too must pass away. Our exaggerated sense of self-importance engenders self-service, self-seeking, self-defensiveness, self-intoxication, self-deception, self-adulation, and self-pity. Grasping produces disrespectful attitudes and discourteous actions toward others. Often we become jealously competitive, needy, and possessive of others. Sometimes we even seek to control other people and subject them to our selfish purposes. We act not altruistically but egocentrically, and the very momentum of our selfish actions ensnares us and propels us toward further rebirth.

Craving is a thirst that consumes us with addictions to bodily pleasures, material possessions, and popular fame. Craving is a lustfulness that inflames us with burning passion, tears us apart with frustration, and breaks our hearts with sorrow upon sorrow. Craving is a covetousness that destroys our peace and chains us to the wheel of reincarnation. The Buddha's Dhamma, however, banishes our ignorance and perverted emotion so that we may extinguish our craving. The Buddha taught his disciples: "When ignorance has been put away, and knowledge has grown, there is no grasping after the pleasures of sense, or after speculations, or after rituals, or after the theory of self" (Majjhima 1.67).

In the Third Noble Truth, Gotama the spiritual physician disclosed the prognosis for our condition. He articulated the foundational hope of Buddhist spirituality: We human beings can surely destroy all pain forever, provided that we take up the work of salvation and eliminate the root cause of all our pain. Our own ignorance generates our craving and our own craving induces our suffering. Conversely, our conquest of ignorance through enlightenment will dislodge our craving and eliminate our suffering. Our endurance of suffering will surely come to an end as our craving ceases to torment us.

The Buddha had discovered this interconnection of cause and effect by minutely analyzing each link in the process:

One who is enlightened knows the fact: These are the Deadly floods [of illusion and defilement]. He knows: This is the origin of the Deadly Floods. He knows: This is the cessation of the Deadly Floods. To him who knows and sees this the heart is set free from the Deadly Taint of Lusts. It is set free from the Deadly Taint of Becomings. It is set free from the Deadly Taint of Ignorance. Being set free there arises in him the knowledge of his freedom and he knows: Rebirth has been destroyed. The higher life has been fulfilled. What had to be done has been done. Now there is no rebirth.

—Digha 1.84

"Dr. Buddha's" medical counsel is cogent and compelling. If we intend to abolish certain phenomena, we must become pro-active and destroy their source. If we are determined to extinguish a fire, we must spring into action and douse the flames with water. If we are resolved to destroy an infection, we must become aggressive and lance the boil. If we seriously seek freedom from our misery, we must focus all our energy upon destroying the walls that imprison us.

As we progress toward disciplined dispassion, we begin to deny ourselves and break out of our self-enclosed cocoon. As we gradually destroy our craving, we begin deliberately to sympathize with others in their sufferings. As we advance in purifying our vision from our alienating conceits, we begin to see others purely through the immaculate lens of the Truth. As we labor to cleanse our hearts from our false ego-centeredness, we begin to embrace others compassionately in their inseparable connection with us.

Buddhist practitioners who appropriate the Third Noble Truth and persevere in applying its logic focus upon the one necessary endeavor for all human beings, and they achieve life's ultimate goal. They conquer the ignorance and perverted emotion that lead to craving. They attain enlightenment and realize Nibbana, dispassion, and disengagement. Enjoying the bliss of Nibbana, the enlightened are free from the karmic fetters that would bind them to the samsaric wheel of rebirth. They have nothing further to learn, and they have no future defilement to incur.

What is the Noble [Aryan] Truth of the stopping of ill? It is the Noble Eightfold Way, namely: Right belief, Right purpose, Right speech, Right action, Right living, Right endeavour, Right mindfulness, Right contemplation. This is the Noble Truth that leads to the stopping of will. From the truth "This is the stopping of ill," by full attention to things unheard of before, there arose in me knowledge, vision, understanding, insight, wisdom and light. I realised unshakeable freedom of heart, through intuitive wisdom.

—Mahavastu 3.333

In the Fourth Noble Truth, Gotama the spiritual physician revealed the treatment for curing our condition. We can achieve the cessation of craving and its resultant suffering provided that we are willing to follow the middle way of the Noble Eightfold Path. Then we can defeat our ignorance and disorderly emotions with their karmic consequences that bind us to the wheel of rebirth. The middle way of the Noble Eightfold Path is an eminently pragmatic method that is completely accessible to us, but we must commit ourselves undividedly to a life of disciplined mind, heart, and activity.

The Buddha's Noble Eightfold Path is not a succession of eight steps in vertical sequence but a simultaneous interplay of eight criteria for the practical guidance of everyday life. The Buddha qualified each of these norms as "right," a kind of Buddhist virtue that translators sometimes render as "perfect," or "full," in the sense of "pure" and "undefiled." People live "rightly" when they detach their minds from all self-centeredness and purge their hearts of all self-interest.

Buddhists sometimes analyze the Buddha's Noble Eightfold Path as the "Threefold Training," the three indispensable dimensions that must characterize our journey if we are to reach enlightenment. The "training in wisdom" includes the two criteria of right knowledge ("right belief") and right intention ("right purpose") toward the practice of the Buddha's Dhamma. These dimensions endow Buddhist spirituality with its intellectual credibility and its directional thrust. The "training in disciplined ethics" comprises the three norms of right speech, right conduct ("right action"), and right livelihood ("right living") toward elimination of grasping and attachment, with their karmic aftermath. These aspects provide Buddhist spirituality with its moral integrity. The "training in meditation" involves the three requirements of right effort ("right endeavour"), right mindfulness, and right concentration ("right contemplation") toward intuitive comprehension of the Truth. These "habits of the heart" crown Buddhist spirituality with its contemplative depth and the twin virtues of wisdom and compassion.

Disciples of the Buddha strive to comprehend universal Reality with "right knowledge." We must work to see things as they really are. We must intellectually appropriate the Buddha's Dhamma as our Truth and assimilate his worldview as our worldview. We must perceive the world as void and ourselves within it as empty so that we may comprehend the Four Noble Truths and attain Nibbana with freedom from rebirth.

Those who seek to enter into the Buddha's Truth must dispose themselves toward life with "right intention." We must make an earnest and deliberate decision to follow the Buddha's Dhamma as we live out our lives. We must involve ourselves wholeheartedly with the Dhamma and all that it requires of us for the future as far as we can control it. We must recognize suffering for what it is, abandon our craving, and attain Nibbana by the practical and faithful cultivation of the Noble Eightfold Path.

Those who quest after enlightenment must communicate with others by "right speech." We must discipline our tongues so that we speak only kindly, justly, significantly, and truthfully. Here we confront the Buddha's profound insight into our human propensity for verbal injury to others. It is not only that we must avoid indulgence in idle chatter and wearisome verbosity. We must also avoid deception, hypocrisy, rash judgment, negative criticism, and gossip as well as detraction, calumny, fraud, and perjury.

Aspirants after enlightenment must live by "right conduct," and Buddhists strongly emphasize the importance of following a life of ethical integrity. The Buddha enunciated Five Precepts that both laypersons and monastics must observe: "How is a disciple accomplished in morality? He refrains from taking life. He abstains from taking what is not given. He abandons unchastity. He abstains from falsehood. He abstains from intoxicants" (Digha 2.77). The Buddha went on to promulgate five further rules for the special guidance of monks and nuns: "He [the disciple] eats only within one meal time. He refrains from seeing dancing, singing and music. He refrains from scents and garlands, from a high or large bed, from accepting gold and silver. He refrains from accepting women, slaves, animals and lands. He refrains from buying and selling, from cheating and fraud, from killing and violence" (Digha 2.77). The pursuit of ethical integrity is indispensable for enlightenment in Buddhist spirituality.

Human beings in pursuit of Nibbana must follow a "right liveli-hood." The Buddha recognized how vitally important it is for us to use our talents and energy for humane service of others. We must engage in occupations that provide social service, such as medicine, statesmanship, and education. We must avoid livelihoods that injure human beings or an-imals, such as soldiering, selling alcohol or deadly weapons, fishing, hunting, tanning, and butchering.

Persons who would achieve wisdom must make a "right effort." The Buddha appreciated the importance of our laboring diligently with minds keenly alert in recollection. We must be vigilant and discriminating in screening our thoughts from any self-orientation. We must be constant in purifying our actions from clinging attachments. We must persevere and not grow weary in disciplining our minds and hearts, lest we fall back into self-delusion with all its calamitous consequences.

Disciples of the Buddha must practice "right mindfulness." As Jews, Christians, and Muslims emphasize the importance in their traditions of remembering, Buddhists stress the necessity of viewing all things through the clarifying lens of the Dhamma. The Buddha emphasized right mind-fulness as a kind of nonviolence of the heart. We must preserve our peace of mind in calm tranquility, free not only from the disturbance of exterior provocations but also from the turbulence of interior confusion and disor-derly passion. We must gently discipline our mind and our appetites so that we may maintain vivid awareness.

Finally and most important of all, those who commit themselves to the Dhamma must engage in "right concentration." Shakya-muni at-tained his Buddhahood by meditative absorption. We must gain insight through right concentration if we are to attain Nibbana during this life-time. We must by a regimen of regular contemplation penetrate the more superficial levels of merely factual information and plumb the depths of the Dhamma's intelligibility. We must by meditation pass from detached assent to personal involvement. We must apply ourselves faithfully to meditative exercises that will overcome our egoistic distractions and elim-inate our craving thirsts. We must seek the ecstatic awareness and height-ened consciousness that transcend all dualisms and illusions. We must center with sharpened focus upon our simple oneness with the flow of all being.

BUDDHIST UNDERSTANDING OF NIBBANA

The ultimately sacred Reality in Buddhism is Nibbana. Herein we con-front an intriguing paradox. Within the vast fluctuating universe of impermanence and no-self, the Buddha did acknowledge the absolute and unconditioned truth of the Dhamma itself. Moreover, the Buddha promised the absolutely permanent state of serene calmness and tranquil peace that is Nibbana. Nibbana is immutable rather than changing, constant rather than fickle, incorruptible rather than fragile, timeless rather than fleeting.

Nibbana is our transforming liberation from all frustration, suffering, and disquiet. Nibbana is our emancipation from the addictions of a self that never existed in the first place. Nibbana is a state of ultimate bliss and immortality, a peace that exceeds our capacity to imagine or understand. Nibbana is not turbulence but serenity and quietude, not commotion but stillness and placidity. Nibbana is the fullness of tranquility, splendidly radiant with boundless light and joy beyond all telling.

Buddhist spirituality results from the pursuit of Nibbana according to the Buddha's Dhamma. Buddhist spirituality is all about following the Noble Eightfold Path in order ultimately to shatter the ego, eliminate all grasping, and arrive at Nibbana, with its freedom from karma and the wheel of rebirth. For the Buddha held out the certain hope of Nibbana for all those who follow the Noble Eightfold Path: "It is said, Nirvana, Nirvana. Now what is Nirvana? Whatever is the extinction of passion, and aversion, and confusion, this is Nirvana. Is there a way for the realisation of this Nirvana? There is. It is the Noble Eightfold Path, which itself is for the realisation of Nirvana" (Samyutta 4.251).

BUDDHIST GROWTH THROUGH THE SAMGHA

The Buddha also guided his disciples toward a congregational dimension in their spirituality. Buddhists experience a bond of solidarity with their fellow practitioners through the centuries and around the world. This feeling of community is especially pronounced at the level of local villages and towns, however, where Buddhists know and interact with one another on a personal basis, as they gather about a central monastery, shrine, or temple. Buddhists come together in order to pay homage to a Buddha or bodhisattva. They assemble in order to receive training in the Buddha's Dhamma, observe a festival, or celebrate a rite of passage. Buddhists may experience an intense dimension of community when they travel together in groups on pilgrimage.

In the first place, when Buddhists follow Gotama's teaching of no-self, they come to view the whole of humankind as one vast network of conditioned interdependence. We must destroy within ourselves any inflated individualism and self-interest in order to be open indiscriminately to all others. We must be generous in our support of all, because our common need for liberation binds us together in the same predicament. We must seek reconciliation with all who feel estranged from us, because we are all wayfarers together on the road to interior peace. Our growth into wisdom necessarily engenders universal compassion. Wise heart and compassionate mind converge.

In the second place, the Buddha embodied his tradition in a vast Samgha (in Sanskrit, *Sangha*, "monastic order") that consists of monks, nuns, and lay affiliates. He strongly affirmed the importance of the Samgha in words such as the following:

I will teach you seven conditions for the welfare of a community: so long
as the brothers foregather often and frequent the formal meetings of the Order
[Samgha]; so long as they meet together in concord and carry out the duties
of the Order in concord; so long as the brothers shall establish nothing that has
not been already prescribed, and act in accordance with the rules; so long as the
brothers honour and support the elders of experience and hearken to their words;
so long as they delight in a life of solitude; so long as they train their minds in
self-possession so that good men may come to them; so long may the brothers
be expected not to decline but to prosper."

—Digha 2.77

The Buddha organized his Samgha in a way that was revolutionary for his society: He treated all people equally and distinguished them not according to their caste or wealth but only according to their level of self-renunciation and detachment in pursuit of enlightenment. Monks and nuns were to observe an order of seniority based only upon their time of higher ordination. For Theravadins, the Samgha is like a pool of mutual needs and resources that interconnects all Buddhists with one another. Even though the monks and nuns are primarily intent upon seeking their own salvation, they also constitute a living fountain of education and merit for the laymen and laywomen. Monks and nuns not only teach the Dhamma to the layfolk but also provide them with opportunities to earn merit by supporting the Samgha materially. For Mahayanists, the Samgha is a vast fellowship of mutual aid, a common treasury of merits that is available for the salvation of all, especially through the compassionate generosity of bodhisattvas.

The Buddha instituted the Samgha as a third haven for those who had given themselves to him and to his Dhamma. The Buddhists speak of the Samgha as one of the **three jewels** that, together with the Buddha and the Dhamma, make up the precious essence of the Buddhist tradition. Shakya-muni announced: "When one thinks that he has unwavering confidence in the Buddha, the Doctrine, and the Order [Samgha], he acquires knowledge of the Doctrine and the delight connected with the Doctrine. Rapture is born from that delight, and so his body is immune to suffering, therefore joy is felt, and the mind is well concentrated" (Majjhima 1.36).

Christians come to the person of Christ as their teacher, to the gospel as his plan of salvation, and to the Church as the congregation of believing communicants. In an analogous way, Buddhists give themselves to the Buddha as their teacher, to the Dhamma as his plan of salvation, and to the Samgha as the community of practitioners, role models, and arahats or bodhisattvas. The person who seeks to become a Buddhist affirms publicly three times: "I come to the Buddha for refuge. I come to the Dhamma for refuge. I come to the Samgha for refuge." Many Buddhists repeat this threefold affirmation repeatedly throughout the day for devotional purposes. All Buddhists belong to the Samgha in some sense, and therefore all Buddhists share in the Samgha's activities in some way. Buddhist laity gain great merit by supporting monastics. Many laypersons, for example, gladly pay the expenses that surround the ordination of a monk or a nun.

Jesus taught his disciples that he would interpret mutual service of one another in their needs as a laudatory service of himself (Matt. 25.31–46). The Buddha spoke similarly to his monks when he announced that their solicitude for one another was truly a caring for him. They cherished words such as these: "You have not a mother or a father who might care for you, O monks. If you do not care for each other, who will care for you? Whosoever would care for me, he should care for the sick" (*Vinaya* 1.302).

FORMATION THROUGH
THE BUDDHIST SCRIPTURES

Since Jews, Christians, and Muslims regard their scriptures as the inspired revelation of a personal God, they utilize them as a canonical standard for their faith commitment. Hindus, on the other hand, revere their Vedic literature as a sacred manifestation of Sanatana Dharma, and they require belief in its supernatural authority. Buddhists, for their part, meditate upon their scriptures not in order to grow in faith but in order to realize the Dhamma's truth within themselves. They are more likely, therefore, to approach their scriptures not as norms of dogmatic belief but as wellsprings for practical guidance toward interior serenity and as texts for devotional chanting or recitation.

The Buddhist scriptures contain the Buddha's Dhamma together with extended analysis, explication, and application. Buddhist scriptures constitute a vast body of literature (several times larger than the Christian Bible) that has evolved extensively over the centuries, and they have played a key role in the Dhamma's endurance through history. Here we can review only some of the more popular texts.

Probably the earliest body of Buddhist writings is the Pali Canon, which is known as the Tipitaka ("three baskets") because it consists of three large collections. The **Vinaya-pitaka** ("basket of discipline") is a compilation of codified precepts for the training of monks and nuns in Buddhist ethics and meditation. It not only recounts the legendary history of the Samgha's beginnings but also presents the Buddha's didactic responses to inquiries about proper behavior according to his middle way. The Vinaya-pitaka guides the minds and hearts of beginners, who must shape their lives according to their sublime quest and its ideals. This collection also reflects the transformation of the advanced, who have persevered along the path to enlightenment. The **Sutta-pitaka** ("basket of discourses") passes on some memorable instructions of the Buddha and his earliest disciples in five major compendia: the Digha, the Majjhima, the Samyutta, the Anguttara, and the Khuddaka, which includes the immensely popular Dhammapada. Buddhist masters find these **suttas** to be especially useful for instructions, and they recite aloud for attentive audiences the suttas that they have memorized so devotedly. In this way, teachers cause the Dhamma to penetrate the hearts of their listeners in practical application to everyday life. The third division of the Tipitaka is the **Abhidhamma-pitaka** ("basket of special teachings"). The Abhidhamma-pitaka is a corpus of philosophical and psychological speculations about Buddhism.

Mahayanists have developed a vast body of profound writings beyond the Pali Canon, known as the Mahayana sutras and shastras. One example would be the Chinese *Mahayanashraddhotpada-shastra,* which tradition ascribes to Ashvaghosha, an outstanding Buddhist poet, philosopher, and sage who lived about 1,900 years ago. Some Mahayanist schools call upon a chosen work such as the immensely popular Lotus Sutra for their primary scripture.

For 2,500 years, Buddhists have drawn inspiring tutelage from their sacred writings as they have developed their spirituality of insightful wisdom and universal compassion. They earn precious merit not only by reading and reciting their scriptures reverently but also by the painstaking act of copying. Buddhist monastics in particular devote their energies to memorizing, preserving, and transmitting their scriptures to succeeding generations. They sometimes engage in strenuous debate and animated dialectic as they seek ever more complete comprehension of the texts. Moreover, scriptures constitute the primary source for Dhamma studies in the monastic schools. Buddhist monasteries function not only as living quarters for the community within but also as educational institutions for the greater community of lay affiliates.

The pursuit of insightful understanding and personal discipline is an integral dimension of all Buddhist spirituality, because seekers must dispel ignorance and unruly emotions. Buddhists find in their scriptures a presentation of the Buddha with his inspiring life, of the Buddha's Dhamma, with his insights into the Truth, and of the Buddha's Samgha, with its institutional structures and its cycle of celebrations. Disciples recall the Buddha's words shortly before he died: "The Buddha said: It may be that in some of you the thought may arise, The word of the Master is ended, we have no longer a teacher! But it is not thus that you should regard it. The Doctrine, and the rules of the Order, which I have set forth and laid down for you all, when I have gone let them be the Teacher to you" (Digha 2.154).

Buddhist scholars investigate their scriptures in order to extract their multilayered meanings, analyze them, and organize them into imposing intellectual systems. Buddhist monasteries provide structured contexts for monastics who work tirelessly to apply the Buddhist scriptures to masterful living of the Dhamma. As a result, Buddhist communities in Asia have maintained significantly high literacy rates. Moreover, monks and nuns meet daily in a kind of worship to chant the texts and appropriate their meaning. Teaching monks interweave scripture and commentary when they explain the Dhamma to novices and to laypeople. All Buddhists may study their scriptures in order personally to assimilate the Dhamma into their lives.

BUDDHIST PURSUIT OF NIBBANA
THROUGH RELIGIOUS PRACTICES
Buddhist Meditation in General

As we have seen, Buddhists recognize Nibbana as the awesome Reality that absolutely transcends this transitory realm of sensory phenomena. Nibbana is mysteriously non-ordinary, ineffable, and ultimate. Monastics and devout laypeople cultivate emotional purification and mental awareness in order to attain this transcendent level of Reality. They pursue the "training in wisdom" (right knowledge and right intention), and they often demonstrate an almost palpable serenity and joy in their everyday demeanor. Of course, they must also be faithful to the "training in disciplined ethics" (right speech, right conduct, and right livelihood), since only persons of unblemished character and selfless service to others are able effectively to meditate.

It is no accident that Buddhists traditionally portray Gotama as seated in a position of *samadhi,* with legs crossed in centered balance, arms extended in relaxed freedom, and half-shut eyes lowered in focused reflection. Serene figures of the meditating Gotama (and of other Buddhas and bodhisattvas in Mahayana lands) reign over the Buddhist world, and Buddhists seek especially by contemplation of these statues and images to follow Gotama's guidance in their own quest. He imparted the following instructions:

He chooses some lonely spot to rest at. He seats himself, when his meal is done, cross-legged, keeping his body erect, and his intelligence alert, intent. Putting away the hankering after the world, he purifies his mind of lusts. Putting away the corruption of the wish to injure, he purifies his mind of malevolence. Putting away torpor of heart and mind, mindful and self-possessed, he purifies his mind of weakness and sloth. Putting away flurry and worry, with heart serene, he purifies himself of irritability and vexation of spirit. Putting away wavering, he remains as one who has passed beyond perplexity. No longer in suspense as to what is good, he purifies his mind of doubt.

—Digha 1.71

Many lay Buddhists are content to observe the Five Precepts and to support the monks and nuns in order to merit a higher rebirth. They know little about the Buddha's Dhamma, and they seldom meditate. Some lay Buddhists, however, do seek to enter Nibbana during this lifetime, and they join with the monastics in setting their sights beyond righteous ethical observance. Such persons cultivate the "training in meditation" (right effort, right mindfulness, and right concentration), and their principal concern is not so much ritual worship or personal prayer as a contemplative cast of mind. They may seek out the experienced wisdom of an accomplished master for guidance.

The Buddha made it clear that we must structure our lives properly for concentration and meditate upon the Dhamma if we are to see things as they really are. We must embrace the Dhamma in calm tranquility, fill our minds with its wisdom, and allow compassion to flood our hearts. Gotama promised: "Putting away all hindrances, he lets his mind full of love pervade one quarter of the world, and so too the second quarter, and so the third, and so the fourth. And thus the whole wide world, above, below, around and everywhere, and altogether he continues to pervade with love-burdened thought, abounding, sublime, beyond measure, free from hatred and ill-will" (Digha 3.49).

The Buddha proposed effective and persevering meditation upon his Dhamma as the sure hope for salvation. If we are finally to pass from ignorance and emotionality to liberating enlightenment, we must tame our minds and pacify our passions. If we are to see the world in its radical impermanence, we must probe its external structure relentlessly until we break through its façade of solid stability. If we are to shatter our inflated egos, we must penetrate into what we really are, no more and no less. We must allow the truth to possess us. We are not self-contained individuals set apart from all others, but part of a vast process of dependent interaction and mutual conditioning. We meditate not that we may receive some new revelation from without but that we may awaken to the reality already within.

Sometimes Buddhists meditate to gain intuitive insight into the **three marks of existence** (impermanence, suffering, and no-self) and the emptiness of the universe. As long as we are unenlightened, we cling to what is pleasing, we turn away from what is displeasing, and we find the neutral to be uninteresting. We must learn to experience things without the judgmental grasping, aversion, and boredom that cause so much suffering. We must see this void universe not through the perverting lens of our preconceived bias, but as it really is in its emptiness.

Buddhists meditate in order to let things simply be, without distortion, free of their addictive craving. Thus, they learn to watch dispassionately and undividedly, with sensitive but cool consciousness of the present moment. They seek to develop a vivid awareness and razor-sharp realization that they are no-self. Thus they gradually disengage themselves in freedom from all that clings to them and the karma that binds them to rebirth.

Often practitioners assume a relaxed position as they turn inward and concentrate their mental energy upon becoming vividly aware, but they may also walk slowly and deliberately. They practice centering with single-pointed focus upon delicate sensations such as the hair on their head, the fingers on a hand, or the toes on a foot, and enter fully into the experience of the present moment—now. As they breathe in, they gently note that fact: "in." As they breathe out, they gently think to themselves: "out." If they are walking during their meditation, they consciously acknowledge each movement one by one as they raise each foot ("up") and replace it on the ground ("down"). Myriad thoughts tumble through their minds, but they do not judge them; they simply acknowledge them for what they are—jealous, affectionate, offended, annoyed, and so on. Physical sensations both pleasant and unpleasant arise, but they do not possess them; they simply recognize them for what they are—fatigue, aching, constraint, itching, and so on.

Second, devotees gently let go of all conscious and half-conscious sentiments such as anxieties, frustrations, and prejudicial notions. They deliberately regulate their breathing as they slowly inhale and exhale. Practitioners begin to note each disquieting idea that invades their consciousness, though they claim none as "theirs." They become alert to each seductive memory or imagining for what it is, though they themselves continue to be coolly detached. They observe all the agitating sentiments and impulses that arise and pass away, though they themselves reserve judgment and remain disengaged. Those who meditate view their unhappiness without being unhappy, their sadness without being sad, their anger without being angry. As they watch their own mental processes, they begin to understand the Buddha's truths of suffering, impermanence, and non-self. As they cultivate right mindfulness, they grow in insight, promote detachment, and advance toward their emancipation.

In another meditative exercise, Buddhists work to reduce the painful burdens of others by assuming them as their own and transforming them as they breathe. First, practitioners call to mind vividly the concrete anguish of some particular persons about whom they have heard. Next, they mentally draw those torments into their own hearts as they breathe inward, slowly and deeply. Then they try to enter into the experience and identify with it so that the individuals concerned may suffer less. At length, they are in a position to "exhale" their compassion upon those persons and encompass them with comfort and consolation.

Zen

Zen, the Japanese rendering of *cha'n* (the Chinese word for "meditative absorption," which is itself derived from the Sanskrit word *dhyana*), designates both a school of Mahayana Buddhists and the unique method by which they pursue enlightenment. When other Buddhists meditate, they usually fix their attention upon a single symbol (perhaps a statue of Gotama or an image of a single lotus in bloom), upon a scriptural verse, or upon an ideal such as Compassion. Zen Buddhists also seek saving enlightenment, but without focusing upon any object or notion. When Zen Buddhists meditate, they strive to go beyond all images, thought patterns, and mental constructs to an intuitive awareness. They radically repudiate all conventional forms of human cognition in favor of nonmediated (non-conceptual) awareness of the Buddha nature within them that is Nibbana.

Christian mystics surrender to the graced sway of Christ's Holy Spirit for a passive purification not only of their senses but also of their spiritual faculties, as they advance toward the state of infused contemplation ("spiritual espousal"). Zen contemplatives also commit themselves to a total purification of their total being. They meditate, however, not by any divine grace from without, but only by their own human efforts toward concentration.

If we want to practice Zen, we may first predispose our bodies for intense centering through zazen, which is the quickest path to alert wakefulness. We must sit down with crossed legs upon a wooden platform, place our hands gently one upon the other (our thumbs barely touching), close our eyes almost completely, and remain still. If we persevere in our practice of zazen, our bodily composure will be conducive to that full attentiveness so indispensable for enlightenment—not as an abstraction, but as the realization of reality.

We must next look within to divest ourselves of our passionate concupiscence, our addictions, and our attachments. By the same token, we must dislodge all our memories of the past, all our distractions of the present, and all our imaginings of the future. It is not sufficient for us merely to attain this sensory level of purification, however. We must probe still more deeply, because we must also terminate any spiritual impediments to our direct encounter with the Absolute. We must restrain our intellectual tendencies toward ideational analyses, synthetic judgments, and the reasoning process itself. We must calm our moral propensity to make decisions and choices. We must transcend all dualisms such as mind-and-body, subject-and-object, good-and-evil, and myself-and-others. Indeed, we must empty our minds of even the most sublime and sacred content. Only then may we receive **satori,** that flash of immediate (that is, unmediated) awareness of the Buddha-nature that is our true Reality, inhering within us and within all beings.

We cannot learn instantaneous insight into the Buddha-nature from the instructions of another. Zen masters can only transmit insight to disciples heart-mind to heart-mind; spoken words cannot communicate it. Nor can we derive intuitive insight into the Buddha-nature from books; written words cannot pass it on to others. We might study, chant, copy, and memorize the Buddhist scriptures, but we would still not awaken to Reality. Zen Buddhists insist that Shakya-muni taught the meaning of enlightenment most effectively to his disciples not verbally by his sermons but wordlessly by simply holding a flower aloft. (The Buddha's gesture that day caused his disciple Kashyapa suddenly to realize the Buddha-nature and smile!)

Disciples look to their *roshis* not for teaching but only for guidance, leadership, and inspiration, since disciples must personally experience the Buddha-nature for themselves. Disciples and *roshis* may engage in one-on-one conferences with question-and-answer dialogues that flout the logic of language and unite contradictions in a higher convergence. *Roshis* may shout outrageous sounds at disciples or even strike them bodily, but this unconventional behavior is only calculated to shock them out of their rationality. *Roshis* may assign to their disciples a **koan** ("paradoxical riddle") to wrestle with, such as the famous question, "What is the sound of one hand clapping?" The whole point of a koan, however, is to serve as a wall against which seekers may shatter their logical processes; only then may they intuit Reality.

Zen is, of course, a much more pervasive Buddhist spirituality than simply the practice of zazen. We learn to meditate in the seated position, but we must be fully mindful in every activity and in every circumstance. Our heightened consciousness must energize and inform our lives. We must walk with awareness, eat with awareness, converse with awareness, work with awareness, and play with awareness. Even though we may follow a secular lifestyle, we must be willing to observe a disciplined regimen. We must make time in the busiest of schedules for daily meditation. We will find it helpful occasionally to go on monastic retreat, where we can concentrate upon study and meditation.

Zen Buddhists have had a broad impact upon Japanese culture by their composure, creativity, and sensitivity to the beauty of nature. Zen painting is characteristically spontaneous, ethereal, and provocative. Zen gardens, flower arranging, and architecture are both simple and profound. Zen poetry captures the sudden impact of the present moment in the **haiku** (a verse of seventeen syllables with the sequence of five, seven, five). The famous tea ceremony is a prescribed ritual that requires deliberate attention to the service of others. Archery, fencing, and even the art of motorcycle repair all deepen the sense of alert awareness in the participants. Such activities help Zen practitioners to realize that they are part of a single process and unitary flow with one another and with their instruments.

Devotions and Rituals

Most religious people require that their experience be not only coolly dispassionate at the deepest level of their spirit but also warmly gratifying at the level of the senses and emotions. Therefore, not only Mahayanists but also Theravadins have fostered humanly satisfying observances that go beyond the austere methods of systematic meditation. Throughout the Buddhist world, we encounter such practices as the recitation of mantras, the offering of prayers, and the celebration of liturgical rituals in the hope of building up merit and receiving blessings.

Devotees of Amitabha Buddha (in Japanese, *Amida*), for example, constantly repeat *"namu Amida Butsu"* ("hail to Amida Buddha") in their faith that Amitabha will keep his promise to deliver them at death into his western paradise. Tibetan Buddhists scarcely ever cease to offer the invocation *"om mani padme hum"* ("hail to the jewel in the lotus") in honor of Avalokitesvara, the bodhisattva who escorts devotees to Amitabha's "pure land." They not only speak and chant this phrase but also spin prayer wheels and string out prayer flags with these words inscribed upon them. Nichiren Buddhists from Japan express their faith in the truth of the Lotus Sutra by chanting over and over the phrase *"namu myoho rengekyo"* ("hail to the wondrous law of the lotus"). Sometimes they travel far in order to promote global peace, and while they pronounce this powerful mantra, they beat their drums and bow to the Buddha-nature in each of the countless persons that they meet.

Buddhists do not have a weekly day of worship similar to the Jewish Sabbath or the Christian Sunday. Buddhists do have the opportunity to visit the monastery or temple for instructions and worship at the first day of the new moon and at the full moon, however, together with the eighth day after each of these. Many take advantage of these opportunities for spiritual refreshment. When Buddhists offer sacred gestures together with flowers, lighted candles, and incense to the image of a Buddha or a bodhisattva, they nourish their devotion and respect that sacred figure. Moreover, their ritual actions create a calming context in which their minds can "wake up" and become more acutely aware. Rites of honor and respect for the Buddha can give way to contemplative reflection upon the Buddha and his holy attributes. Worshippers renew their commitment at least to observing Buddhist ethics and supporting the monastics more generously, but they may also give themselves to the practice of resolute meditation. They may express their gratitude for blessings received or offer their petitions for new blessings such as abundant crops, physical health, and familial prosperity.

The most important festival of Buddhism occurs at the full moon of April for Theravadins and at the full moon of May for Mahayanists: the thrice-significant day of Gotama's birth, enlightenment, and final passage into Nibbana. Another major festival in China and Japan is Ullambana, a commemoration that assists the "hungry ghosts." In Theravada countries,

Buddhists joyfully celebrate the New Year during April as a water festival at the end of the dry season, and people playfully splash one another with water for a purification from their bad karma.

Many Buddhists need to do more than travel the interior journey of the heart that actualizes the transforming Buddha-truth within themselves. They need also to walk the exterior journey of the legs that realizes the energizing Buddha-power available at cosmic peaks. Pilgrimage, therefore, is also a "skillful means," a meritorious work that can play a significant role in the spirituality of Buddhists.

Sometimes, pilgrims seek out a **stupa** (mound-shaped temple) that contains, perhaps, a relic of the Buddha such as a hair or a splinter of bone. A stupa may also enshrine something the Buddha used, such as his begging bowl, or an imprint of the Buddha's presence, such as his footprint or his shadow. On other occasions, pilgrims laboriously climb "natural stupas" such as Japan's Mount Fuji. At still other times, Buddhist pilgrims travel to a memorial site such as Lumbini in Nepal, where Gotama was born, to Bodh-Gaya in India, where Gotama received his enlightenment, or to Deer Park at Sarnath near Varanasi in India, where Gotama preached his first sermon. On every occasion, Buddhists pay homage to the Buddha with bows, prostrations, prayers, and gift offerings.

A woman from a town in Thailand begins her day by bowing to a statue of the meditating Gotama that stands prominently on a small table in her home. She reverently offers some freshly cut flowers from her garden, some food, and some water to the Buddha. The woman lights some candles and ignites three sticks of incense as an offering in honor of the three jewels. Clouds of fragrant smoke fill the room as she acknowledges her threefold refuge in the Buddha, the Dhamma, and the Samgha. The woman covers her face with her hands, and she prostrates herself before the sacred image. She may recite her small Buddhist rosary (monks use a large rosary of 108 beads, with two halves of 54 beads each, representing the 54 stages of becoming a Buddha). She offers her prayers and recites her scriptural texts, not because she believes Gotama is present to hear her but because she seeks blessings for her household and she wishes to gain merit.

A householder in a Burmese town hears someone approach her front door, and she immediately procures the pot of rice and vegetables that she has freshly prepared on the stove. She is delighted to find that one of the monks has come to her door in order to beg for his food. The woman opens the door and ladles a whole day's nourishment into the monk's begging bowl. The monk in no way acknowledges her generosity, because he knows it is she who is in debt to him. For he has favored her with an opportunity to gain rich merit. The monk departs with his eyes cast down; he will eat his meal before noon, deliberately taking no pleasure in the taste. The householder has launched her day.

During August, a man from a small town in Sri Lanka makes his yearly pilgrimage to Kandy and ascends the steps to the Temple of the Tooth for which Kandy is so renowned. His most awe-inspiring experience will be the privilege of entering the actual presence of a tooth of the Buddha that lies secreted within the sanctuary. For ten days, the man will thrill to the pandemonium and carnival atmosphere of this greatest of Asian festivals. He will hear the deafening drums, enjoy the dancers in their elaborate costumes, and laugh at the clowning. The man will watch the colorful procession that parades daily through Kandy's streets during the festival: monks, nuns, and laypeople; elephants and other animals; and large wagons festooned with myriads of flowers. Finally, he will join with many thousands of other Buddhists in fixing his fascinated gaze upon the privileged elephant that carries a casketed symbol of the relic on its garlanded back. Transformed by the Buddha's blessings, the man will return to his home jubilant, his hands filled with merit and his heart filled with joyful hope.

Buddhists make much of the celebration of death, since they focus upon delivery from the wheel of rebirth as their one priority. They view death as the irrepressible reminder of the fleeting transience of life. Buddhists are especially concerned that they and their relatives should die well, because their state of mind at death can greatly influence their next rebirth. Therefore, the family of a dying relative summons the monks to chant the scriptures in the sickroom until the person has finally departed. Then they wash the body and shave the head of the deceased man or woman. Monks (or priests) conduct the funeral with more chanting and the burning of incense, while friends and relatives stand by in attendance. The service concludes with a procession to the burial ground or crematorium, but rites and prayers will follow at regular intervals thereafter, even on an annual basis. Buddhists want their dear ones above all to be free from possibly woeful rebirths.

The consideration of Buddhist death with its concern for ensuring a favorable reincarnation or avoiding rebirth altogether takes us back to the heart and core of all Buddhist spirituality. Despite its diverse shapes and expressions, it is finally reducible to the basic solution that Gotama originally offered for the human problem. After we have recognized that all things are impermanent, including ourselves, we must follow the middle way of the Eightfold Path to ensure that we eliminate all grasping, with its karmic bonds to the wheel of rebirth. Only in this way may we enter into Nibbana, with its liberation from reincarnation and its indescribable peace.

MATERIAL FOR DISCUSSION

1. What are the principal themes in the spirituality of Theravada Buddhism?

2. What are the principal themes in the spirituality of Mahayana Buddhism?

3. In what ways can the person of no religious persuasion benefit from the study of Buddhist spirituality generally?

4. In what ways can persons of monotheistic religious persuasion profit from the study of Buddhist spirituality generally?

SUGGESTIONS FOR FURTHER READING

Borg, Marcus, ed. *Jesus and Buddha: The Parallel Sayings.* Berkeley, Calif.: Seastone, 1997. An interesting comparison of teachings attributed to Jesus and the Buddha that shows fascinating similarities in their spiritual insights, ethical concerns, and practical counsels, although their ways and goals differ decisively.

Boucher, Sandy. *Discovering Kwan Yin, Buddhist Goddess of Compassion.* Boston: Beacon Press, 1999.

Buddhist Studies at Nyingma Institute. *Ways of Enlightenment.* Berkeley, Calif.: Dharma, 1993. An authoritative and most useful presentation of Buddhist themes, concepts, terminology, and techniques for the independent student.

Conze, Edward, ed. and trans. *Buddhist Scriptures.* London: Penguin, 1959. A classical anthology of Buddhist scriptures in English, selected from Theravada and Mahayana collections.

Fischer-Schreiber, Ingrid, Franz-Karl Ehrhard, and Michael S. Diener. *The Shambhala Dictionary of Buddhism and Zen.* Trans. Michael H. Kohn. Boston: Shambhala, 1991. A small encyclopedic dictionary of Buddhism that presents both the Sanskrit and the Pali terms together with concise yet ample explanations of their significance.

Guruge, Ananda W. P. *Buddhism: The Religion and Its Culture.* 2nd ed. Colombo, Sri Lanka: The World Fellowship of Buddhists, 1984. A marvelously organized introduction to the concrete experience of Buddhist life and practice.

Hanh, Thich Nhat. *Zen Keys.* Rev. ed. New York: Doubleday, 1995. A superbly clear and illuminating work on Zen Buddhism by an accomplished practitioner and leading spokesperson for Vietnamese Buddhism in the West.

Mitchell, Donald W., and James A. Wiseman. *The Gethsemani Encounter: A Dialogue on the Spiritual Life by Buddhist and Christian Monastics.* New York: Continuum, 1999. A groundbreaking treasury of forty-eight talks delivered by Buddhist and Christian monks, nuns, and scholars in the course of a historic and global conference of the Monastic Interreligious Dialogue at Gethsemani Abbey during the week of July 22–27, 1996.

Parrinder, Geoffrey, ed. *The Sayings of the Buddha.* Hopewell, N.J.: Ecco Press, 1998. A most helpful compilation of poignant sayings that have been ascribed to the Buddha, selected from the Pali Canon and presented in smooth English translation.

Watson, Burton, trans. *The Lotus Sutra.* New York: Columbia University Press, 1993. An English translation of the most popular and widely read of the scriptures among Mahayana Buddhists.

Glossary

Abba "Daddy" (Aramaic).

'Abd al-Rahman In Islam, "servant of the merciful One" (Arabic).

Abhidhamma-pitaka In Buddhism, the basket of special teachings (Pali).

Adonai In Judaism, LORD (Hebrew).

agape In Christianity, an unconditional love that seeks no return (Greek).

Agni In Hinduism, the god of fire.

ahimsa In Hinduism and Buddhism, nonviolence (Sanskrit).

Allah In Islam, "the God" (Arabic); the God of Abraham.

Allahu akbar In Islam, "God is greater" (Arabic).

almsgiving Sharing one's material goods with the poor and needy.

al-Rahim In Islam, the merciful One (Arabic).

al-Rahman In Islam, the compassionate One (Arabic).

ananda In Hinduism, unmitigated bliss (Sanskrit).

anatta In Buddhism, no-self (Pali).

anawim Poor and lowly in spirit (Hebrew).

anicca In Buddhism, impermanence (Pali).

anointing of the sick In Catholic Christianity, a sacred rite for the healing and strengthening of sick persons; one of the seven **sacraments.**

anthropomorphic In the form of a human being.

apostle In Christianity, a disciple with a solemn commission, particularly the Twelve Apostles of Jesus.

arahat In **Theravada** Buddhism, a person who has become realized through enlightenment (Pali).

Aranyakas In Hinduism, a **Vedic** collection of mystical treatises by forest-dwelling holy men.

ark   In Judaism, a container (for the **Torah** scrolls).

artha   In Hinduism, material wealth (Sanskrit).

asceticism   The disciplined practice of self-denial.

Ashkenazim   In Judaism, European Jews who have observed the customs of Jews from medieval Germany (Hebrew).

ashram   In Hinduism, a dwelling set apart where members of a community may practice meditation and observe a simple and meditative lifestyle (Sanskrit).

ashramas   In Hinduism, the four stages of life (Sanskrit).

atman   In Hinduism, the self or soul (Sanskrit).

avatars   In Hinduism, descents or incarnations (Sanskrit).

avijja   In Buddhism, ignorance (Pali).

baptism   In Christianity, a symbolic washing with water; one of the **sacraments.**

bar mitzvah   In Judaism, "son of commandment" (Hebrew); the ceremonial admission of a boy to legal adulthood.

bat mitzvah   In Judaism, "daughter of commandment" (Hebrew); the ceremonial admission of a Jewish girl to legal adulthood.

beatitudes   In Christianity, declarations of blessedness or happiness.

berakhah   In Judaism, a blessing (Hebrew).

Bhagavad Gita   In Hinduism, "The Song of the Divine Lord," a popular subdivision of an immense Indian epic, the Mahabharata.

bhaktas   In Hinduism, those who follow the way of devotion (Sanskrit).

bhakti marga   In Hinduism, the way of devotion (Sanskrit).

bimah   In Judaism, a pulpit (Hebrew).

Blessed Sacrament   In Catholic and Anglican Christianity, the **sacramental** presence of the risen Christ under the appearances of bread and wine.

Blessed Trinity   In Christianity, the life of the one God in three distinct, co-equal, and co-eternal persons: the Father, the Son, and the Holy Spirit.

bodhisattva   In **Mahayana** Buddhism, a person who enjoys the transcendent powers of an enlightened being and is destined for **Nibbana** (Sanskrit).

born-again Christians   In Protestant Christianity, believers who have experienced a second birth of the Holy Spirit.

Brahma   In Hinduism, God the Creator.

brahmacharya   In Hinduism, the student stage (Sanskrit).

Brahman   In Hinduism, the impersonal Godhead.

Brahmanas   In Hinduism, a **Vedic** collection of general doctrinal texts for priests.

Brahman-atman   In Hinduism, the one universal and absolute Self.

Brahmins   In Hinduism, the priestly caste (Sanskrit).

brit milah   In Judaism, circumcision (Hebrew).

Buddha   In Buddhism, the Enlightened One (Sanskrit).

Buddhahood   In Buddhism, the state of being an enlightened one.

Buddhist spirituality   The inner meaning of human experience as shaped by the pursuit of transformation under the impact of the Buddha's **Dhamma.**

canon   Definitive edition.

catechumens   In Christianity, individuals who are being prepared for entrance into the **Church.**

cenobitical   Life in common, as in monasticism.

Chanukah   In Judaism, the Festival of Dedication (Hebrew).

charismatics   In Christianity, believers who are especially devoted to the Holy Spirit and the Spirit's gifts.

chit   In Hinduism, pure consciousness (Sanskrit).

Chrismation   In Eastern Orthodox Christianity, the same as the **sacrament** of **confirmation.**

Christ   In Christianity, the Anointed One (from the Greek rendering of the Jewish notion of the **Messiah**).

Christian spirituality   The inner meaning of human experience as shaped by the pursuit of transformation under the impact of the way of Jesus' discipleship.

Church   In Christianity, the assembled community of believers.

communion of saints   In Christianity, the shared life and union between believers on earth and those who have died in Christ.

confirmation   In Catholic and Anglican Christianity, a **sacrament** for the sealing and completion of baptism.

covenant   In Judaism and Christianity, an alliance or agreement.

crucifix   In Catholic Christianity, a cross with an image of the nailed Jesus upon it.

Daibutsu   In Buddhism, "the great Buddha" (Japanese), a massive statue of Amitabha Buddha at Kamakura, Japan.

Dar al-Harb   In Islam, the dwelling place of struggle (Arabic).

Dar al-Islam   In Islam, the dwelling place of peace (Arabic).

darshan   In Hinduism, a view (of a god or goddess) (Sanskrit).

Dhamma   In Buddhism, the Buddha's message of universal Truth (Pali).

Dharma   In Hinduism, law/duty (Sanskrit).

dhikr   In Islam, remembrance (Arabic).

Divali   In Hinduism, the Festival of Lights.

Divine Liturgy   In Eastern Orthodox Christianity, the celebration of the **Holy Eucharist,** or Lord's Supper.

dogma   A doctrinal formulation.

dukkha   In Buddhism, suffering (Pali).

Durga   In Hinduism, a form of **Shakti,** the Goddess consort of **Shiva.**

dvijas   In Hinduism, the twice-born (Sanskrit).

Easter   In Christianity, the festival that commemorates the resurrection of Jesus from the dead.

echad   In Judaism, one (Hebrew).

ecumenical councils   In Christianity, universal assemblies of bishops.

eirene   Peace (Greek).

ekklesia kyriake   In Christianity, "Lordly assembly" (Greek).

'emet   In Judaism, fidelity (Hebrew).

Epistles   In Christianity, letters; books of the New Testament attributed to Paul the Apostle and others.

evangelicals   In Protestant Christianity, those who emphasize a conservative faith based solely upon the Bible.

Exodus   In Judaism, the escape from slavery in Egypt and also the biblical book that narrates that event (Greek).

fasting   Abstinence from food; can be a form of spiritual exercise.

Ganesha   In Hinduism, the elephant-headed god.

Garuda   In Hinduism, **Vishnu's** eagle vehicle.

Gemara   In Judaism, "completion" (Hebrew); part of the Talmud.

ghaflah   In Islam, heedlessness (Arabic).

ghats   Steps (Sanskrit); the dead are cremated in pyres on the ghats along the banks of the Ganges.

glossolalia   Speaking in tongues.

gopala   A cowherd (Sanskrit).

gopi   A cowherdess (Sanskrit).

gospel   In Christianity, the good news (about God's reign in the risen Jesus).

Gospels   In Christianity, four scriptural accounts of the life and teachings of Jesus: Matthew, Mark, Luke, and John.

grace   In Christianity, God's sanctifying action.

grihasthya   In Hinduism, the householder stage (Sanskrit).

guru   In Hinduism, a spiritual instructor (Sanskrit).

hadith   In Islam, the collection of words and events from the life of Muhammad (Arabic).

hadith qudsi   In Islam, a non-Quranic revelation of God that Muhammad handed on to the Muslims in his own words (Arabic).

Haggadah   In Judaism, narrative (Hebrew).

haiku   In Zen Buddhism, a verse of seventeen syllables with the sequence of five, seven, five (Japanese).

hajj   In Islam, pilgrimage (Arabic); one of the Five Pillars of Islam.

Ha Shem   In Judaism, the Name (of God) (Hebrew).

Hasids   In Judaism, the "pious ones," who cultivate direct and joyful experience of God's presence (Hebrew).

Hebrew Bible   In Judaism, the collection of thirty-nine books in Hebrew that are officially recognized as biblical in Jewish tradition.

henotheism   In Hinduism, the recognition of one God or Goddess as the greatest deity among many gods and godesses (Sanskrit).

hesed   In Judaism, steadfast love (Hebrew).

heterodoxy   A belief system that differs from that of a religious tradition's mainstream.

hijra   In Islam, the emigration (of Muhammad to Medina) (Arabic).

Hindu spirituality   The inner meaning of human experience as shaped by the pursuit of transformation under the impact of the ways of **Sanatana Dharma.**

hodos   A way (Greek).

Holy Communion   In Christianity, the encounter with the risen Jesus through participation in a **sacramental** meal that memorializes Jesus' last supper.

Holy Eucharist   In Christianity, the **sacramental** memorial of Jesus' last supper in the form of bread and wine.

holy orders   In Catholic, Anglican, and Eastern Orthodox Christianity, the **sacrament** by which an individual is initiated into sacred ministry as a deacon, priest, or bishop.

Host   In Catholic Christianity, the consecrated bread that has been changed into the **sacramental** presence of the risen Christ (from the Latin *hostia,* "victim").

huppah   In Judaism, a canopy (Hebrew).

Iblis   In Islam, the devil (Arabic).

icons   In Eastern Orthodox Christianity, holy images created by monks.

Id al-Adha   In Islam, the Festival of the Sacrifice, a feast at the conclusion of the pilgrimage to Mecca (Arabic).

Id al-Fitra   In Islam, the Festival of the Breaking of the Fast (Arabic), a feast at the conclusion of the Ramadan fast.

ijma   In Islam, communal consensus (Arabic); one of the four authoritative sources that determine the laws of shariah.

imam   In Islam, a leader of prayer (Arabic).

immanent   Abiding within.

ineffable   Beyond adequate human expression.

infallible   In Christianity, the belief that doctrines are divinely protected from teaching error.

inspiration of the Bible   In Christianity, the belief that God is the principal author of the Scriptures.

Ishtadeva   In Hinduism, God of choice (Sanskrit).

Islam   In Islam, "submission" (Arabic), the name of the religious tradition instituted through Muhammad.

Islamic spirituality   The inner meaning of human experience as shaped by the pursuit of transformation under the impact of the straight path of submission to Allah.

Jewish spirituality   The inner meaning of human experience as shaped by the pursuit of transformation under the impact of the way of the **Torah.**

jihad   In Islam, a struggle (Arabic).

jnana marga   In Hinduism, the way of knowledge (Sanskrit).

justification   In Christianity, the process of being made righteous by God for Jesus' sake.

Kaba   In Islam, "cube" (Arabic); at Mecca, the most sacred Islamic sanctuary.

Kabbalah   In Judaism, a medieval movement of esoteric mysticism (Hebrew).

Kalam Allah   In Islam, "the Word of God" (Arabic).

Kali   In Hinduism, a form of **Shakti,** the Goddess consort of **Shiva.**

kama   In Hinduism, pleasure or happiness (Sanskrit).

Kamakshi   In Hinduism, "the Great Mother."

kamma   In Buddhism, the same as **karma,** "action, consequence of action" (Pali).

karma   In Hinduism, an action or the consequence of an action (Sanskrit).

karma marga   In Hinduism, the way of action (Sanskrit).

kashrut   In Judaism, the collection of dietary precepts (Hebrew).

Ketuvim   In Judaism, the Writings (Hebrew).

khalifa   In Islam, a successor to Muhammad (Arabic).

Kitab al-Allah   In Islam, the Book of God (Arabic).

K'lal Yisrael   In Judaism, catholic Israel (Hebrew).

koan   In Zen Buddhism, a paradoxical riddle (Japanese).

Kol Nidrei   In Judaism, "all vows" (Hebrew); the hymn that introduces Yom Kippur.

kosher   In Judaism, "clean" (Hebrew); refers to Jewish dietary laws.

Krishna   In Hinduism, an incarnation of the God **Vishnu** (Sanskrit).

Kshatriyas   In Hinduism, the warrior caste (Sanskrit).

Lakshmi   In Hinduism, **Vishnu's** Goddess consort and chief queen.

Laws of Manu   In Hinduism, a practice manual of daily duties according to class and stage of life.

lectio divina   In Catholic Christianity, a divine reading (Latin).

Lent   In Catholic Christianity, the forty days of preparation for the solemn feast of **Easter.**

lila   Whimsical and purposeless play (Sanskrit).

linga   A phallic symbol (Sanskrit).

liturgy   Public and communal worship through a sacred rite.

Lord   In Christianity, a title for Jesus as Absolute Sovereign.

magga   In Buddhism, a way (Pali).

magisterium   In Catholic Christianity, the teaching authority of the Church.

Mahadeva   In Hinduism, a supreme God (Sanskrit).

Mahadevi   In Hinduism, a supreme Goddess (Sanskrit).

Mahayana   "The great vehicle" (Sanskrit); Northern and Eastern Buddhism.

Mahayogi   In Hinduism, the great ascetic (Sanskrit).

maitri   In Hinduism, friendly love (Sanskrit).

manna   In Judaism and Christianity, a breadlike substance (Aramaic).

mantra   In Hinduism, a sacred word or phrase (Sanskrit).

marga   In Hinduism, a way (Sanskrit).

maror   In Judaism, bitter herbs (Hebrew).

masjid   In Islam, a "place of prostration," or mosque (Arabic).

Mass   In Catholic Christianity, the central celebration of worship in commemoration of Jesus' last supper.

matzah   In Judaism, unleavened bread (Hebrew).

Maulid al-Nabi   In Islam, the festival of Muhammad's birthday (Arabic).

Medina al-Nabi   In Islam, the city of the Prophet (Arabic).

Messiah   In Judaism and Christianity, the Anointed One.

mezuzah   In Judaism, a small scroll receptacle (Hebrew).

minaret   In Islam, a tower attached to a mosque (Arabic).

minyan   In Judaism, a quorum of ten men (Hebrew).

Mishnah   In Judaism, "repetition" (Hebrew); part of the Talmud.

mitzvah   In Judaism, a commandment; plural, **mitzvot** (Hebrew).

moksha   In Hinduism, "liberation" (Sanskrit), salvation from the wheel of rebirth.

monotheism   The recognition of one God or one Goddess alone.

muezzin   In Islam, a person who summons to prayers (Arabic).

Muslim   In Islam, "one who submits" (Arabic); those who practice the religion of Islam.

murti   In Hinduism, an image of a god or holy person (Sanskrit).

mystery   A notion that surpasses human capacity to comprehend; in Eastern Orthodox Christianity, one of seven **sacraments.**

mystic   One who by meditation seeks and cultivates direct experience of the ultimate Absolute.

myth   A vividly imaginative story.

nafs   In Islam, the lower self or soul (Arabic).

Nandi   In Hinduism, the white bull that is **Shiva's** vehicle.

Nataraja   In Hinduism, the Lord of the Dance (Sanskrit).

neti, neti   In Hinduism, "not this, not that" (Sanskrit).

Nevi'im   In Judaism, the Prophets (Hebrew).

New Testament   In Christianity, a collection of scriptures that supplements the Jewish scriptures in constituting the Bible.

Nibbana   In Buddhism, "state of being blown-out, cool" (Pali), a liberation from the wheel of rebirth.

Nicene Creed   In Christianity, a classical statement of Christian doctrines.

Nirguna Brahman   In Hinduism, **Brahman**-without-qualities (Sanskrit).

numinous   Pertaining to the divinely Other.

Old Testament   In Christianity, Jewish scriptures interpreted in light of faith in Christ.

Om   In Hinduism, the primordial syllable that symbolizes God and also the sacred sound through which the cosmos came into being (Sanskrit).

original sin   In Christianity, state of estrangement from God inherited from our first parents.

orthodoxy   Right faith (Greek).

orthopraxis   Right practice (Greek).

Pali Canon   In Buddhism, the earliest collection of scriptures, written in the Pali language.

parable   A story with a lesson.

paradigm   A model or pattern.

Parinibbana   In Buddhism, the state of **Nibbana** that an enlightened being realizes after death (Pali).

Parvati   In Hinduism, the Goddess consort of **Shiva.**

parve   In Judaism, neutral (Hebrew); refers to dietary laws.

Pentateuch   In Judaism and Christianity, the first five books of the Bible.

Pentecostals   In Protestant Christianity, those who cultivate special devotion to the Holy Spirit.

Pesah   In Judaism, the Festival of Passover (Hebrew).

phala   In Hinduism, a fruit (Sanskrit).

prayer   A religious act by which human beings individually or communally carry on a dialogue with the divinely sacred.

prophecy   In Judaism, Christianity, and Islam, a message spoken on behalf of God.

prophesy   In Judaism, Christianity, and Islam, to speak on behalf of God.

puja   In Hinduism, worship (Sanskrit).

Purim   In Judaism, the Festival of Lots (Hebrew).

Purusha   In Hinduism, a divine being that the gods dismembered in a cosmic sacrifice.

qiyas   In Islam, "an analogy" (Arabic); one of the authoritative sources for the laws of shariah.

Quakers   In Christianity, members of the Society of Friends.

Quran   In Islam, the "recital," the book of scripture given to Muhammad (Arabic).

Quraysh   In Islam, Muhammad's clan.

Radha   In Hinduism, an avatar of **Lakshmi,** a Goddess consort of **Vishnu.**

Rama   In Hinduism, an avatar of **Vishnu.**

Ramadan   In Islam, the month of fasting (Arabic).

rasul   In Islam, a messenger (Arabic).

rasuliyyah   In Islam, messengerhood (Arabic).

rebbe   In Hasidic Judaism, a teacher (Yiddish).

reconciliation   In Catholic, Anglican, and Eastern Orthodox Christianity, a **sacrament** for the forgiveness of sins committed after baptism.

recto tono   In Catholic Christianity, a style of chanting in a single note (Latin).

reign   In Christianity, God's dominion.

religion   The pursuit of transformation under the impact of a sacred worldview.

religious spirituality   The inner meaning of human experience as shaped by the pursuit of transformation under the impact of a sacred worldview.

rishis   In Hinduism, seers (Sanskrit).

rita   In Hinduism, right order (Sanskrit).

Rosh Hashanah   In Judaism, the "head of the year," or the New Year (Hebrew).

roshi   In Japanese Buddhism, an aged teacher (Japanese).

ruh   In Islam, the higher self or spirit (Arabic).

sabda   In Hinduism, a sound (Sanskrit).

saccidananda   In Hinduism, the transforming experience of actualized existence, pure consciousness, and unmitigated bliss (Sanskrit).

sacrament   In Christianity, a visible sign of God's invisible and sanctifying **grace** instituted by Christ.

sacramentalize   In Catholic, Anglican, and Eastern Orthodox Christianity, to communicate through visible signs.

sacred   Nonordinary, venerable, set apart.

sadhu   In Hinduism, a just man or saint (Sanskrit).

Saguna Brahman   In Hinduism, **Brahman**-with-qualities (Sanskrit).

salam   Peace (Arabic).

salat   In Islam, prayers (Arabic); one of the Five Pillars of Islam.

samadhi   In Hinduism, deep meditation (Sanskrit).

Samgha   In Buddhism, the monastic order (Pali).

Samhitas   In Hinduism, sacred collections that include the Rig-Veda, the Sama-Veda, the Yajur-Veda, and the Atharva-Veda (Sanskrit).

samsara   In Hinduism, the impermanence of the universe, the cycle of rebirth (Sanskrit).

Sanatana Dharma   In Hinduism, eternal law or duty (Sanskrit).

sanctuary lamp   In Catholic Christianity, a candle that burns continuously to symbolize the sacramental presence of the risen Christ under the appearance of bread.

sannyasa   In Hinduism, the renunciate stage (Sanskrit).

sannyasin   In Hinduism, a holy man who has embraced the fourth stage of life as a renunciate (Sanskrit).

santi   In Buddhism, peace (Pali).

sat   In Hinduism, actualized existence (Sanskrit).

Satan   In Judaism, Christianity, and Islam, the devil.

satori   In Zen Buddhism, an awakening to immediate awareness of the Buddha-nature that is our true Reality, inhering within us and within all beings (Japanese).

sawm   In Islam, fasting (Arabic); one of the Five Pillars of Islam.

seder In Judaism, the Passover service (Hebrew).

Sephardim In Judaism, Jews of Mediterranean and Arab countries who have observed the customs of medieval Spanish Jews (Hebrew).

service of the Eucharist In Christianity, a structured thanksgiving that includes an account of Jesus' last supper and concludes with the distribution of Holy Communion; part of the liturgy.

service of the Word In Christianity, a structured series of prayers, scripture readings, and sermon; part of the liturgy.

Shabbat In Judaism, "Sabbath," or Saturday (Hebrew).

shahadah In Islam, a witness (Arabic); one of the Five Pillars of Islam.

Shaivas In Hinduism, devotees of **Shiva.**

Shaivism In Hinduism, the worship of **Shiva** the Destroyer.

Shakers In Protestant Christianity, a community of those who dance and shake when they experience the Holy Spirit.

Shaktas In Hinduism, devotees of **Shakti.**

Shakti In Hinduism, the Goddess who personifies the Feminine Dynamic Energy.

Shaktism In Hinduism, the worship of **Shakti,** the Feminine Dynamic Energy.

Shakya-muni In Buddhism, the sage of the Shakyas (Sanskrit).

shalom Peace (Hebrew).

shanti Peace (Sanskrit).

shariah In Islam, a "way" (Arabic), religious law.

Shavuot In Judaism, the Festival of Weeks (Hebrew).

shaykh In Islam, a leader (Arabic).

Shekhinah In Judaism, the presence of God (Hebrew).

Shema In Judaism, the confession of faith that the LORD God is one (Hebrew).

Shi'ite Islam In Islam, a significant minority of Muslims, who believe that Muhammad appointed 'Ali and his blood descendants as his legitimate successors.

Shiva In Hinduism, God the Destroyer.

Shruti   In Hinduism, (the Revelation that) has been heard (Sanskrit).

Shudras   In Hinduism, the servant caste.

Siddur   In Judaism, a prayer book (Hebrew).

Simhat Torah   In Judaism, the ceremony of Rejoicing in the **Torah** (Hebrew).

sin   In Judaism, Christianity, and Islam, a moral evil that offends God.

Sita   In Hinduism, an avatar of **Lakshmi,** Goddess consort of **Vishnu.**

Smriti   In Hinduism, (the Revelation that) has been remembered (Sanskrit).

soul   The animating principle in living beings.

spirit   The inner foundation for properly human experience.

spirituality   The inner meaning of human experience under the impact of a humane worldview.

stations of the cross   In Catholic Christianity, fourteen places along the way between Jesus' condemnation and his crucifixion.

stupa   In Buddhism, a mound-shaped temple (Sanskrit).

Sufis   In Islam, Muslims who seek and cultivate direct experience of God (Arabic).

Sukkot   In Judaism, the Festival of Booths (Hebrew).

sunna   In Islam, customary practice (Arabic).

sunnata   In Buddhism, emptiness (Pali).

Sunni Islam   In Islam, the majority of Muslims, who depend upon the **Quran,** the customary practice of Muhammad, and the community for their guidance.

sura   In Islam, a **Quranic** chapter (Arabic).

Sutta-pitaka   In Buddhism, the basket of discourses (Pali).

suttas   In Buddhism, discourses (Pali).

tabernacle   In Catholic Christianity, the boxlike receptacle in which the sacramental presence of the risen Christ is reserved for the Holy Communion of the sick.

Talmud   In Judaism, a compendium of authoritative commentary on the Bible (Hebrew).

Tanakh   In Judaism, the Bible (Hebrew).

tanha   In Buddhism, craving desire (Pali).

taqwa   In Islam, righteousness, piety (Arabic).

Tathagata   In Buddhism, one who has been thus perfected (Sanskrit).

Tat tvam asi   "That thou art" (Sanskrit).

tefillin   In Judaism, leather boxes containing inscriptions from the **Torah** with straps for binding to the forehead, the left hand, and the left arm (Hebrew).

tetragrammaton   In Judaism, the word of four letters that is God's name, YHWH, or **Yahweh** (Greek).

theophany   An appearance of God.

theosis   In Eastern Orthodox Christianity, the divinization of the believer (Greek).

Theravada   The "teaching of the elders" (Sanskrit), Southeast Asian Buddhism.

three jewels   In Buddhism, the Buddha, the **Dhamma,** and the **Samgha;** the same as the Three Refuges.

three marks of existence   In Buddhism, impermanence, suffering, and no-self.

tikkun haolam   In Judaism, the restoration of the world (Hebrew).

Tipitaka   In Buddhism, "three baskets," the book of scriptures in the Pali language.

tirthas   Pilgrimage sites (Sanskrit).

tirthayatra   A pilgrimage (Sanskrit—literally, a "tour to a ford").

Tishri   In Judaism, September (Hebrew).

tithe   In Judaism and Christianity, donating one tenth of one's income to charitable and religious causes.

Torah   In Judaism, the teaching of God to Israel through Moses (Hebrew).

traif   In Judaism, unclean; literally, "torn" (Hebrew); refers to dietary laws.

transcendent   Exceeding limits, surpassing.

Trinity   In Christianity, three equal and eternal persons in one God: the Father, the Son, and the Holy Spirit.

tritheism   The belief in three gods.

tzaddik   In Judaism, a righteous man (Hebrew); plural, *tzaddikim.*

tzedakah   In Judaism, righteousness (Hebrew).

'ubadiyah   In Islam, being the servant of God (Arabic).

umma   In Islam, the community of Muslims (Arabic).

unction   In Anglican and Eastern Orthodox Christianity, the same **sacrament** as the **anointing of the sick.**

upanayana   In Hinduism, sacramental initiation into **Vedic** study (Sanskrit).

Upanishads   In Hinduism, a collection of late **Vedic** scriptures (Sanskrit).

utsava   In Hinduism, a festival (Sanskrit).

vade mecum   A handbook (Latin).

Vaishnavas   In Hinduism, devotees of **Vishnu.**

Vaishnavism   In Hinduism, the worship of **Vishnu** the Preserver or one of his **avatars.**

Vaishyas   In Hinduism, the business and agricultural caste (Sanskrit).

Vajrayana   In Buddhism, the "diamond vehicle," the Tibetan school (Sanskrit).

vanaprasthya   In Hinduism, the forest-dweller stage (Sanskrit).

varna   In Hinduism, a social class or caste (Sanskrit).

Vedanta   In Hinduism, the "end of the **Vedas,**" the **Upanishads.**

Vedas   In Hinduism, the collection of ancient scriptures (Sanskrit).

Vespers   In Christianity, the celebration of communal evening prayers.

Vinaya-pitaka   In Buddhism, the basket of discipline (Pali).

Vishnu   In Hinduism, God the Preserver.

walayah   In Islam, being the friend of God (Arabic).

worldview   A perspective through which one approaches and interprets reality.

yad   In Judaism, a pointer (Hebrew).

Yahweh   In Judaism, God's own name, as revealed to Moses and Israel (Hebrew).

yana   In Buddhism, a vehicle (Sanskrit).

yetzer ha ra   In Judaism, bad tendencies (Hebrew).

yetzer ha tov   In Judaism, good tendencies (Hebrew).

yoga   In Hinduism, a system for religious growth (Sanskrit).

yogis   In Hinduism, practitioners of yoga (Sanskrit).

Yom Kippur   In Judaism, the Day of Atonement, the penitential day of absolute fasting (Hebrew).

zakat   In Islam, almsgiving (Arabic); one of the Five Pillars of Islam.

zazen   In Japanese Buddhism, "sitting meditation" (Japanese).

Zen   In Japanese Buddhism, "meditation" (Japanese).

Bibliography

Aitken, Robert. *The Practice of Perfection: The* Paramitas *from a Zen Buddhist Perspective.* New York: Pantheon Books, 1994.

Akira, Hirakawa. "Stupa Worship." Translated by Paul Groner. In *The Encyclopedia of Religion.* Vol. 14. New York: Macmillan, 1987, 92–96.

Ali, Ahmed. *Al-Qur'an: A Contemporary Translation.* Princeton: Princeton University Press, 1984.

Berger, Peter L. *The Sacred Canopy: Elements of a Sociological Theory of Religion.* Garden City, N.Y.: Doubleday, 1969.

Beyer, Stephan. *The Buddhist Experience: Sources and Interpretations.* Encino, Calif.: Dickenson, 1974.

———. *The Cult of Tara: Magic and Ritual in Tibet.* Berkeley: University of California Press, 1978.

Bhardwaj, Surinder M. "Hindu Pilgrimage." In *The Encyclopedia of Religion.* Vol. 11. New York: Macmillan, 1987, 353–54.

Blau, Joseph L. *Modern Varieties of Judaism.* New York: Columbia University Press, 1964.

Borg, Marcus, and Ray Riegert, eds. *Jesus and Buddha: The Parallel Sayings.* Berkeley, Calif.: Seastone, 1997.

Borowitz, Eugene B. "Judaism: An Overview." In *The Encyclopedia of Religion.* Vol. 8. New York: Macmillan, 1987, 127–48.

Boucher, Sandy. *Discovering Kwan Yin, Buddhist Goddess of Compassion.* Boston: Beacon Press, 1999.

Browne, Lewis, ed. *The World's Great Scriptures: An Anthology of the Sacred Books of the Ten Principal Religions.* New York: Macmillan, 1946.

Buber, Martin. *Moses: The Revelation and the Covenant.* New York: Harper Torchbooks, 1958.

Buddhist Studies at Nyingma Institute. *Ways of Enlightenment.* Berkeley, Calif.: Dharma, 1993.

Burke, T. Patrick. *The Major Religions: An Introduction with Texts.* Cambridge, Mass.: Blackwell, 1996.

Cameli, Louis J. "Spirituality in the Western Catholic Tradition." *Chicago Studies* 36 (1997): 5–15.

Campbell, Joseph. *The Hero with a Thousand Faces.* New York: Bollingen Foundation, 1949.

Carmody, Denise L., and John T. Carmody. *Interpreting the Religious Experience: A Worldview.* Englewood Cliffs, N.J.: Prentice-Hall, 1987.

———. *Mysticism: Holiness East and West.* New York: Oxford University Press, 1996.

———. *Ways to the Center: An Introduction to World Religions.* 4th ed. Belmont, Calif.: Wadsworth, 1993.

Chaudhuri, Nirad C. *Hinduism: A Religion to Live By.* New York: Oxford University Press, 1979.

Cohn-Sherbok, Dan, ed. *The Sayings of Moses.* Hopewell, N.J.: Ecco Press, 1991.

Conze, Edward, ed. and trans. *Buddhist Scriptures.* London: Penguin, 1959.

Coomaraswamy, Ananda K. *Buddha and the Gospel of Buddhism.* New York: Harper and Row, 1964.

Corrigan, John A., et al. *Readings in Judaism, Christianity, and Islam.* Upper Saddle River, N.J.: Prentice-Hall, 1998.

Cragg, Kenneth. *The House of Islam.* 2nd ed. Encino, Calif.: Dickenson, 1975.

Cragg, Kenneth, and Marston Speight. *Islam from Within: Anthology of a Religion.* Belmont, Calif.: Wadsworth, 1980.

Cross, F. L., ed. *The Oxford Dictionary of the Christian Church.* London: Oxford University Press, 1958.

Cunningham, Lawrence. *The Catholic Faith: An Introduction.* New York: Paulist Press, 1987.

Cunningham, Lawrence S., and Keith J. Egan. *Christian Spirituality: Themes from the Tradition.* New York: Paulist Press, 1996.

Cunningham, Lawrence S., et al. *The Sacred Quest: An Invitation to the Study of Religion.* 2nd ed. Englewood Cliffs, N.J.: Prentice-Hall, 1995.

Dalai Lama. *The Bodhgaya Interviews*. Edited by Jose Ignacio Cabezon. Ithaca, N.Y.: Snow Lion Publications, 1988.

Davies, J. G. *The New Westminster Dictionary of Liturgy and Worship*. Westminster, Pa.: Westminster Press, 1986.

Denny, Frederick M. *Islam and the Muslim Community*. San Francisco: HarperSanFrancisco, 1987.

Dillenberger, John, and Claude Welch. *Protestant Christianity: Interpreted Through Its Development*. 2nd ed. New York: Macmillan, 1988.

Dosick, Wayne D. *Living Judaism: The Complete Guide to Jewish Belief, Tradition, and Practice*. San Francisco: HarperSanFrancisco, 1995.

Downey, Michael. *Understanding Christian Spirituality*. New York: Paulist Press, 1997.

Dunne, Carrin. *Buddha and Jesus: Conversations*. Springfield, Ill.: Templegate, 1975.

Dupre, Louis, and Don E. Saliers, eds. *Christian Spirituality: Post-Reformation and Modern*. Vol. 18 of *World Spirituality: An Encylopedic History of the Religious Quest*. New York: Crossroad, 1989.

Eastman, Roger, ed. *The Ways of Religion: An Introduction to the Major Traditions*. 2nd ed. New York: Oxford University Press, 1993.

Eck, Diana. *Darsan: Seeing the Divine Image in India*. New York: Columbia University Press, 1996.

———. *Encountering God: A Spiritual Journey from Bozeman to Banaras*. Boston: Beacon Press, 1993.

Eiki, Hoshino. "Buddhist Pilgrimage in East Asia." In *The Encyclopedia of Religion*. Vol. 11. New York: Macmillan, 1987, 349–51.

Eliade, Mircea, ed. *The Encyclopedia of Religion*. 16 vols. New York: Macmillan, 1987.

Ellwood, Robert S. *Introducing Religion: From Inside and Outside*. 3rd ed. Englewood Cliffs, N.J.: Prentice-Hall, 1993.

———. *Mysticism and Religion*. Englewood Cliffs, N.J.: Prentice-Hall, 1980.

Epstein, Isidore. *Judaism: A Historical Presentation*. Harmondsworth, Middlesex: Penguin, 1959.

Erndl, Kathleen M. *Victory to the Mother: The Hindu Goddess of Northwest India in Myth, Ritual, and Symbol*. New York: Oxford University Press, 1993.

Esposito, John L. *Islam: The Straight Path*. 3rd ed. New York: Oxford University Press, 1998.

Fischer-Schreiber, Ingrid, Franz-Karl Ehrhard, and Michael S. Diener. *The Shambhala Dictionary of Buddhism and Zen*. Translated by Michael H. Kohn. Boston: Shambhala, 1991.

Fisher, Mary Pat. *Living Religions*. 3rd ed. Upper Saddle River, N.J.: Prentice-Hall, 1997.

Glazer, Nathan. *American Judaism*. 2nd ed., rev. Chicago: University of Chicago Press, 1957.

Green, Arthur, ed. *Jewish Spirituality: From the Bible Through the Middle Ages*. Vol. 13 of *World Spirituality: An Encyclopedic History of the Religious Quest*. New York: Crossroad, 1986.

——, ed. *Jewish Spirituality: From the Sixteenth Century Revival to the Present*. Vol. 14 of *World Spirituality: An Encyclopedic History of the Religious Quest*. New York: Crossroad, 1987.

Guillaume, Alfred. *Islam*. Harmondsworth, Middlesex: Penguin, 1954.

Gunaratana, Henepola. *The Path of Serenity and Insight: An Explanation of the Buddhist Jnanas*. Delhi: Motilal Banarsidass, 1985.

Guruge, Ananda W. P. *Buddhism: The Religion and Its Culture*. 2nd ed. Colombo, Sri Lanka: The World Fellowship of Buddhists, 1984.

Haberman, David L. *Journey Through the Twelve Forests: An Encounter with Krishna*. New York: Oxford University Press, 1994.

Hanh, Thich Nhat. *Living Buddha, Living Christ*. London: Rider, 1995.

——. *Peace Is Every Step: The Path of Mindfulness in Everyday Life*. Edited by Arnold Kotler. New York: Bantam, 1992.

——. *Zen Keys: A Guide to Zen Practice*. New York: Doubleday, 1974.

Happel, Stephen, and David Tracy. *A Catholic Vision*. Philadelphia: Fortress Press, 1984.

Heschel, Abraham Joshua. *The Earth Is the Lord's* and *The Sabbath*. New York: Harper Torchbooks, 1966.

Hiltebeitel, Alf. "Hinduism." In *The Encyclopedia of Religion*. Vol. 6. New York: Macmillan, 1987, 336–60.

Holmes, Urban T. *A History of Christian Spirituality: An Analytical Introduction*. New York: Seabury Press, 1981.

Hopfe, Lewis M., and Mark R. Woodward. *Religions of the World*. 7th ed. Upper Saddle River, N.J.: Prentice-Hall, 1998.

Hopkins, Thomas J. *The Hindu Religious Tradition*. Encino, Calif.: Dickenson, 1971.

Jagannathan, Shakunthala. *Hinduism: An Introduction*. Bombay: Vakils, Feffer and Simons, 1984.

Jeffery, Arthur, ed. *Islam: Muhammad and His Religion*. Indianapolis: Bobbs-Merrill, 1958.

Johnston, William. *The Mirror Mind: Spirituality and Transformation*. San Francisco: Harper and Row, 1981.

Jomier, Jacques. *How to Understand Islam*. New York: Crossroad, 1989.

Jones, Alexander, ed. *The Jerusalem Bible*. Garden City, N.Y.: Doubleday, 1966.

Jones, Cheslyn, et al. *The Study of Spirituality*. New York: Oxford University Press, 1986.

Katz, Nathan. "Bhakti." In *The Encyclopedia of Religion*. Vol. 2. New York: Macmillan, 1987, 130–34.

Kennedy, Richard. *The International Dictionary of Religion: A Profusely Illustrated Guide to the Beliefs of the World*. New York: Crossroad, 1984.

Keyes, Charles F. "Buddhist Pilgrimage in South and Southeast Asia." In *The Encyclopedia of Religion*. Vol. 11. New York: Macmillan, 1987, 347–49.

King, Winston L. "Religion." In *The Encyclopedia of Religion*. Vol. 12. New York: Macmillan, 1987, 282–93.

Kinsley, David R. *Hinduism: A Cultural Perspective*. Englewood Cliffs, N.J.: Prentice-Hall, 1982.

Klostermaier, Klaus K. *A Survey of Hinduism*. 2nd ed. Albany: State University of New York Press, 1994.

LaFleur, William R. *Buddhism*. Englewood Cliffs, N.J.: Prentice-Hall, 1988.

Lane, Dermot A. *The Reality of Jesus*. New York: Paulist Press, 1975.

Leclercq, Jean. *The Love of Learning and the Desire for God: A Study of Monastic Culture*. Translated by Catharine Misrahi. New York: Fordham University Press, 1961.

Lefebure, Leo D. "Buddhism and Catholic Spirituality." *Chicago Studies* 36 (1997): 47–61.

Levinson, David. *Religion: A Cross-Cultural Dictionary.* New York: Oxford University Press, 1996.

Livingston, James C. *Anatomy of the Sacred: An Introduction to Religion.* 3rd ed. Upper Saddle River, N.J.: Prentice-Hall, 1998.

Ludwig, Theodore M. *The Sacred Paths: Understanding the Religions of the World.* 2nd ed. Upper Saddle River, N.J.: Prentice-Hall, 1996.

Markham, Ian S., ed. *A World Religions Reader.* Cambridge, Mass.: Blackwell, 1996.

Martin, Richard C. *Islam: A Cultural Perspective.* Englewood Cliffs, N.J.: Prentice-Hall, 1982.

Martos, Joseph. *Doors to the Sacred: A Historical Introduction to Sacraments in the Catholic Church.* Liguori, Mo.: Triumph Books, 1991.

Matthews, Warren. *World Religions.* St. Paul: West, 1991.

McGinn, Bernard, and John Meyendorff, eds. *Christian Spirituality: Origins to the Twelfth Century.* Vol. 16 of *World Spirituality: An Encyclopedic History of the Religious Quest.* New York: Crossroad, 1985.

McKenzie, Peter. *The Christians: Their Beliefs and Practices.* Nashville: Abingdon Press, 1988.

Meeks, Wayne A., ed. *The HarperCollins Study Bible: New Revised Standard Version with the Apocryphal/Deuterocanonical Books.* London: Harper-Collins, 1989.

Mitchell, Donald W., and James Wiseman, eds. *The Gethsemani Encounter: A Dialogue on the Spiritual Life by Buddhist and Christian Monastics.* New York: Continuum, 1999.

Mitchell, Stephen. *The Enlightened Heart: An Anthology of Sacred Poetry.* New York: HarperCollins, 1993.

Monk, Robert C., et al. *Exploring Religious Meaning.* 5th ed. Upper Saddle River, N.J.: Prentice-Hall, 1998.

Monroe, Charles R. *World Religions: An Introduction.* Amherst, N.Y.: Prometheus Books, 1995.

Myerhoff, Barbara G., Linda A. Camino, and Edith Turner. "Rites of Passage: An Overview." In *The Encyclopedia of Religion.* Vol. 12. New York: Macmillan, 1987, 380–86.

Narayan, Kirin. *Storytellers, Saints, and Scoundrels: Folk Narrative in Hindu Religious Teaching*. Philadelphia: University of Pennsylvania Press, 1989.

Nasr, Seyyed Hossein. *Islamic Art and Spirituality*. Albany: State University of New York Press, 1987.

———, ed. *Islamic Spirituality: Foundations*. Vol. 19 of *World Spirituality: An Encyclopedic History of the Religious Quest*. New York: Crossroad, 1987.

———, ed. *Islamic Spirituality: Manifestations*. Vol. 20 of *World Spirituality: An Encyclopedic History of the Religious Quest*. New York: Crossroad, 1991.

Neusner, Jacob. *Between Time and Eternity: The Essentials of Judaism*. Encino, Calif.: Dickenson, 1975.

———. *The Way of Torah: An Introduction to Judaism*. 5th ed. Belmont, Calif.: Wadsworth, 1993.

Nigosian, S. A. *World Faiths*. 2nd ed. New York: St. Martin's Press, 1994.

Noss, David S., and John B. Noss. *A History of the World's Religions*. 9th ed. New York: Macmillan, 1994.

Novak, Philip, ed. *The World's Wisdom: Sacred Texts of the World's Religions*. San Francisco: HarperSanFrancisco, 1994.

O'Flaherty, Wendy Doniger, trans. *The Rig Veda, An Anthology: One Hundred and Eight Hymns Selected, Translated, and Annotated*. New York: Penguin, 1981.

O'Grady, John F. "Spirituality Without Religion." *Chicago Studies* 36 (1997): 87–101.

Olivelle, Patrick, trans. *The Early Upanisads: Annotated Text and Translation*. New York: Oxford University Press, 1998.

Organ, Troy Wilson. *Hinduism: Its Historical Development*. Woodbury, N.Y.: Barron's, 1974.

Otto, Rudolf. *The Idea of the Holy*. Translated by John W. Harvey. 2nd ed. London: Oxford University Press, 1950.

Parrinder, Geoffrey. *Mysticism in the World's Religions*. New York: Oxford University Press, 1976.

———, ed. *The Sayings of the Buddha*. Hopewell, N.J.: Ecco Press, 1991.

————. *Worship in the World's Religions.* Totowa, N.J.: Littlefield, Adams, 1976.

Pelikan, Jaroslav. "Christianity: An Overview." In *The Encyclopedia of Religion.* Vol. 3. New York: Macmillan, 1987, 348–62.

————. *Jesus Through the Centuries: His Place in the History of Culture.* New Haven: Yale University Press, 1985.

Pieper, Josef. *Leisure: The Basis of Culture.* Translated by Alexander Dru. New York: New American Library, 1952.

Pilgrim, Richard B. *Buddhism and the Arts of Japan.* Chambersburg, Pa.: Anima Books, 1981.

Porterfield, Amanda. *The Power of Religion: A Comparative Introduction.* New York: Oxford University Press, 1998.

Rahman, Fazlur. *Islam.* Garden City, N.Y.: Doubleday, 1966.

————. "Islam: An Overview." In *The Encyclopedia of Religion.* Vol. 7. New York: Macmillan, 1987, 304–22.

Raitt, Jill, ed. *Christian Spirituality: High Middle Ages and Reformation.* Vol. 17 of *World Spirituality: An Encyclopedic History of the Religious Quest.* New York: Crossroad, 1989.

Ray, Reginald A. *Buddhist Saints in India: A Study in Buddhist Values and Orientations.* New York: Oxford University Press, 1994.

Renard, John. "Islamic Spirituality." *Chicago Studies* 36 (1997): 62–73.

————. *Seven Doors to Islam: Spirituality and the Religious Life of Muslims.* Berkeley: University of California Press, 1996.

Reynolds, Frank E., and Charles Hallisey. "Buddhism: An Overview." In *The Encyclopedia of Religion.* Vol. 2. New York: Macmillan, 1987, 334–51.

Rice, Edward. *Eastern Definitions.* Garden City, N.Y.: Doubleday, 1980.

Robinson, Neal, ed. and trans. *The Sayings of Muhammad.* Hopewell, N.J.: Ecco Press, 1991.

Sax, William S. "Kumbha Mela." In *The Encyclopedia of Religion.* Vol. 8. New York: Macmillan, 1987, 401–402.

Schallman, Herman E. "Judaic Spirituality." *Chicago Studies* 36 (1997): 39–46.

Schillebeeckx, Edward. *Christ, The Sacrament of the Encounter with God.* Translated by Paul Barrett. English text revised by Mark Schoof and Laurence Bright. New York: Sheed and Ward, 1963.

————. *Jesus.* New York: Seabury Press, 1979.

Schimmel, Annemarie. *Mystical Dimensions of Islam.* Chapel Hill: University of North Carolina Press, 1975.

Schmidt, Roger. *Exploring Religion.* Belmont, Calif.: Wadsworth, 1980.

Seneviratne, H. L. *Rituals of the Kandyan State.* London: Cambridge University Press, 1978.

Shearer, Alistair. *Buddha: The Intelligent Heart.* London: Thames and Hudson, 1992.

Sivaraman, Krishna, ed. *Hindu Spirituality: Vedas through Vedanta.* Vol. 6 of *World Spirituality: An Encyclopedic History of the Religious Quest.* New York: Crossroad, 1989.

Smart, Ninian. *The Religious Experience.* 5th ed. Upper Saddle River, N.J.: Prentice-Hall, 1996.

————. *Worldviews: Crosscultural Explorations of Human Beliefs.* 2nd ed. Englewood Cliffs, N.J.: Prentice-Hall, 1995.

Smart, Ninian, and Richard D. Hecht, eds. *Sacred Texts of the World: A Universal Anthology.* New York: Crossroad, 1982.

Smith, Jonathan, and William Scott Green, eds. *The HarperCollins Dictionary of Religion.* San Francisco: HarperSanFrancisco, 1995.

Sundarajan, K. R., and Bithika Mukerji, eds. *Hindu Spirituality: Postclassical and Modern.* Vol. 7 of *World Spirituality: An Encyclopedic History of the Religious Quest.* New York: Crossroad, 1991.

Suzuki, Shunryu. *Zen Mind, Beginner's Mind: Informal Talks on Zen Meditation and Practice.* Edited by Trudy Dixon. New York: Weatherhill, 1970.

Swartz, Merlin L., trans. and ed. *Studies on Islam.* New York: Oxford University Press, 1981.

Swearer, Donald. "Buddhism in Southeast Asia." In *The Encyclopedia of Religion.* Vol. 2. New York: Macmillan, 1987, 285–400.

————. *The Buddhist World of Southeast Asia.* Albany: State University of New York Press, 1995.

Teasdale, Wayne. "The Eternal Religion: Spirituality in Hinduism." *Chicago Studies* 36 (1997): 74–86.

Tremmell, William Calloley. *Religion: What Is It?* 2nd ed. New York: Holt, Rinehart and Winston, 1984.

Trepp, Leo. *Judaism: Development and Life.* 2nd ed. Encino, Calif.: Dickenson, 1974.

Tugwell, Simon. *Ways of Imperfection: An Exploration of Christian Spirituality.* Springfield, Ill.: Templegate, 1985.

Turner, Edith. "Pilgrimage: An Overview." In *The Encyclopedia of Religion.* Vol. 11. New York: Macmillan, 1987, 327–30.

Turner, Victor. *The Ritual Process: Structure and Anti-Structure.* Ithaca: Cornell University Press, 1969.

Van Buitenen, J. A. B. *The Bhagavadgita in the Mahabharata: Text and Translation.* Chicago: University of Chicago Press, 1981.

Van Ness, Peter H., ed. *Spirituality and the Secular Quest.* Vol. 22 of *World Spirituality: An Encyclopedic History of the Religious Quest.* New York: Crossroad, 1996.

Van Voorst, Robert E. *Anthology of World Scriptures.* Belmont, Calif.: Wadsworth, 1994.

Wainwright, Geoffrey. "Christian Spirituality." In *The Encyclopedia of Religion.* Vol. 3. New York: Macmillan, 1987, 452–60.

Ware, Timothy. *The Orthodox Church.* Baltimore: Penguin, 1972.

Watson, Burton, trans. *The Lotus Sutra.* New York: Columbia University Press, 1993.

Watt, W. Montgomery. *Muhammad: Prophet and Statesman.* London: Oxford University Press, 1961.

Weaver, Mary Jo. *Introduction to Christianity.* Belmont, Calif.: Wadsworth, 1984.

Weborg, John. "Protestant Spirituality: A Reprise." *Chicago Studies* 36 (1997): 26–38.

Webster's New World Dictionary of the American Language. Second College Edition. Cleveland: William Collins.

Whitmyer, Claude, ed. *Mindfulness and Meaningful Work: Explorations in Right Livelihood.* Berkeley, Calif.: Parallax Press, 1994.

Wiesel, Elie. *Souls on Fire: Portraits and Legends of Hasidic Masters*. Translated by Marion Wiesel. New York: Random House, 1972.

Wilson, Andrew, ed. *World Scripture: A Comparative Anthology of Sacred Texts*. New York: Paragon House, 1995.

Wilson, John E. *Religion: A Preface*. Englewood Cliffs, N.J.: Prentice-Hall, 1982.

Yamaguchi, Susumu. *Mahayana Way to Buddhahood*. Translated and edited by Buddhist Books International. Los Angeles: Buddhist Books International, 1982.

Young, William A. *The World's Religions: Worldviews and Contemporary Issues*. Englewood Cliffs, N.J.: Prentice-Hall, 1995.

Zaehner, R. C., ed. *The Concise Encyclopedia of Living Faiths*. Boston: Beacon Press, 1959.

Index